# *Microsoft® Excel 7.0 for Windows® 95*

# Microsoft® Excel 7.0 for Windows® 95

Sarah E. Hutchinson

Glen J. Coulthard

THE IRWIN ADVANTAGE SERIES FOR COMPUTER EDUCATION

**IRWIN**

Chicago • Bogotá • Boston • Buenos Aires • Caracas • London • Madrid • Mexico City • Sydney • Toronto

**Irwin Book Team**

Publisher: *Tom Casson*
Sponsoring editor: *Garrett Glanz*
Developmental editor: *Kristin Hepburn*
Associate marketing manager: *Michelle Hudson*
Project editor: *Jane Lightell*
Production supervisor: *Pat Frederickson*
Art director: *Keith McPherson*
Assistant manager, graphics: *Charlene R. Perez*
Compositor: *Graphic Typesetting Service*
Typeface: *11/13 Bodoni Book*
Printer: *Webcrafters, Inc.*

**Times Mirror**
**Higher Education Group**

***Library of Congress Cataloging-in-Publication Data***

Hutchinson, Sarah E.
Microsoft Excel 7.0 for Windows 95 / Sarah E. Hutchinson, Glen J. Coulthard.
p. cm. — (The Irwin advantage series for computer education)
Includes index.
ISBN 0-256-22049-2
1. Microsoft Excel for Windows. 2. Business—Computer programs. 3. Electronic spreadsheets. I. Coulthard, Glen J. II. Title. III. Series.
HF5548.4.M523H875 1996
005.369—dc20 96–13557

*Printed in the United States of America*
1 2 3 4 5 6 7 8 9 0 WC 3 2 1 0 9 8 7 6

# Contents

## SESSION 1

### *Fundamentals*



## SESSION 2

### *Working with Spreadsheets*

# SESSION 3

## *Increasing Your Productivity*



# SESSION 4

## *Managing a Workbook*

## SESSION 5
### *Creating Charts*



## APPENDIX

# USING THIS GUIDE

Welcome to the Irwin Advantage Series! This tutorial is one in a series of learning guides that lead you through the most popular microcomputer software programs available. The following features are incorporated into each session of our guides to ensure that your learning experience is as productive and enjoyable as possible:

- Each session begins with a real-world ***case scenario*** that introduces you to a fictitious person or company and describes their immediate problem or opportunity. During the session, you obtain the knowledge and skills necessary to define and solve the problem or take advantage of the opportunity. At the end of the session, you are invited to solve problems directly related to the case scenario.
- ***Concepts, skills, and procedures*** are grouped into session topics and are presented in a logical and structured manner.
- ***In Addition boxes*** are placed strategically throughout the guide to provide information about topics related to the current discussion, but beyond the scope of the text.
- Commands and procedures are introduced using ***hands-on examples in a step-by-step format***, and students are encouraged to perform the steps along with the guide.
- Each session concludes with ***short answer questions and hands-on exercises.*** These exercises are integrated with the session's objectives; they were not added as an afterthought. The exercises are comprehensive and meaningful, and they provide students with an opportunity to practice the session material. For maximum benefit, students should complete all the exercises at the end of each session.
- For each of the learning guides, an instructor's resource kit is available with suggested answers to the questions, exercises, and case problems appearing at the end of each session. In addition, the resource kit provides a test bank of additional questions and exercises.

The exercises and examples in this guide use several standard conventions to indicate menu options, keystroke combinations, and command instructions.

## MENU INSTRUCTIONS

In Windows 95, all Menu bar options and pull-down menu commands have an underlined or highlighted letter in each option. When you need to execute a command from the Menu bar—the row of menu choices across the top of the screen—the tutorial's instruction line separates the Menu bar option from the command with a comma. Notice also that the word "CHOOSE" is always used for menu commands. For example, the command for quitting an application is shown as:

CHOOSE: File, Exit

This instruction tells you to choose the File option on the Menu bar and then to choose the Exit command from the File pull-down menu. The actual steps for choosing a menu command are discussed later in this guide.

## KEYSTROKES AND KEYSTROKE COMBINATIONS

When two keys must be pressed together, the tutorial's instruction line shows the keys joined with a plus (+) sign. For example, you can execute a Copy command in Windows by holding down CTRL and then pressing the letter **c**.

The instruction for this type of keystroke combination follows:

PRESS: CTRL +**c**

## COMMAND INSTRUCTIONS

This guide indicates with a special typeface data that you are required to type in yourself. For example:

TYPE: **Income Statement**

When you are required to enter unique information, such as the current date or your name, the instruction appears in italics. The following instruction directs you to type your name in place of the actual words "your name."

TYPE: ***your name***

## ADVANTAGE DISKETTE

The Advantage Diskette provided with this guide or by your instructor contains the files that you use in each session and in the hands-on exercises. ***This diskette is extremely important to your success with the guide.*** If you are using this guide in a self-study program, we suggest that you make a copy of the Advantage Diskette. When the guide asks you to insert the Advantage Diskette, you insert and work with the copied diskette instead. By following this procedure, you will be able to work through the guide again at a later date using a fresh copy of the Advantage Diskette. If you want to copy the contents of the Advantage Diskette to a permanent storage device, such as a network drive, ensure that the storage device allows for Windows' long file names.

## ACKNOWLEDGMENTS

This series of learning guides is the direct result of the teamwork and heart of many people. We sincerely thank the reviewers, instructors, and students who have shared their comments and suggestions with us over the past few years.

We do read them! With their valuable feedback, our guides have evolved into the product you see before you. We also appreciate the efforts of the instructors and students from the Vernon Continuing Education division of Okanagan University College who classroom tested our guides to ensure accuracy, relevancy, and completeness.

We also give many thanks to Tom Casson from Richard D. Irwin for his skillful management of this text. Special recognition goes to Stacey Sawyer for her original design work on the series and for being just so talented! Finally, to the many others who weren't directly involved in this project but who have stood by us the whole way, we appreciate your patience, support, and understanding.

## WRITE TO US

We welcome your response to this book, for we are trying to make it as useful a learning tool as possible. Write to us in care of Thomas Casson, Publisher, Richard D. Irwin, 1333 Burr Ridge Parkway, Burr Ridge, IL 60521. Thank you.

***Sarah E. Hutchinson***

***Glen J. Coulthard***

# Microsoft Excel 7.0 for Windows 95

## *Fundamentals*

## SESSION OUTLINE



## INTRODUCTION

Be thankful for the electronic spreadsheet, one of the most commonly used business software tools! Just a few years ago, a spreadsheet existed only in paper form and its 7,500 or so tiny spaces had to be filled in by hand. Many a manager, accountant, and business planner wore down several pencils (and erasers) revising this paper instrument. Today, electronic spreadsheets such as Microsoft Excel enable you to insert and change numbers with ease. This session shows you how to begin using this valuable tool.

## CASE STUDY THE BONDABLE GROUP

Started in the spring of 1994, The Bondable Group is composed of three friends who formed a partnership after graduating together with degrees in business administration. The group offers investment advice to individuals wanting to expand their portfolios into the bond and stock markets. Jennifer Spalding is the undisputed leader of the group, having graduated with a Finance major. Although they don't possess the same financial skills as their associate, Pancho Valdez and Mackenzie Sherwood are definitely the sales backbone. Both Pancho and Mackenzie are marketing majors with excellent communication and presentation skills.

The group agreed recently to purchase notebook computers for Pancho and Mackenzie, since most of their work entails visiting clients' homes in the evening. To prepare for the arrival of their new computers, Jennifer suggested that the two men develop a simple financial planning tool using Microsoft Excel for Windows 95. Pancho and Mackenzie could use this tool to explain different investment strategies to their clients. Unfortunately, neither of the two has ever used Microsoft Excel and they don't know the first thing about creating an electronic spreadsheet.

In this session, you and our two friends are led step-by-step through one of the most popular spreadsheet programs available, Microsoft Excel. You will initially concentrate on spreadsheet fundamentals like entering text, numbers, dates, and formulas. By the end of the session, you will know how to effectively design, create, and save a spreadsheet. You will also know how to retrieve advice from Excel's Help system and how to use the Undo command for reversing data entry and editing mistakes.

## WORKING WITH ELECTRONIC SPREADSHEETS

The electronic spreadsheet has been available for personal computers since the introduction of VisiCalc in 1978. The arrival of Lotus 1-2-3 in 1983 launched the second generation of spreadsheet software, expanding the perceived use of the spreadsheet from a visual calculator (VisiCalc) to an all-around business tool. Microsoft Excel for Windows 95 is helping lead the electronic spreadsheet into its third generation, adding an easy-to-use graphical interface, spreadsheet publishing capabilities, and single-step functionality.

For years, people have used calculators and rolls of paper to perform numerical calculations. With the recent advancements in computers and electronic spreadsheets, these manual tools may soon be considered obsolete. Accountants, statisticians, and business people now use spreadsheets to analyze their financial and statistical data. However, spreadsheets are much more than glorified calculators; often they are the primary financial tool for a small business.

An electronic spreadsheet is similar to a manual worksheet or an accountant's ledger (Figure 1.1.) With a manual worksheet, you write descriptive labels down the first column or along the top row. An electronic spreadsheet is also composed of columns and rows. You create a spreadsheet in much the same way as before, by entering information into cells, or intersections of the columns and the rows.

**FIGURE 1.1** PARTIAL VIEW OF AN ACCOUNTANT'S MANUAL WORKSHEET

| Date | Item | Debit | Credit |
|---|---|---|---|
| 19-Jun-96 | Sold photocopy machine | | |
| | Dr. Cash in Bank | 750.00 | |
| | Cr. Equipment | | 750.00 |
| | | | |
| 25-Jun-96 | Sold 20 units of inventory | | |
| | Dr. Accounts Receivable | 1000.00 | |

One of the primary advantages of an electronic spreadsheet over a manual worksheet is the ability to perform **what-if analysis.** The term *what-if* refers to your ability to change a value in the spreadsheet and immediately see the effects it has on other calculations. For example, *"What if my annual sales were only 5,000 units? How would that affect my net income?"* or *"What if the interest rate was 7.5%? How would that affect my mortgage payment?"* This capability makes the electronic spreadsheet one of the most valuable planning tools available.

Some additional advantages of using electronic spreadsheets are these:

- *Electronic spreadsheets are much larger than manual worksheets.*
  While manual worksheets are limited by paper size, electronic spreadsheets typically contain hundreds of columns and thousands of rows. This expansive area allows you to keep related information together and to produce reports that are larger than a normal page.
- *Electronic spreadsheets can perform mathematical, statistical, and financial calculations quickly and accurately.*
  The primary use of a spreadsheet is to calculate **formulas,** such as 200 + 350, that are entered into its cells.

- *Cells in electronic spreadsheets can use information from other cells.* A formula may consist solely of numbers or it may refer to other cells in the spreadsheet. Rather than entering the values 200 + 350, a formula can reference the cells in a worksheet that contain these numbers. With a manual worksheet, changing a single number can mean hours of extra work in recalculating figures. Changing a number in an electronic spreadsheet, however, immediately produces a ripple effect of recalculations for all formulas dependent upon that value.

- *Electronic spreadsheets can be stored and retrieved for repeated use.* You can permanently save electronic spreadsheets onto diskettes, hard disks, or other types of media for safe storage. Rather than searching through endless filing cabinets for handwritten worksheets, you can use your computer's electronic filing system to retrieve files instantaneously. An electronic spreadsheet can be retrieved, edited, updated, printed, and then saved under a new name quickly and easily.

## PLANNING YOUR SPREADSHEET

Would you start building a house or an office building before receiving an architect's plans? Hopefully not! Even experienced builders rely heavily on the planning phase before breaking new ground. Likewise, you wouldn't want to create a spreadsheet without first having a clear objective. This section provides some guidelines to help you plan and develop your electronic spreadsheets.

Use the following steps to create a spreadsheet:

1. *Establish your objectives.* Ask yourself why you are creating a spreadsheet. Is it to save time on lengthy calculations or to provide a regular template for a monthly report? By clearly stating your objectives, you will gain a better understanding of the requirements of the spreadsheet.
2. *Define the output requirements.* Since the layout or structure of a spreadsheet is largely determined by the type of reports required, you should mock up the reports on paper before creating the spreadsheet on the computer.
3. *Construct the spreadsheet.* Having completed your needs assessment, you now construct the spreadsheet. Most people prefer to enter the known information first (row and column headings) and then create the formulas.
4. *Test and use the spreadsheet.* Testing involves performing manual calculations on various parts of the spreadsheet and then comparing those values with the spreadsheet's results. Don't take it for granted that a spreadsheet's calculations are correct—a simple typing mistake can cause numerous errors. A spreadsheet is a dynamic tool and must be updated and maintained to remain relevant.

5. *Document the spreadsheet.* A spreadsheet can become quite complex. Proper documentation is essential, especially when the spreadsheet is used by several different people. Documentation consists of on-screen and paper instructions specifying where and how information is to be entered and outlining the formulas used to perform calculations.

## THE WINDOWS ADVANTAGE

As of this writing, the most recent version of Microsoft Windows is Windows 95. A microcomputer operating system, Windows 95 is the successor to MS-DOS and Windows 3.1. Microsoft focused its development efforts for Windows 95 on three main usability areas: making it easier to learn, making it easier to understand, and making it faster and more responsive. Windows 95 provides a standardized interface for all programs, whether they are word processing, spreadsheet, or database applications. As a result, you can use the knowledge acquired from one Windows product in working with other Windows products.

Some advantages of using Windows 95 include these factors:

- *The ability to run more than one application at a time.* Windows 95 is a **multitasking** environment whereby more than one application or program may be running at the same time. For example, multitasking allows you to simultaneously receive an electronic mail message, calculate an Excel spreadsheet, and print a report.
- *The ability to copy and move information among applications.* Windows 95 provides a program called Clipboard that lets you copy and move information within an application or among applications. For example, it's easy to copy a budget from an Excel spreadsheet to the Clipboard and then paste that budget into a Word document.
- *The ability to link or embed objects from one application into another.* Many Windows 95 applications have the ability to integrate applications using a feature called OLE (pronounced Olé) or Object Linking and Embedding. This feature enables you to embed an object created in one application into another application and facilitates sharing and manipulating information. An object may be a document, worksheet, chart, picture, or even a sound recording or movie.
- *The ability to display on the screen what you will get from the printer.* This feature is called **WYSIWYG** ("What You See Is What You Get"); it allows different fonts, borders, and graphics to be displayed on the screen at all times.

## INTRODUCING MICROSOFT OFFICE 95

Microsoft Office for Windows 95 combines the most popular and exciting software programs available into a single suite of applications. In the Standard edition, Office 95 includes Microsoft Word, Microsoft Excel, Microsoft PowerPoint, and the all-new Schedule+. In the Professional edition, you also get Microsoft Access and Microsoft Bookshelf® '95[1]. In addition to these primary applications, Office 95 provides shared applications (sometimes called "servers") that let you insert clip art, word art, charts, and mathematical equations into your documents.

First introduced in 1988, Microsoft Office has sold over 11 million copies worldwide and enjoys an 80 to 90 percent market share against other application software suites. This number is significant considering that over 60 percent of all word processing and spreadsheet software is now sold in suites.

All software products are born with specific design goals. For Office 95, Microsoft concentrated on rewriting and optimizing Office for use in Windows 95's 32-bit environment. In addition to enjoying performance improvements, Office 95 benefits from many of Windows 95's usability enhancements. For example, you can now name your documents using up to 250 characters, place shortcuts to documents directly on the desktop, use the Windows Briefcase program to compare and synchronize files, and multitask your applications with single-click functionality from the taskbar. Office 95 lets users focus on their work and not on their software.

Further blurring the line between applications, the new Microsoft Binder allows you to assemble, print, and distribute collections of varied documents. Like working with a real three-ring binder, you can insert and withdraw documents that you create in Word, Excel, and PowerPoint into a single binder document. Then, you can print the contents of the binder complete with consistent headers and footers and with consecutive page numbering. A binder document also provides an easy way to transfer information from one computer to another, since all the documents are stored in a single file.

## FEATURES OF MICROSOFT EXCEL 7.0

At the time of this writing, the latest release of Microsoft Excel is version 7.0 for Windows 95. To ensure its competitiveness in the marketplace, Microsoft increased Excel's performance by up to 50 percent in some areas and intro-

[1] Microsoft Bookshelf® '95 is provided on the CD ROM version only of Microsoft Office 95 Professional Edition.

duced several significant new features. This section highlights some of the main features and enhancements available in Microsoft Excel 7.0.

- Excel 7.0 files are called *workbooks*. Each workbook may contain worksheets, chart sheets, macro sheets, and Visual Basic programming modules. The number of worksheets you can create and store in a workbook is limited only by the memory within your computer.
- Excel 7.0 introduces several new templates and wizards that make creating personal and business worksheets as simple as double-clicking the mouse. For example, you can easily create the following spreadsheet solutions using Excel's pre-built templates: Business Planner, Loan Manager, Expense Statement, Invoice, and Purchase Order.
- Excel 7.0 lets you access context-sensitive commands on a shortcut menu by pointing at an item, such as a cell or chart, with the mouse pointer and clicking the right mouse button. You no longer have to search for commands in the Menu bar.
- Excel 7.0 provides eight primary toolbars for single-step mouse access to formatting, drawing, charting, and other menu commands. You can display more than one toolbar at a time and hide, move, and customize toolbars as required.
- Excel 7.0 provides wizards that simplify the process of entering functions, analyzing your data, importing text, and working with databases. The TipWizard even watches your keystrokes while you work, offering helpful shortcuts and other suggestions.
- Excel 7.0 provides productivity enhancement tools with the AutoCalculate, AutoComplete, AutoCorrect, AutoFilter, and AutoFormat features. These commands take the "work" out of creating "worksheets."
- Excel 7.0 incorporates the standard Windows 95 dialog box enhancements for opening, saving, and managing your worksheet documents. In addition, Excel 7.0 provides an improved file-search utility.
- Excel 7.0 introduces the new Data Map utility that lets you create geographical maps and pinpoint demographic information (such as age, income, and education statistics) and analyze regional trends using numerical worksheet information.

If you are new to electronic spreadsheet programs, you may not understand all of the terms used in the above discussion. Don't despair—you'll definitely understand the importance and utility of these features by the end of this guide. Now, let's begin our journey through Microsoft Excel 7.0.

## WORKING WITH MICROSOFT EXCEL

Microsoft Excel for Windows 95, Version 7.0, is a complex yet easy-to-learn program. As you proceed through this guide, you will find that there are often three methods for performing the same command or procedure in Excel:

- Menu — Select a command or procedure from the Menu bar.
- Mouse — Point to and click a toolbar button.
- Keyboard — Press a keyboard shortcut (usually CTRL + *letter*).

Although this guide concentrates on the quickest and easiest methods, we recommend that you try the others and decide which you prefer. *Don't memorize all of the methods and information in this guide! Be selective and find your favorite methods.*

## HOW THE MOUSE IS USED

Although you may use Excel with only a keyboard, much of the program's basic design relies on using a mouse. Regardless of whether your mouse has two or three buttons, you will use the left or primary mouse button for selecting workbook items and menu commands and the right or secondary mouse button for displaying shortcut menus.

The most common mouse actions used in Excel are these:

- Point — Slide the mouse on your desk to position the tip of the mouse pointer over the desired object on the screen.
- Click — Press down and release the left mouse button quickly. Clicking is used to select a cell in the worksheet and to choose menu commands.
- Right-Click — Press down and release the right mouse button. Right-clicking the mouse pointer on a cell or an object displays a context-sensitive shortcut menu.
- Double-Click — Press down and release the mouse button twice in rapid succession. Double-clicking is used to perform in-cell editing and to modify the worksheet tab names in a workbook.
- Drag — Press down and hold the mouse button as you move the mouse pointer across the screen. When the mouse pointer reaches the desired location, release the mouse button. Dragging is used to select a group of cells and to copy or move data.

You may notice that the mouse pointer changes shape as you move it over different parts of the screen. Each mouse pointer shape has its own purpose and may provide you with important information. There are five primary mouse shapes that appear in Excel:

| | | |
|---|---|---|
|  | arrow | Used to choose menu commands, access the toolbars, and complete dialog boxes. |
|  | cross | Used to select cells and groups of cells in a worksheet. |
|  | hourglass | Informs you that Excel is occupied with another task and requests that you wait. |
|  | I-beam | Used to modify and edit text in the Formula bar and in a cell. |
|  | hand | In a Help window, the hand is used to select shortcuts and display definitions. |

As you proceed through this guide, other mouse shapes will be explained in the appropriate sections.

### HOW THE KEYBOARD IS USED

Aside from being the primary input device for creating a worksheet, the keyboard offers shortcut methods for performing commands and procedures. For example, several menu commands have shortcut key combinations listed to the right of the command in the pull-down menu. Therefore, you can perform a command by simply pressing the shortcut keys rather than accessing the Menu bar. Many of these shortcut key combinations are available throughout Windows applications.

## STARTING EXCEL

This session assumes that you are working on a computer with Windows 95 (or Microsoft Windows NT 3.51 or later) and Microsoft Excel 7.0 loaded on the hard disk drive. Because Windows 95 is an operating system, it is loaded automatically into the computer's memory when you turn on the computer.

Perform the following steps to load Windows 95.

1. Turn on the power switches to the computer and monitor. After a few seconds, the Windows 95 desktop will appear (Figure 1.2). (*Note:* The desktop interface on your computer may look different from Figure 1.2.)

FIGURE 1.2 THE WINDOWS 95 DESKTOP

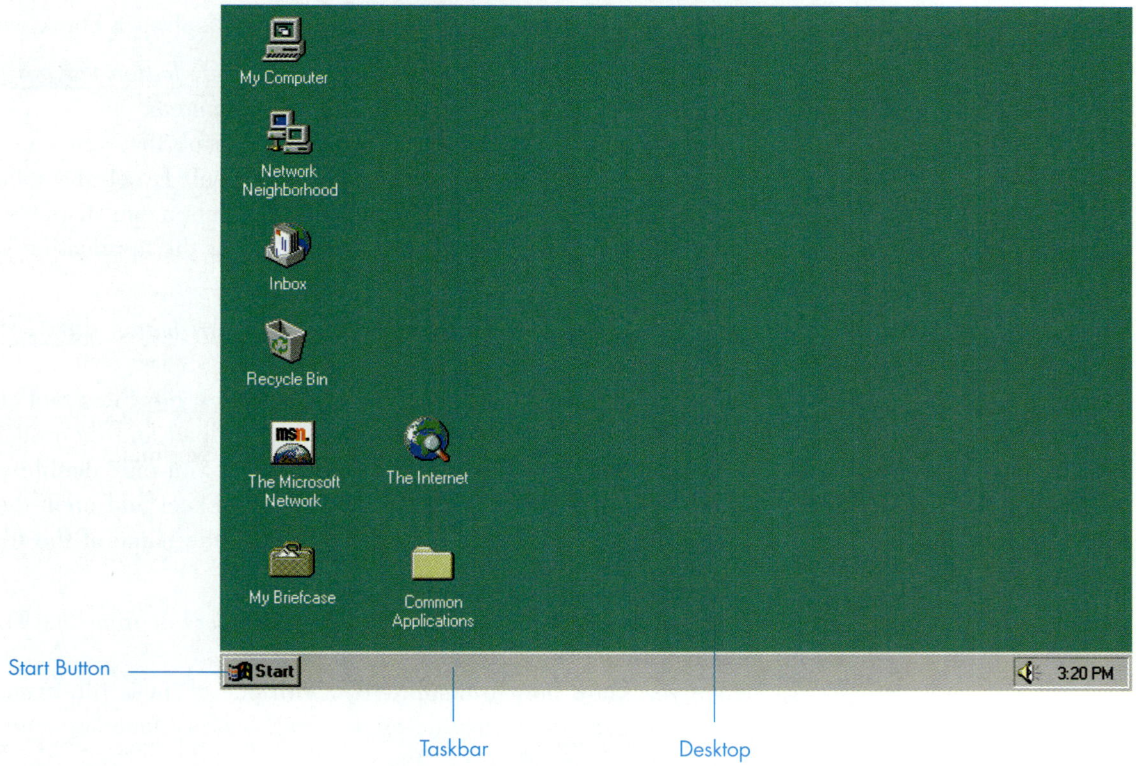


2. If a "Welcome to Windows 95" dialog box appears, do the following:
CLICK: Close button (☒) in the top right-hand corner of the window

| QUICK REFERENCE Loading Windows 95 | **Turn on your computer to load Microsoft Windows 95 (or Microsoft Windows NT 3.51 or later).** |
|---|---|

## LOADING APPLICATIONS IN WINDOWS 95

Microsoft introduced the Start button (Start) in Windows 95. This button contains 99 percent of the functionality required by novice users to manage their computer data. Using the mouse, you click the Start button (Start) once to access your favorite programs, documents, and system management tools.

We summarize some of the more common methods for launching application programs, such as Microsoft Excel, on the next page.

- *Load a program by clicking the Start button (Start) on the taskbar and then choosing the Programs command.*
  After you choose Programs, click Microsoft Excel on the Programs cascading menu. This method loads Excel and displays a blank worksheet.
- *Open an existing document by clicking the Start button (Start) on the taskbar and then choosing the Documents command.*
  After you choose Documents, click the workbook that you want to open from the menu list. This method loads Microsoft Excel and then displays the workbook that you selected. The Documents menu displays the last 15 files that you've worked with, regardless of the application you used to create them.
- *Open an existing document by clicking the Start button (Start) on the taskbar and then choosing the Find command.*
  After you choose Find on the Start menu, click the Files or Folders command. Type the name of the file you want to load and then click the Find Now command button. Once a file is located, you may double-click its filename in the dialog box to load Microsoft Excel and open the workbook. This method is useful when you know the name of the file but don't know where it is located on the hard disk.
- *Open an existing document from "My Computer" or from the Windows Explorer.*
  Once you know how to display files with one of these file-management tools, you can simply double-click a workbook's filename or icon to load it into Microsoft Excel.
- *If Microsoft Office is loaded on your computer, open a document or application directly from the Start menu.*
  If you have installed Microsoft Office on your computer, you will see two new menu items called New Office Document and Open Office Document on the Start menu. To load Microsoft Excel and display a blank worksheet window, choose the New Office Document command and then double-click the Blank Workbook icon ( ) on the General tab.

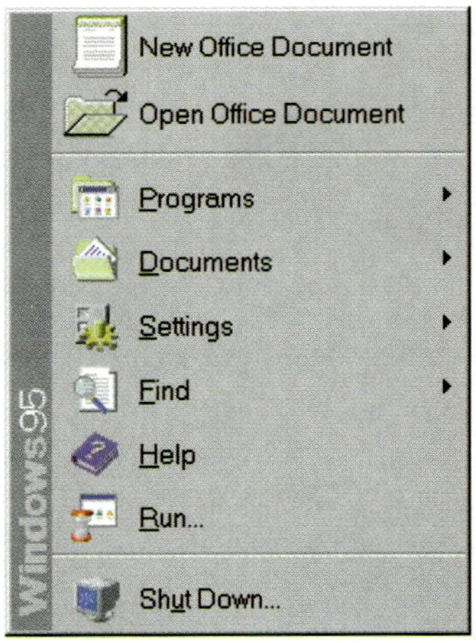


  To load Microsoft Excel and open an existing workbook, choose the Open Office Document command and select the desired file from the Open dialog box. We describe how to use the Open dialog box later in this session.
- *If Microsoft Office is loaded on your computer, open a document or application from the Microsoft Office Shortcut Bar.*
  The Microsoft Office Shortcut Bar provides a Start a New Document

button (▢) and an Open a Document button (▢). These two buttons provide the same functionality as the two Start menu commands that we described previously.

### LOADING MICROSOFT EXCEL 7.0

Perform the following steps to load Microsoft Excel.

1. Point to the Start button (Start) on the taskbar and then click the left mouse button once. The Start menu appears as a pop-up menu.
2. Point to the Programs command using the mouse. Notice that you do not need to click the left mouse button to display the list of programs in the fly-out or cascading menu.
3. Move the mouse pointer horizontally to the right until it highlights an option in the Programs menu. You can now move the mouse pointer up and down the Programs menu. Notice that you still haven't clicked the left mouse button.
4. Point to the Microsoft Excel menu item and then click the left mouse button once to execute the command. After a few seconds, the Microsoft Excel screen appears.

**QUICK REFERENCE**
Loading Microsoft Excel 7.0

1. **CLICK: Start button (Start)**
2. **CHOOSE: Programs, Microsoft Excel**

## THE GUIDED TOUR

Software programs designed for Microsoft Windows 95, such as Excel, have many similarities in screen design and layout. Each program operates in its own application window, while the spreadsheets, letters, and brochures you create appear in separate document windows. This section describes the various parts of Excel, including the tools for manipulating application and document windows.

### APPLICATION WINDOW

When you first load Excel, the screen displays the **application window** and a maximized **document window.** The application window (Figure 1.3) contains the Title bar, Menu bar, Standard toolbar, Formatting toolbar, Formula bar and Name box, and Status bar. You create new worksheets or open existing workbooks in the document area. In Figure 1.3, the document area is covered by a maximized document window.

**FIGURE 1.3** MICROSOFT EXCEL'S APPLICATION WINDOW

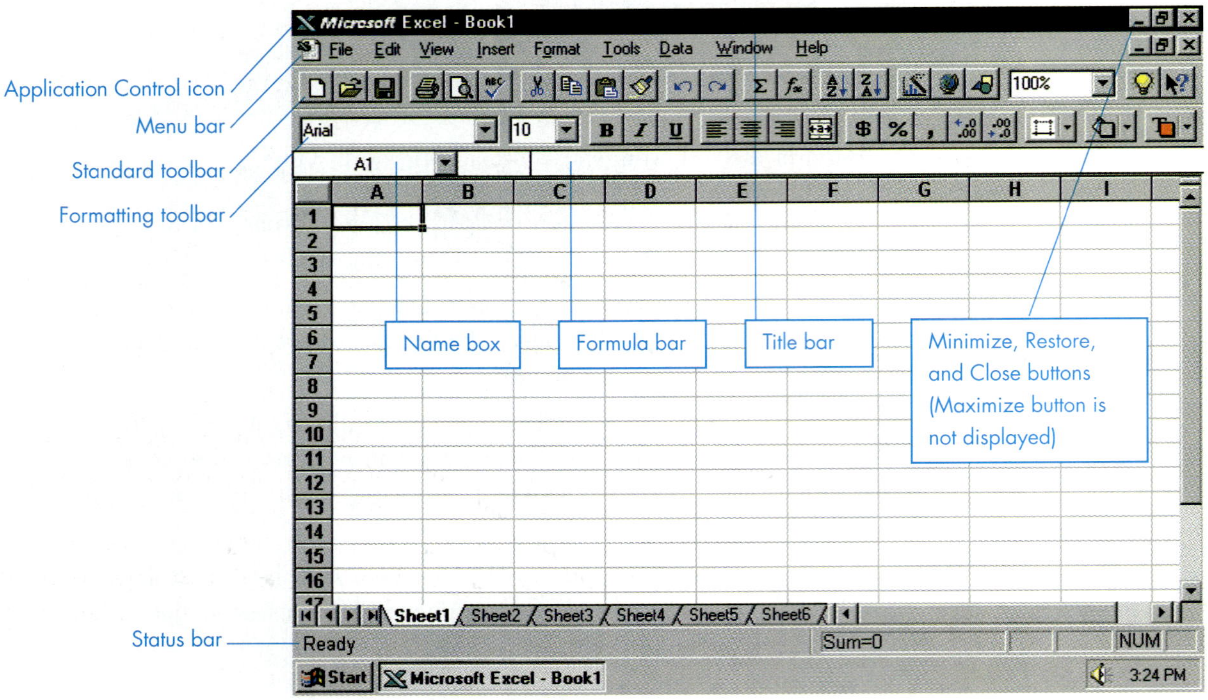


The primary components of the application window are:

| | |
|---|---|
| Application Control icon ( ) | Used to identify the application and to size and position the application window using the keyboard. (*Note:* Use the mouse to perform the same options available in the Control menu.) |
| Minimize ( ) and Maximize ( ), Restore ( ), and Close ( ) icons | Located in the top right-hand corner of the application window, these icons are used to control the display of the application window using the mouse. (*Note:* Since the window is already maximized, the Maximize icon does not appear in Figure 1.3.) |
| Title bar | The Title bar contains the name of the program or workbook file. Using a mouse, you can move a window by dragging its Title bar. |
| Menu bar | Contains the Excel menu commands. |
| Standard toolbar | Displays buttons for opening and saving workbooks, copying and moving information, and accessing special features using a mouse. |
| Formatting toolbar | Displays buttons for accessing character and cell formatting commands using the mouse. |

| | |
|---|---|
| Formula bar | The Formula bar appears below the toolbars and includes the Name box, which shows your current location on the worksheet. |
| Status bar | Located at the bottom of the application window and above the taskbar, the Status bar displays the status or mode and other helpful information. |

Although the application window is usually maximized, you can reduce it to a window that appears on the desktop. You can then size, move, and manipulate the application window to customize your work environment in Windows 95. In this guide, we assume that the Excel application window is always maximized.

## DOCUMENT WINDOW

You create and store related worksheets, charts, and macros in a special file called a **workbook.** You can think of an Excel workbook as a three-ring binder with tabs at the beginning of each new section or topic. In a workbook, you can add and delete sheets, copy information from one sheet to another, and organize your information into logical sections. Each workbook appears in its own document window which can be minimized to an icon, maximized to fill the entire document area, or displayed as a window.

A worksheet (Figure 1.4) is the most common sheet that you will create in an Excel workbook file. Other sheets may include chart sheets and macro or module sheets. Each new workbook contains 16 blank worksheets labeled Sheet1,

FIGURE 1.4 A DOCUMENT WINDOW

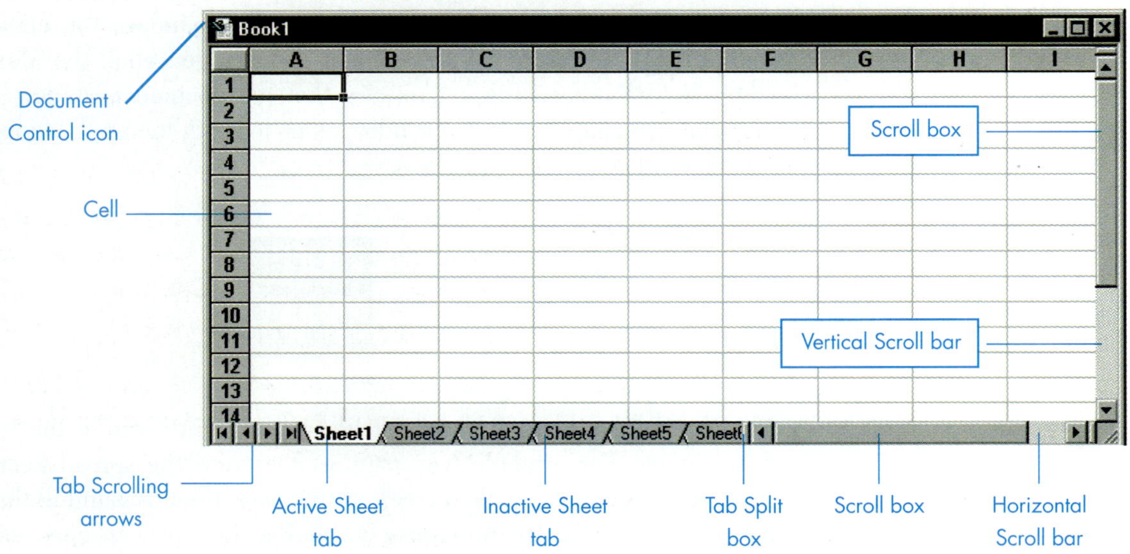

Sheet2, and so on to Sheet16. Similar to a large piece of ledger paper, a worksheet is divided into vertical columns and horizontal rows. The 16,384 rows are numbered and the 256 columns are labeled from A to Z, then AA to AZ, and so on to column IV. The intersection of a column and a row is called a **cell.** Each cell is given a **cell address,** like a post office box number, consisting of its column letter followed by its row number (for example, B4 or FX400).

A document window consists of the following parts:

| | |
|---|---|
| Document Control icon ( ) | Used to size and position the window using the keyboard. (*Note:* Use the mouse to perform the same options available in the Control menu.) |
| Scroll bars | Placed at the right and bottom borders of the document window, scroll bars facilitate moving around a worksheet using the mouse. |
| Sheet tabs | Sheet tabs identify the various pages in a workbook. Using the mouse, you click a tab to move to that particular page or double-click a tab to rename it. |
| Tab Split box | Using the mouse, you drag the tab split box to increase or decrease the space shared by the sheet tabs and the horizontal scroll bar. |
| Tab Scrolling arrows | Using the mouse, you click the tab scrolling arrows to move quickly to the first sheet, previous sheet, next sheet, or last sheet in a workbook file. |

You should recognize some familiar components in the document window that appear in all windows (see the diagram below). For example, the Minimize, Maximize, and Close buttons appear in the top right-hand corner of the document window. To restore a maximized document to a window, you click the Restore button ( ). To maximize a document window, you click the Maximize button ( ). Before proceeding, make sure that the document window is maximized and that you can identify the window icons for both the application and the document window (as shown below):

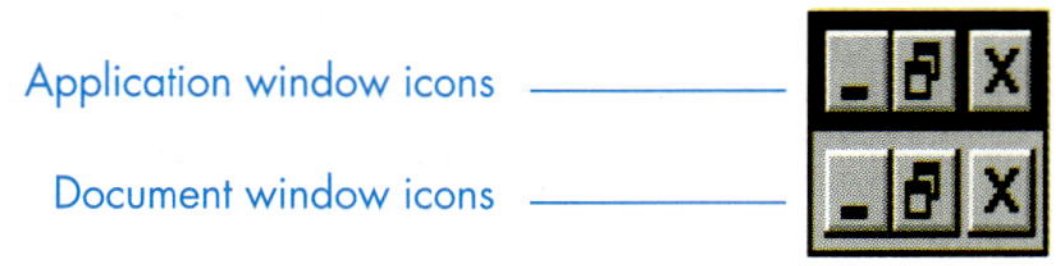


You can display several workbook files concurrently within the Excel application window. For example, you may want to view the spreadsheet results from various departments on the screen at the same time. Assuming that the departmental data is divided into separate workbooks, you can open each file in its own document window. Another method for accomplishing this type of summary view is to create and store multiple worksheets in a single workbook. Similar to peeling off pages from a notepad, you enter each department's data on its own worksheet and then consolidate the data in a separate summary worksheet. In Session 4, you learn how to work with multiple workbook files and multiple-sheet workbooks.

## MENU BAR

Excel commands are grouped together on the Menu bar, as shown in the example provided below.

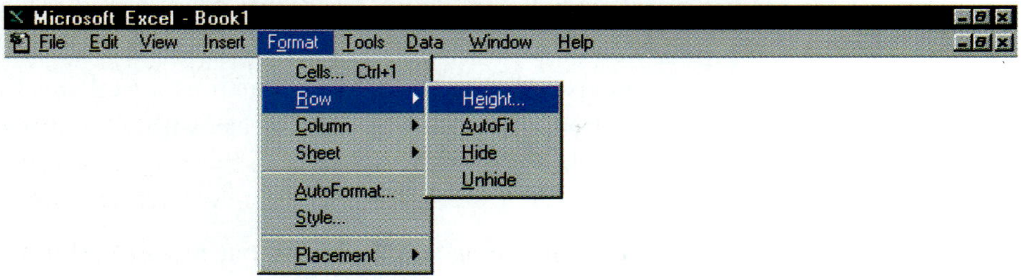


Commands in this guide are written in the following form: Format, Row, where Format is the Menu bar option and Row is the command to be selected from the pull-down menu. To execute a command, click once on the Menu bar option and then click once on the pull-down menu command. Commands that are not available for selection appear dimmed. Commands that are followed by an ellipsis (Height..., for example) require further information to be collected in a dialog box.

To practice accessing the Menu bar, perform the following steps on your computer.

1. To choose the Help command, position the tip of the mouse pointer on the word Help in the Menu bar and click the left mouse button once. A pull-down menu appears below the Help option.
2. To see the pull-down menus associated with other menu options, drag the mouse pointer slowly to the left over the additional options on the Menu bar. (*Note:* You need not hold down the left mouse button as you move the mouse pointer.)
3. To leave the Menu bar without making a command selection, position the pointer in a blank area of the Title bar and click once. You can also click the selected menu item, such as Help, to remove the pull-down menu. On your own, try clicking the Help menu item repeatedly and notice how the pull-down menu appears and disappears.

4. To display the pull-down menu for the File option:
   CHOOSE: File
   This instruction tells you to click the left mouse button once with the pointer on the File option in the Menu bar. (*Note:* All menu commands that you execute in this guide begin with the word "CHOOSE.")

5. To leave the Menu bar without making a selection:
   CHOOSE: File
   (*Note:* As demonstrated previously, clicking the menu option twice removes the pull-down menu.)

## SHORTCUT MENUS

Excel provides context-sensitive shortcut menus for quick access to menu commands. Rather than searching for commands in the Menu bar, you position the mouse pointer on an object, such as a worksheet cell, and click the right mouse button. A pop-up menu appears with the most commonly selected commands for the object.

To practice accessing a shortcut menu, perform the following steps.

1. To display a shortcut menu, position the mouse pointer over any button on the Standard toolbar and click the right mouse button. The shortcut menu at the right should appear.

2. To remove the shortcut menu from the screen:
   PRESS: ESC
   The shortcut menu disappears.

**QUICK REFERENCE**
Using Shortcut Menus

1. **Position the mouse pointer over an item, such as a toolbar button.**
2. **CLICK: the right mouse button to display a shortcut or pop-up menu**
3. **CHOOSE: a command from the menu, or**
   **PRESS: ESC to remove the menu**

## TOOLBARS

Assuming that you haven't yet customized your Excel screen, you will see the Standard and Formatting toolbars appear below the Menu bar. Excel provides eight primary toolbars and hundreds of buttons[2] for quick and easy mouse access to its more popular features. Don't worry about memorizing the button

[2] Sometimes called *icons.*

names appearing in the following graphics—the majority of these buttons are explained elsewhere. You can also point at any toolbar button and pause until a ToolTip label appears with the button's name.

The Standard toolbar (Figure 1.5) provides access to file management and editing commands, in addition to special features like the Function Wizard and the ChartWizard:

**FIGURE 1.5** STANDARD TOOLBAR

The Formatting toolbar (Figure 1.6) lets you access character and cell formatting commands:

**FIGURE 1.6** FORMATTING TOOLBAR

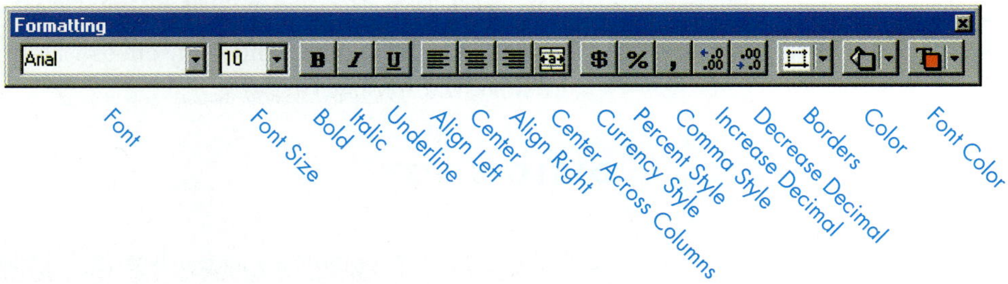


To select additional toolbars, you point to an existing toolbar and click the right mouse button. From the shortcut menu that appears, you can display and hide toolbars by choosing their names in the pop-up menu. If a toolbar is currently being displayed, a check mark appears beside its name.

To practice displaying and hiding toolbars, perform the following steps.

1. Position the mouse pointer over any button on the Standard toolbar.
2. CLICK: right mouse button to display the shortcut menu

3. To display the Drawing toolbar:
   CHOOSE: Drawing
   The new toolbar appears, usually in its own window as shown below:

4. If the Drawing toolbar appears in a window as shown here, move to Step 5. If, on the other hand, the toolbar appears "docked" against a border of the application window, you must drag it away from the border to make it a free-floating window. To un-dock a toolbar, position the mouse pointer on any part of the toolbar that is not a button or drop-down list. Once positioned, click the left mouse button and hold it down and then drag the toolbar to the center of the application window. The toolbar turns into a window, complete with a Title bar and Control menu.
5. To move the Drawing toolbar:
   DRAG: the toolbar's Title bar around the application window
   This instruction tells you to position the mouse pointer over the toolbar's Title bar, click the mouse button and hold it down, and then move the mouse pointer to move the window.
6. To remove the Drawing toolbar:
   CLICK: the toolbar's Close button (☒) once
   The toolbar disappears from the application window. (*Note:* You can also right-click the toolbar and then choose Drawing on the shortcut menu to remove the toolbar.)

## DIALOG BOX

A dialog box is a common mechanism in Windows applications for collecting information before processing a command or instruction (Figure 1.7). In a dialog box, you indicate the options you want to use and then click the OK command button when you're finished. Dialog boxes are also used to display messages or to ask for confirmation of commands.

A dialog box uses several methods for collecting information. We describe each method in Table 1.1.

Most dialog boxes provide a question mark icon (?) near the right side of the Title bar. If you have a question about an item in the dialog box, click the question mark and then click the item to display a pop-up window. You should also know that dialog boxes have a memory. For example, the tab that appears when you exit the dialog box will be selected the next time you open the dialog box.

**FIGURE 1.7** A DIALOG BOX

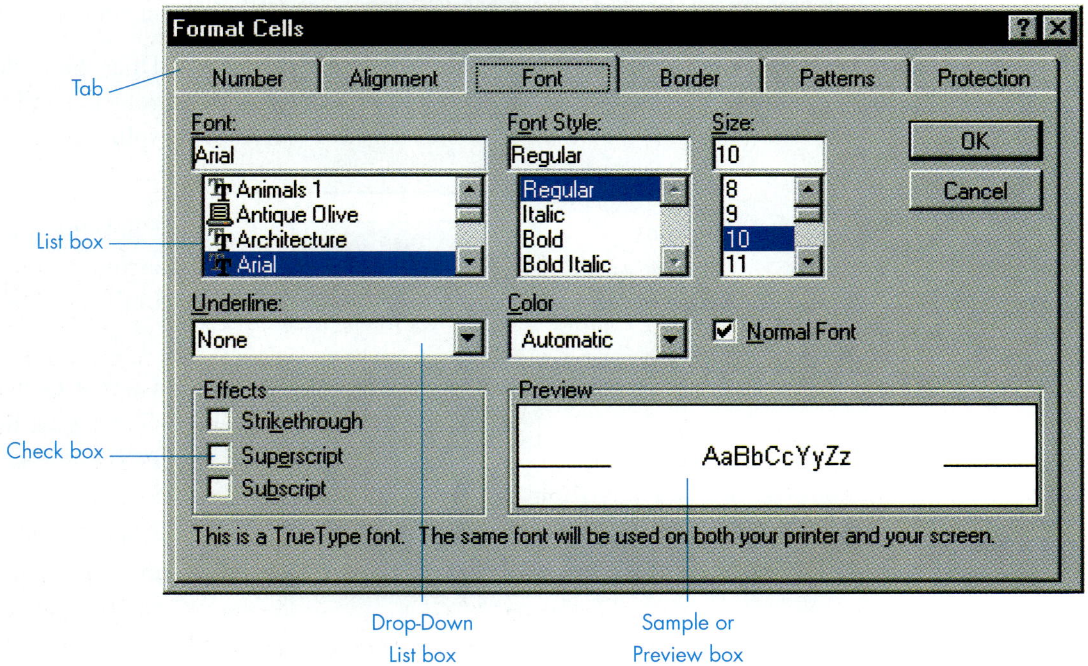


**TABLE 1.1**

Parts of a Dialog Box

| *Name* | *Example* | *Action* |
|---|---|---|
| Check box |   | Click an option to turn it on or off. The option is turned on when an "×" or "✓" appears in the box. |
| Command button | 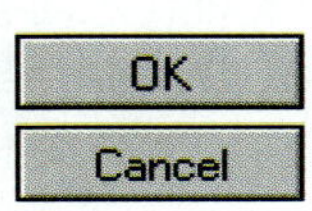  | Click a command button to execute an action. You accept or cancel the selections in a dialog box by clicking the OK or Cancel command buttons, respectively. |
| Drop-down List box | 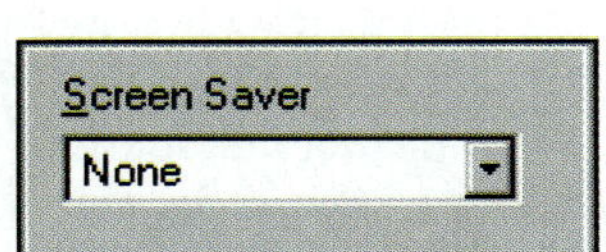  | Make a choice from the list that appears when you click the down arrow next to the box; only the selected choice is visible. |
| List box | 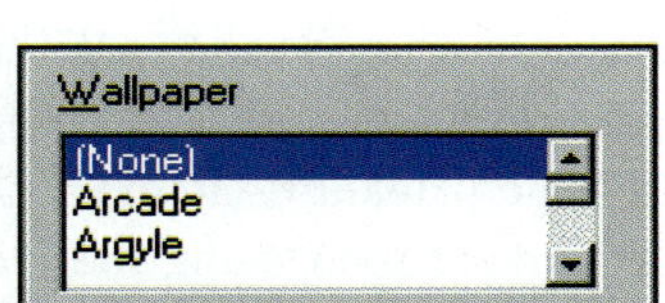  | Make a choice from the scrollable list; several choices, if not all, are always visible. |

**TABLE 1.1**
***Continued***

| *Name* | *Example* | *Action* |
|---|---|---|
| Option button |   | Select an option from a group of related options. |
| Slide box | 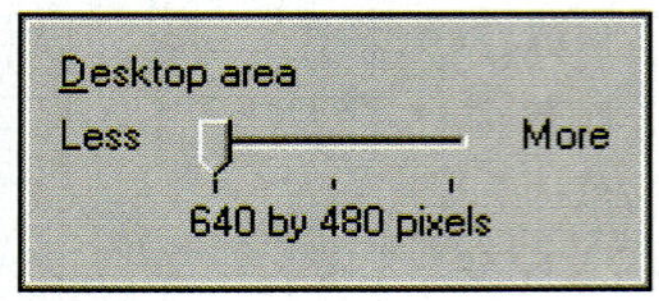  | Drag the slider bar to make a selection, like using a radio's volume control. |
| Spin box | 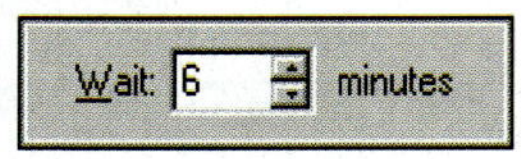  | Click the up and down arrows to the right of the box until the number you want appears. |
| Tab |   | Click a named tab at the top of the window to access other pages of options in the dialog box. |
| Text box |   | Click inside the text box and then type the desired information. |

### THE WINDOWS TASKBAR

The Windows taskbar is usually located on the bottom of your screen below the Status bar. (*Note*: We say "usually" because you can move the taskbar on your desktop.) Each application that you are currently working with is represented by a button on the taskbar. Switching between open applications on your desktop is as easy as clicking the appropriate button on the taskbar, like switching channels on a television set. At this point, you should see a button for Microsoft Excel on the taskbar.

## GETTING HELP

Excel provides several **context-sensitive help** features and a comprehensive library of online documentation. Like many developers trying to minimize the retail price of software and maximize profits, Microsoft has stopped shipping volumes of print-based documentation in favor of disk-based Help systems. However, a Help system is only as good as the search tools that it provides. Fortunately for us, Windows 95 gives developers the tools and capability to create consistent and easy-to-use Help systems. This section describes the context-sensitive help features found in Excel and then describes where to find more detailed information using the Help Topics window.

## CONTEXT-SENSITIVE HELP

Context-sensitive help refers to a software program's ability to retrieve and present helpful information reflecting your current position in the program. In Excel, you can access context-sensitive help for menu options, toolbar buttons, and dialog box items. The help information is presented concisely in a small pop-up window that you can remove with the click of the mouse. This type of help lets you access information quickly and then continue working without interruption. Table 1.2 describes some methods for accessing context-sensitive help while working in Excel.

**TABLE 1.2**

Displaying Context-Sensitive Help Information

| *To display . . .* | *Do this . . .* |
|---|---|
| A description of a dialog box item | Click the question mark button (?) in a dialog box's Title bar and then click an item in the dialog box. A helpful description of the item appears in a pop-up window. Additionally, you can often right-click a dialog box item to display its description. |
| A description of a menu command | Click the Help button (?) on the Standard toolbar and then choose the desired command using the question mark mouse pointer. Rather than executing the command, a helpful description of the command appears in a pop-up window. |
| A description of a toolbar button | Point to a toolbar button to display its ToolTip label; a full description of the toolbar button also appears in the Status bar. You can also click the Help button (?) and then click a toolbar button to display more detailed help information in a pop-up window. |

Perform the following steps to access context-sensitive help.

1. In the next few steps, you use the Help button (?) on the Standard toolbar to access help for the File, New command and a toolbar button. Let's start with the File, New command. Position the tip of the mouse pointer over the Help button (?) on the Standard toolbar. To activate the question mark mouse pointer, do the following:
   CLICK: Help button (?) once
   Your mouse pointer should now appear with an attached question mark.
2. Using the question mark mouse pointer (and not the keyboard):
   CHOOSE: File, New
   Rather than executing the command, Excel provides a description of the command in a pop-up window.
3. After reading the description, close the pop-up window by clicking on it once.

4. To display a ToolTip for a toolbar button, position the mouse pointer over the AutoSum button (Σ) on the Standard toolbar. After a second or two, a ToolTip will appear showing the button's name. Also, the button's description "Inserts SUM function and proposes sum range" displays in the Status bar.

5. To display additional information for the AutoSum button:
CLICK: Help button () once
CLICK: AutoSum button (Σ)
The following pop-up window appears:

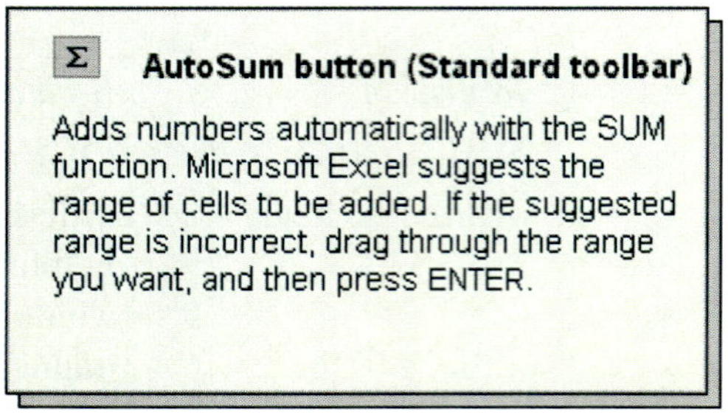


6. CLICK: the pop-up window once to remove it

7. Excel also provides a special Help tool called the TipWizard. The TipWizard watches your keystrokes as you work and offers suggestions and shortcuts. To display the TipWizard Box:
CLICK: TipWizard button () on the Standard toolbar
One example of the TipWizard box appears below:

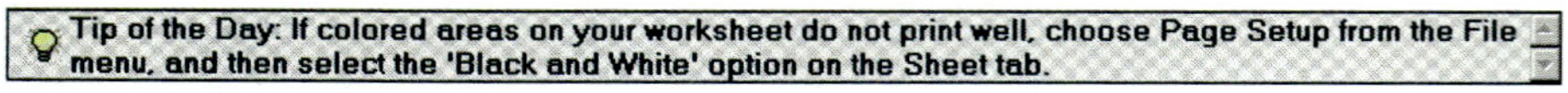


You may have noticed that this toolbar button sometimes appears as an illuminated light bulb. This is Excel's way of telling you it has a new tip or suggestion to display in the TipWizard box. When the light bulb appears pale or "turned off," there is nothing new to report. However, you can always refer back to previous tips by clicking the spin arrows at the right side of the TipWizard box.

8. To remove the TipWizard box:
CLICK: TipWizard button ()
The toolbar button should now appear "turned off."

**QUICK REFERENCE**
Displaying Context-Sensitive Help

1. **CLICK: Help button ( ) once**
2. **Using the question mark mouse pointer, select the desired item for which you want to display a help pop-up window:**
   - **CHOOSE: a menu command, or**
   - **CLICK: a toolbar button, or**
   - **CLICK: a dialog box item**

## HELP TOPICS WINDOW

The primary way that you access Excel's Help system is by choosing the Help, Microsoft Excel Help Topics command from the menu. This command displays the Help Topics window, as shown in Figure 1.8. You can think of the Help Topics window as the front door to Excel's vast help resources.

**FIGURE 1.8** HELP TOPICS WINDOW: *CONTENTS* TAB

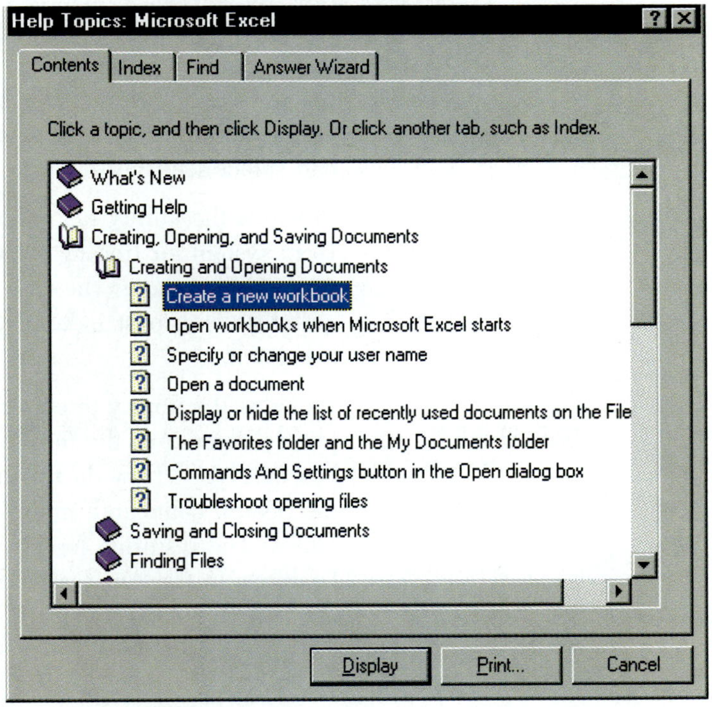


The Help Topics window provides four different tools, each on its own tab, to help you find the information you need quickly and easily. You point to and click a tab using the mouse to make the tab active in the window. Refer to the following tab descriptions to determine which tool you should use when requiring assistance:

| | |
|---|---|
| Contents tab | Displays a list of help topics organized as a hierarchy of books and pages. Think of this tab as the Table of Contents for the entire Help system. You navigate through categories by double-clicking book icons ( ) until reaching the desired help topic ( ). Notice in Figure 1.8 that there are three different types of icons displayed:<br>represents a help category; double-click a book icon to view the books and topics it contains<br>represents an open category that is currently displaying its contents; double-click an open book icon to close (or collapse) the book<br>represents a help topic; double-click a topic icon to display a help window |
| Index tab | Displays an alphabetical list of keywords and phrases, similar to a traditional book index. To search for a topic using this tab, you type a word (or even a few letters) into the text box which, in turn, makes the list box scroll to the first matching entry in the index. When the desired entry appears in the list box, double-click it to display the help topic. If a keyword has more than one associated topic, a Topics Found window appears and you can select a further topic to narrow your search. |
| Find tab | Provides the ability to conduct a full-text search of the Help system for finding a particular word or phrase. Although similar to the Index tab, this tab differs in its ability to look past indexed keywords and search the help text itself. |
| Answer Wizard tab | Provides the ability to conduct a search using an English phrase entered in the form of a question. For example, you can type "How do I print a chart?" and then click the Search command button to display suggested help topics. The resulting topics are organized under three headings in the Answer Wizard's list box, as follows:<br>• "How Do I" section lists topics that provide step-by-step help<br>• "Tell Me About" section lists topics that provide textual and visual explanations<br>• "Programming and Language Reference" section lists topics that provide detailed help for Visual Basic for Applications |

When you double-click a help topic, it is displayed in a *secondary* window. You may find that secondary windows include some unfamiliar buttons, like [»] and [↖], embedded in the help text. The [»] symbol, which we'll call the Chiclet button, represents a "See Also" link that you can click to move to a related help topic. You may also notice that some words or phrases in the help window have a dotted underline. If you click such a word or phrase, a definition pop-up window appears.

Perform the following steps to access the Help Topics window.

1. To access the Help Topics window:
   CHOOSE: Help, Microsoft Excel Help Topics
   (*Note:* Rather than choosing the menu command, you can also double-click the Help button ([?]) to display the Help Topics window.)
2. CLICK: Contents tab
   Your screen should now appear similar to Figure 1.8, except that your book categories will appear collapsed. (*Note:* The Help Topics window remembers the tab that was selected when it was last closed. It will automatically return to this tab the next time you access the Help system. For example, if you close the Help Topics window with the Index tab active, it will again appear active the next time you display the window.)
3. To display the contents of a book:
   DOUBLE-CLICK: "Entering, Selecting, and Editing Data" book
   (*Note:* You can double-click the book icon ( ) or the book's title. If you find it difficult to double-click using the mouse, you can also select or highlight the book by clicking it once and then click the Display command button.) This particular book contains one topic page and four additional book categories.
4. To further clarify the search:
   DOUBLE-CLICK: "Entering Data in a Worksheet" book
   Notice that this book contains multiple topics.
5. To display a help topic:
   DOUBLE-CLICK: "[?] Entering text" topic
   The Help Topics window is removed from view and a secondary window appears with the topic information.
6. To print the help topic:
   RIGHT-CLICK: anywhere in the help text of the secondary window
   CHOOSE: Print Topic (as shown in Figure 1.9)
   (*Note:* You can also print help information directly from the Contents tab. If you select a book by clicking on it once and then click the Print command button, the entire book—including the additional book categories that may be contained within the book—is sent to the printer. If you select an individual topic and click Print in the Help Topics window, only the highlighted topic is sent to the printer.)

**FIGURE 1.9** DISPLAYING A HELP TOPIC AND A SHORTCUT MENU

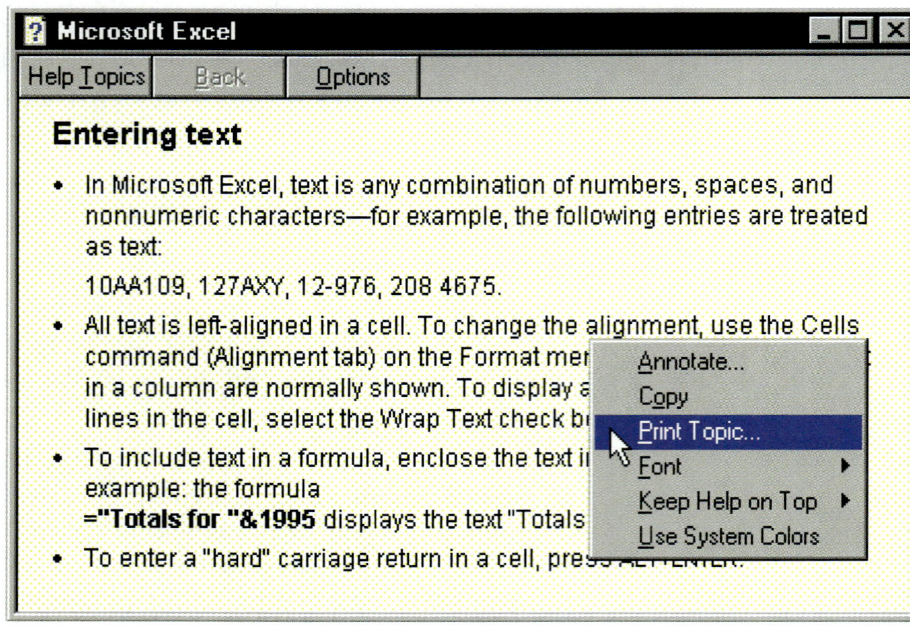


7. In the Print dialog box that appears:
   - CLICK: OK command button to print the topic, or
   - CLICK: Cancel command button if you do not have a printer

   Whatever your selection, you are returned to the secondary window. (*Note:* If you selected to print the topic and your computer does not have a printer connected, you may be returned to Excel with an error message. In this case, double-click the Help button ( ) to redisplay the Help Topics window and then proceed to Step 10.)

8. To close the secondary window and return to the Help Topics window:
   CLICK: Help Topics button (immediately under the Title bar)

9. To close the current book:
   CLICK: on the vertical scroll bar repeatedly
   DOUBLE-CLICK: " Entering, Selecting, and Editing Data" book
   Notice that the list of books and topics is collapsed under the book icon.

10. Let's search for some information using the keyword index:
    CLICK: Index tab

11. To find the topics related to formatting a worksheet:
    TYPE: **formatting**
    The list automatically scrolls to display the first occurrence of the word "formatting."

12. To display one of the sub-topics under the "formatting" heading:
    DOUBLE-CLICK: autoformats
    Notice that a new window appears called the Topics Found dialog box.

Your screen should now appear similar to Figure 1.10.

FIGURE 1.10 INDEX TAB AND THE TOPICS FOUND DIALOG BOX

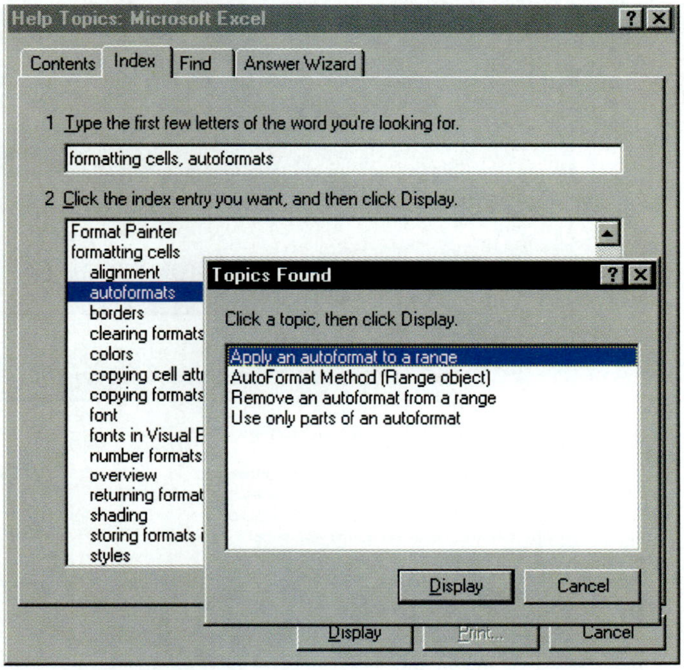


13. DOUBLE-CLICK: "Apply an autoformat to a range" topic
    A secondary window appears with help information.
14. You may have noticed that there are two terms in this secondary window that appear with a dotted underline. To view one of these definition terms, do the following:
    CLICK: "autoformat" with the hand mouse pointer (☝)
    A pop-up window appears with a definition.
15. After reading the help text, remove the definition pop-up window:
    CLICK: the pop-up window once
16. To return to the Help Topics window:
    CLICK: Help Topics button
17. To perform a search using the Answer Wizard:
    CLICK: Answer Wizard tab
18. In the Answer Wizard, you type the request just as you would ask the question out loud. For this example, let's find out what a "function" is in an Excel worksheet. Do the following:
    TYPE: **What is a function?**
    (*Note:* You need not be concerned about typing your questions using perfect grammar and punctuation.)

19. To display the results:
    CLICK: Search command button
    Notice that the resulting topics are organized under three headings: *How Do I, Tell Me About,* and *Programming and Language Reference.* Your screen should appear similar to Figure 1.11.

**FIGURE 1.11** RESULTS OF A SEARCH USING THE ANSWER WIZARD

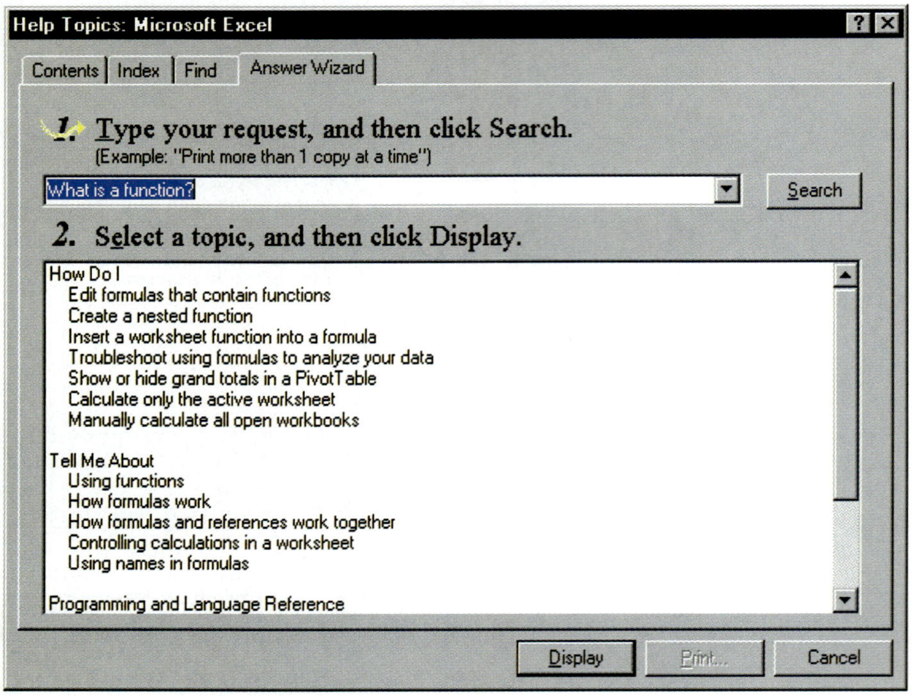


20. Rather than viewing another topic in a secondary window, let's close the Microsoft Excel Help system. To do so:
    CLICK: Cancel command button (in the lower right-hand corner)
    The Help Topics window is removed. *(Remember:* The next time you open the Help Topics window, the Answer Wizard tab will be selected.)

**QUICK REFERENCE**
Searching for Help Using the Help Topics Window

1. **To display the Help Topics window:**
   **DOUBLE-CLICK: Help button (?), or**
   **CHOOSE: Help, Microsoft Excel Help Topics**
2. **CLICK: Contents tab to navigate a hierarchical Help system**
   **CLICK: Index tab to search for a word or phrase in a keyword index**
   **CLICK: Find tab to conduct a full-text search of the Help system**
   **CLICK: Answer Wizard tab to enter your search request using phrases and sentences**

## MOVING THE CELL POINTER

When you first open a new workbook, the **cell pointer** is positioned on cell A1 in Sheet1. For your convenience, Excel displays the current cell address in the Name box at the left-hand side of the Formula bar. In this section, you learn how to move the cell pointer around the worksheet using the mouse and keyboard. Although rudimentary, these skills are vital for efficiently creating and viewing worksheets.

Perform the following steps, starting at cell A1.

1. To move the cell pointer to cell G4 using the keyboard:
   PRESS: → six times
   PRESS: ↓ three times
   Notice that the cell address appears in the Name box.
2. To move to cell E12 using a mouse:
   CLICK: cell E12
   (*Hint:* Position the cross mouse pointer over cell E12 and click the left mouse button once.)
3. To move to cell E24 using the keyboard:
   PRESS: ↓ 12 times
   You may notice that the first few rows scroll off the top of the screen.
4. To move to cell E124 using the keyboard, there is an easier method than pressing the ↓ key 100 times. The PgUp and PgDn keys are used to move up and down a worksheet by as many rows as fit in the current document window. In other words, if the document window displays 15 rows of your worksheet, pressing PgDn will move you down 15 rows at a time. To move to cell E124, do the following:
   PRESS: PgDn until cell E124 is in view
   PRESS: ↑ or ↓ arrow keys to move to cell E124
5. To move back to cell E24 using the mouse:
   CLICK: ▲ on the vertical scroll bar and hold down the left mouse button
   CLICK: cell E24 when it appears after scrolling
   (*Note:* You can also drag the scroll box (□) on the vertical scroll bar.)
6. To move to cell AE24:
   CLICK: ▶ on the horizontal scroll bar and hold down the left mouse button
   CLICK: cell AE24 to move the cell pointer
7. To move back to cell E24:
   DRAG: scroll box (□) to the left on the horizontal scroll bar
   Notice that a Scroll Tip appears showing the column letter as you drag the mouse. When you see "Column: E" in the Scroll Tip, stop dragging and proceed to Step 8.

8. CLICK: cell E24 to move the cell pointer
9. To move to the first cell (A1) in the worksheet using the keyboard:
   PRESS: CTRL + HOME
10. To move the cell pointer in any direction until the cell contents change from empty to filled, filled to empty, or until a border is encountered, press CTRL with an arrow key. To move to column IV:
    PRESS: CTRL + →
11. To move to row 16,384 (the last cell at the bottom of the worksheet):
    PRESS: CTRL + ↓
12. You can also use the Name box to move directly to any cell in the worksheet. To move to cell AA100, for example:
    CLICK: Name box
    The cell address in the Name box will appear highlighted.
13. TYPE: **aa100**
    PRESS: ENTER
    You are taken immediately to cell AA100.
14. To move back to cell A1:
    PRESS: CTRL + HOME

## OVERVIEW OF DATA ENTRY

You create a worksheet by entering information into the individual cells. A worksheet can be as simple as a five-item household budget or as complex as an order entry and invoicing application. The remainder of this session explores the basic building blocks for creating a worksheet from scratch using Excel, including entering, editing, and deleting cell information.

There are several types of information that may be entered into a worksheet cell: text, numbers, dates and times, formulas, and functions. Regardless of the type of information, you enter data by moving the cell pointer to a cell and then typing what you want to place into the cell. The information that you type appears in Excel's Formula bar. To transfer the information from the Formula bar into the cell, you press ENTER or an arrow key. You can also click on another cell using the mouse or click the ✓ button in the Formula bar.

To practice entering information, you will create the worksheet appearing in Figure 1.12 by the completion of this section.

FIGURE 1.12 SAMPLE WORKSHEET

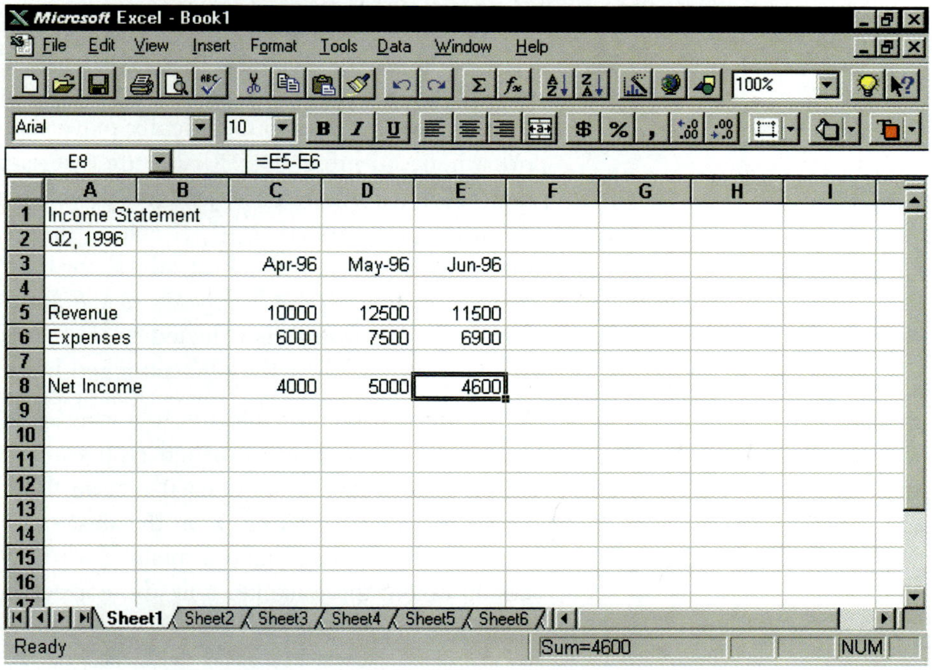


## ENTERING TEXT

Text labels enhance the readability of a worksheet with headings, instructions, and descriptive information. Although a typical worksheet column is only eight or nine characters wide, a single cell in a worksheet can hold hundreds of characters. With longer entries, the text spills over into the next cell, if it is empty. Later, you will learn how to emphasize important text using different fonts and alignment options.

To begin creating the worksheet, perform the following steps.

1. Move to cell A1. (*Hint:* CTRL + HOME)
   For the remainder of this guide, you can use either the keyboard or mouse to move the cell pointer.

2. As you type the following text, watch the Formula bar. Enter the following heading for the worksheet:
   TYPE: **Income Statement**
   Notice that there is an ☒ and a ☑ to the left of the text in the Formula bar. Rather than pressing ENTER to accept the entry or ESC to cancel the entry, you can click the ☑ and ☒ symbols respectively.

3. To accept the entry and deposit it into the current cell:
   PRESS: ENTER
   Notice that the words do not fit in a single cell and must spill over into column B. This is acceptable as long as you do not want to place any information into cell B1. Otherwise, you would have to increase the width of column A. Session 2 discusses changing a column's width.
   (*Note:* Excel 7.0 can automatically move the cell pointer down to the next row when you press ENTER. For the exercises in this guide, we assume that you have this feature selected. If your cell pointer did not move to A2 when you pressed ENTER, choose the Tools, Options command from the menu and select the Edit tab. From the resulting dialog box page, make sure that an "X" appears in the *Move Selection after Enter* check box and that "Down" is selected in the *Direction* drop-down list box. When finished, click the OK command button.)

4. Move the cell pointer into the following cells and type in the corresponding text. When you are finished typing a label, you press ENTER or a cursor-movement key to deposit it from the Formula bar to the active cell. Using the mouse, you click on the next cell after you have finished typing the label. If you make a mistake while typing, press the BACKSPACE key to delete the mistake, type the correct information, and then press ENTER.

   Enter the following text:

| *Move to Cell* | *Type* |
|---|---|
| A2 | **Q2, 1996** |
| A5 | **Revenue** |
| A6 | **Expenses** |
| A8 | **Net Income** |

All the text data has now been entered into the worksheet.

## ENTERING DATES

You enter dates as values in order to perform date arithmetic, such as calculating how many days have elapsed between two dates. Dates are typically entered into cells using the following formats: mm/dd/yy (for example, 12/31/96) or dd-mmm-yy (for example, 31-Dec-96). If you need to display monthly headings across the top of a column, you can enter a date as mmm-yy (for example, Dec-96). Although dates can be displayed in a variety of formats, Excel stores each date internally as the number of days elapsing since January 1, 1900.

Perform the following steps to enter dates into the worksheet.

1. Move to cell C3.
2. TYPE: **Apr-96**
   PRESS: ➔
3. Move the cell pointer into the following cells and type in the corresponding dates:

| *Move to Cell* | *Type* |
|---|---|
| D3 | **May-96** |
| E3 | **Jun-96** |

With the cell pointer positioned on cell E3, you will notice that the Formula bar contains 6/1/1996. This is one example of the difference between the appearance of a cell and its actual contents. You will encounter other examples later in this session.

All the dates have now been entered into the worksheet.

## ENTERING NUMBERS

Numbers are entered into the worksheet for use in formulas and reports. Whereas text is initially left-aligned with the cell border, numbers and dates are right-aligned. When the cell pointer is positioned on a cell that contains a number, the raw form of the number usually appears in the Formula bar. In other words, the cell may read 8.50% in the worksheet but the value in the Formula bar reads .085. Phone numbers, Social Security numbers, and zip codes are not considered numeric values, since they are never used in mathematical calculations.

Perform the following steps.

1. Move to cell C5.
2. TYPE: **10000**
   PRESS: ➔

3. Move the cell pointer into the following cells and type in the corresponding numbers:

| *Move to Cell* | *Type* |
|---|---|
| D5 | **12500** |
| E5 | **11500** |

All the numeric data has now been entered into the worksheet. You are ready to enter formulas to calculate the remaining values.

**QUICK REFERENCE**
Entering Data

1. **Move the cell pointer to the desired cell location.**
2. **Type the information into the Formula bar. If you make a typing or spelling mistake, press the BACKSPACE key to erase the mistake.**
3. **To deposit the information into the cell, press ENTER or an arrow key, or click on a new cell using the mouse.**

## ENTERING FORMULAS

A formula is a mathematical calculation that may contain numbers, cell references, and mathematical operators. The basic mathematical operators and rules of precedence apply to an Excel formula. These operators are similar to those found in most electronic spreadsheets (and high school algebra textbooks). For example, in the formula $(3+4)*5$, the $3+4$ operation is performed before multiplying the sum by 5 because it appears in parentheses. Table 1.3 lists the common mathematical operators. As for the rules of precedence, Excel calculates what appears in parentheses first, multiplication and division operations (from left to right) second, and, lastly, addition and subtraction (again from left to right).

**TABLE 1.3**
Basic Mathematical Operators

| | *Symbol* | *Description* |
|---|---|---|
| | ( ) | Parentheses |
| | * | Multiplication |
| | / | Division |
| | + | Addition |
| | − | Subtraction |
| *Additional Operators* | % | Percentage |
| | ^ | Exponentiation |

You enter a formula into the worksheet by positioning the cell pointer where you want the result to appear and then preceding the expression with an equal sign (=). The expression itself can be entered either by typing the equation or by using a method called pointing. With pointing, you use the keyboard or mouse to point to or select cell addresses while constructing the formula.

In this exercise, you enter a formula that calculates Expenses as 60% of Revenue. Your first step is to move the cell pointer to where you want the result to appear and then enter the formula into the cell.

Perform the following steps.

1. Move to cell C6.
2. TYPE: **=c5*60%**
   PRESS: →
   In this expression, "c5" represents the cell address in the worksheet.
3. Move the cell pointer into the following cells and type in the corresponding formulas.

| *Move to Cell* | *Type* |
|---|---|
| D6 | **=d5*60%** |
| E6 | **=e5*60%** |

4. Let's create a second formula to subtract Expenses from Revenue, yielding Net Income. When constructing the formula, glance at the Formula bar to see the results of your mouse clicks and keystrokes. To begin:
   CLICK: cell C8
5. In this step, you build a formula by pointing using the mouse:
   TYPE: =
   CLICK: cell C5
   TYPE: −
   CLICK: cell C6
   CLICK: ✓ in the Formula bar
   The answer 4000 should now appear in the cell.
6. Repeat the process for cells D8 and E8. Your worksheet should now appear similar to Figure 1.12.

**QUICK REFERENCE**
Entering a Formula

1. **Select the cell to contain the formula.**
2. **TYPE: = (an equal sign)**
3. **Enter the desired expression (for example, A4+B4) by typing or by pointing to the cells using the mouse.**
4. **PRESS: ENTER or CLICK: ✓ in the Formula bar**

# EDITING A CELL

What if you type a label, a number, or a formula into a cell and then decide it needs to be changed? Novices and experts alike make data entry errors when creating a worksheet. Fortunately, Excel provides several options for editing information that has already been entered.

The primary methods for editing information are these:

- Before you press ENTER or click on another cell to deposit an entry, you can correct a typing or spelling mistake using BACKSPACE.
- You can replace a cell's contents by selecting the cell and typing a new entry. When you press ENTER or click on another cell, the new information replaces the original cell's contents.
- If a cell's entry is too long or complicated to re-type, you can edit the entry by double-clicking the cell or by selecting the cell and pressing F2. A flashing vertical bar appears in the cell, advising you that the entry may be modified. After making the necessary changes, you press ENTER to overwrite the original cell or ESC to abort the modifications.
- You can also select a cell and then move the mouse pointer into the Formula bar area until it changes into an I-beam. At this point, click the left mouse button once to begin editing the contents of the Formula bar. Clicking ✓ performs the same function as pressing ENTER and clicking ✗ performs the same function as pressing ESC.

Practice editing information in the worksheet.

1. CLICK: cell A1
2. TYPE: **Profit/Loss Report**
   PRESS: ENTER
3. To modify the entry in cell A2 to read "Quarter 2" instead of "Q2":
   DOUBLE-CLICK: cell A2
   (*Note:* You can also press F2 to enter Edit mode.)
4. Using the ← and → keys or the mouse, position the flashing vertical bar between the "Q" and the "2".
5. TYPE: **uarter**
   PRESS: Space bar
   PRESS: ENTER
6. DOUBLE-CLICK: cell A5
7. To change the word "Revenue" to "Sales":
   DOUBLE-CLICK: Revenue (using the I-beam mouse pointer)

8. TYPE: Sales
PRESS: ENTER or CLICK: ✓
Notice that the word "Revenue" is replaced with "Sales."

**QUICK REFERENCE**
Editing a Cell's Contents

1. **DOUBLE-CLICK: the cell that you want to edit (or PRESS: F2)**
2. **Use the mouse and arrow keys to edit the entry.**
3. **PRESS: ENTER or CLICK: ✓**

## ERASING A CELL

Excel allows you to quickly erase a single cell, a group of cells, or the entire worksheet with a few simple keystrokes. To erase a cell's contents, highlight the cell and press the DELETE key. If you would like to delete only the formatting of a cell, you choose Edit, Clear from the Menu bar to display further commands (listed in Table 1.4) on a cascading menu.

**TABLE 1.4**
Edit, Clear Commands

| *Command* | *Description* |
|---|---|
| All | Removes the cell contents, formatting (for example, boldface and italic), and notes (reminders that can be attached to a cell that do not appear when printed). |
| Formats | Removes the cell formatting only, leaving the contents and attached cell notes intact. |
| Contents | Removes the cell contents only, leaving the formatting and attached cell notes intact; same as DELETE. |
| Notes | Removes the cell notes only, leaving the cell contents and formatting intact. |

In the next exercise, you practice erasing information from the worksheet.

1. Move to cell A2.
2. PRESS: DELETE to remove the information from the cell
3. Move to cell A8.
4. CHOOSE: Edit, Clear
   CHOOSE: All from the cascading menu
   Do not perform another command until proceeding to the next section, where you learn how to undo a command.

**QUICK REFERENCE**
Erasing a Cell

1. **SELECT: the cell that you want to erase**
2. **PRESS: DELETE**

## USING THE UNDO COMMAND

The **Undo command** allows you to cancel the last command you performed in the worksheet. There are three methods for executing the Undo command. You can choose Edit, Undo from the menu, press the keyboard shortcut of CTRL + z, or click the Undo button () on the Standard toolbar. Let's practice two of these methods in the next exercise.

Perform the following steps.

1. To undo the last command that you executed in the previous section:
   CLICK: Undo button ()
   The words "Net Income" reappear in the worksheet.
2. SELECT: cell A1
3. PRESS: DELETE
4. To undo the command executed in the last step:
   PRESS: CTRL + z
   The title should reappear on the worksheet.

**QUICK REFERENCE**
Undo a Command

- **CHOOSE: Edit, Undo, or**
- **PRESS: CTRL + z, or**
- **CLICK: Undo button () on the Standard toolbar**

## SAVING, CLOSING, AND OPENING WORKBOOKS

When you are creating a workbook, it exists only in the computer's RAM (random access memory), which is highly volatile.[3] To permanently store your work, you must save the workbook to the hard disk or to a floppy diskette. Saving your work to a disk is similar to placing it into a filing cabinet. For important workbooks (ones that you cannot risk losing), you should save your work every 15 minutes, or whenever you're interrupted, to protect against an unexpected power outage or other catastrophe.

---

[3] RAM is wiped clean when you turn off the computer or experience a power failure.

To save a workbook to a disk, click the Save button () on the Standard toolbar or select the File, Save command from the menu. If you haven't saved the document before, a dialog box appears with a suggested filename. You can either accept the suggested filename or type in a new name. When naming a file for use with Windows 95, you can use up to 255 characters, including spaces. You can't use the following characters in filenames:

\ / : * ? " < > |

When you are finished typing the filename, press **ENTER** or click the Save command button. As the workbook is being written to the disk, a series of boxes appears in the Status bar indicating its progress.

Perform the following steps to save the current workbook.

1. Make sure that the Advantage Diskette is placed in the diskette drive.
2. CLICK: Save button ()
   Excel displays a dialog box similar to the one shown in Figure 1.13; the filenames and directories may differ from your dialog box.

**FIGURE 1.13** SAVE AS DIALOG BOX

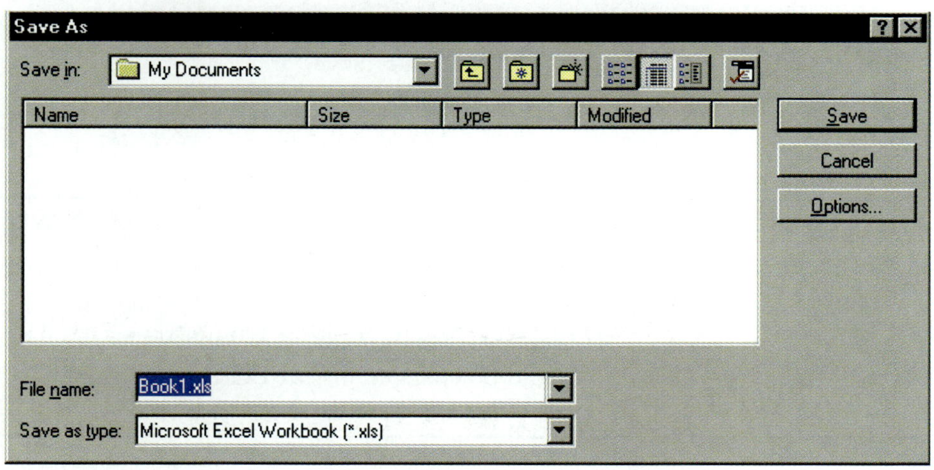


3. To specify a filename for the workbook:
   TYPE: **My First Workbook**
4. To specify that the workbook be saved onto the Advantage Diskette:
   CLICK: down arrow beside the *Save in* drop-down list box
   SELECT: 3½ Floppy (A:)
   If your Advantage Diskette is located in drive B:, select "3½ Floppy (B:)" in this step.

5. To proceed with saving the workbook:
   PRESS: ENTER or CLICK: Save command button

6. When you are finished working with a workbook, you should close the file to free up valuable RAM. To close the "My First Workbook" file:
   CHOOSE: File, Close
   (*Note:* You can also close a workbook by clicking its Close button (☒). If, however, you click the Close button for the application window by mistake, Excel will close.)

7. To open a new workbook:
   CLICK: New Workbook button (🗋)
   (*Note:* You can also choose File, New from the menu and then double-click the blank Workbook template icon (icon) to load a new workbook.)

There are times when you'll want to save an existing workbook under a different filename. For example, you may want to keep different versions of the same workbook on your disk. Or, you may want to use one workbook as a template for future workbooks that are similar in style and format. Rather than retyping an entirely new workbook, you can retrieve an old workbook file, edit the information, and then save it under a different name using the File, Save As command. If you want to replace the old file instead, choose File, Save or click the Save button (💾).

**QUICK REFERENCE**
Saving a File

- **CLICK: Save button (💾), or**
- **CHOOSE: File, Save, or**
- **CHOOSE: File, Save As**

**IN ADDITION**

USING LONG FILENAMES IN DOS (AND WINDOWS 3.1)

Because DOS can't understand filenames that are longer than eight characters, it changes a Windows 95 filename when it tries to use a file with a long filename. For example, the Windows 95 filename "Multitasking Document" would be changed to "MULTIT~1.DOC" in DOS or when saved to a network drive that did not support long filenames.

**QUICK REFERENCE**
Closing a File

- **CHOOSE: File, Close, or**
- **CLICK: Close button (☒)**

**QUICK REFERENCE**
Opening a New Workbook

- **CLICK: New Workbook button (🗋), or**
- **CHOOSE: File, New**
  **DOUBLE-CLICK: Workbook template icon (icon)**

Now that your workbook is stored in this electronic filing cabinet called a disk, how do you retrieve it for editing? To modify or print an existing workbook, click the Open button () on the Standard toolbar or choose File, Open from the Menu bar. Once the Open dialog box appears, you select the file's location by clicking in the *Look in* drop-down list box. You then double-click the workbook's name appearing in the file list.

Perform the following steps.

1. Ensure that the Advantage Diskette is placed in the diskette drive.
2. To practice using the Open dialog box:
   CLICK: Open button () on the Standard toolbar
3. To view the files on the Advantage Diskette:
   CLICK: down arrow beside the *Look in* drop-down list box
   SELECT: 3½ Floppy (where the Advantage Diskette is located)
   Your screen should now appear similar to Figure 1.14.

**FIGURE 1.14** OPEN DIALOG BOX

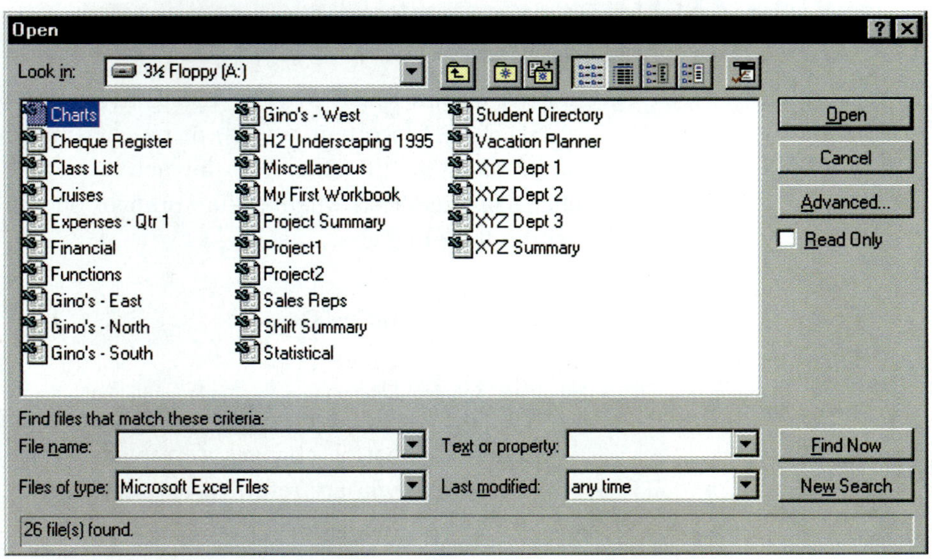


4. To change the display in the Open dialog box, try the following:
   CLICK: Detail button () to see each workbook's file size and last modification date
   CLICK: Properties button () to see summary information for the selected workbook
   CLICK: Preview button () to see a preview of the selected workbook
   CLICK: List button () to see workbook icons and names in a multiple-column format

5. Let's open our workbook:
   DOUBLE-CLICK: My First Workbook
   The workbook is loaded into Excel's application window.

**QUICK REFERENCE**
Opening a Workbook

1. **CLICK: Open button ( ), or**
   **CHOOSE: File, Open from the Menu bar**
2. **CLICK: down arrow beside the *Look in* drop-down list box**
3. **SELECT: a file location**
4. **DOUBLE-CLICK: the desired workbook**

**IN ADDITION**

OPENING A WORKBOOK FROM THE WINDOWS DESKTOP

From the Windows 95 desktop, you can open a workbook that you've worked with recently. Click the Start button on the taskbar and then choose the Documents command. Then, choose the document's name from the cascading menu. The application you used to create the document loads automatically.

## LEAVING EXCEL

When you are finished using Excel, save your work and exit the program by clicking the Close button ( ) or by choosing the File, Exit command. If you have made modifications to the active worksheet and have not saved the changes, Excel asks whether the workbook should be saved or abandoned before exiting the program.

Perform the following steps.

1. To exit Excel:
   CLICK: Close button ( ) of the Excel application window
   Assuming that no changes were made to the workbook, the application is closed and you are returned to the Windows desktop.
2. To exit Windows 95:
   CHOOSE: Start, Shut Down
   SELECT: *Shutdown the computer?* option button
   CLICK: Yes command button

**QUICK REFERENCE**
Exiting Excel

**CLICK: Close button ( ), of the Excel application window or**
**CHOOSE: File, Exit**

## SUMMARY

This session introduced you to working with spreadsheet programs, specifically Microsoft Excel 7.0 for Windows 95. We began the session exploring the advantages of electronic spreadsheets over manual worksheets, comparing the size of work areas and the speeds at which calculations and corrections are performed. The importance of planning the construction of a spreadsheet was also emphasized.

After you loaded Windows 95 and Excel, this session presented an overview of Excel's major components, including the application and document windows. As well, you were introduced to data entry techniques for entering text, numbers, and formulas into the worksheet cells. Because even experts require some assistance now and then, this session also demonstrated Excel's Help system.

For easy reference, many of the commands and procedures appearing in this session are provided in Table 1.5, the Command Summary.

**TABLE 1.5**

Command Summary

| *Command* | *Description* |
|---|---|
| Edit, Clear | Erases the contents and formatting of a cell. |
| Edit, Undo (↶) | Reverses the last commands executed. |
| File, Close | Closes a workbook file. |
| File, Exit (or ☒) | Leaves Excel. |
| File, New (🗋) | Creates a new workbook file. |
| File, Open (📂) | Opens an existing workbook file. |
| File, Save (💾) | Saves a workbook file to the disk. |
| File, Save As | Saves a workbook file, specifying the filename. |
| Help, Microsoft Excel Help Topics | Displays the Help Topics window. |

## KEY TERMS

**application window**
In Microsoft Windows, each running application program appears in its own application window. These windows can be sized and moved anywhere on the Windows desktop.

**cell**

In a spreadsheet program, this marks the intersection of a column and a row.

**cell address**

The location of a cell on a spreadsheet given by the intersection of a column and a row. Columns are usually labeled using letters. Rows are numbered. A cell address combines the column letter with the row number (for example, B9 or DF134).

**cell pointer**

The cursor on a spreadsheet that points to a cell. The cell pointer is moved using the arrow keys or the mouse.

**context-sensitive help**

A pop-up window that provides concise help information for a particular menu option, toolbar button, or dialog box item.

**document window**

In Microsoft Excel, each open workbook file appears in its own document window. These windows can be sized and moved anywhere within the Excel application window.

**formulas**

Mathematical expressions that define the relationships among various cells in an electronic spreadsheet.

**multitasking**

Activity in which more than one task or program is executed at a time. A small amount of each program is processed, and then the CPU moves to the remaining programs, one at a time, processing small parts of each.

**Undo command**

In a software application program, a command that makes it possible to reverse the last command executed.

**what-if analysis**

Also called *scenario analysis.* The ability to change the values of independent variables and immediately see the effects of those changes on dependent formulas or calculations.

**workbook**

The Excel file where you create your work. A workbook appears in a document window and may contain worksheets, chart sheets, and programming modules (also called macro sheets).

**WYSIWYG**

Acronym for *What You See Is What You Get.* Page description software that allows the user to see the final version of a document on the screen before it is printed out.

# EXERCISES

## SHORT ANSWER

1. What is the procedure for loading Microsoft Excel?
2. What is a cell? a cell address?
3. What advantages do electronic spreadsheets have over manual worksheets?
4. Explain the term *context-sensitive help.*
5. How do you reverse the last command executed?
6. Describe the different methods for moving around the worksheet.
7. What is a toolbar? How is it accessed?
8. What is the significance of an ellipsis (...) after a menu option?
9. What is a formula? Provide an example.
10. What must you type first to inform Excel that you are entering a formula?

## HANDS-ON

1. This exercise produces a worksheet to help manage your personal credit card balances and limits. The tasks include entering text and numbers and then editing data.

   *a.* Load Windows and Excel to begin working with a new workbook.

   *b.* Move the cell pointer to the following cells: (a) A21, (b) K50, (c) IV50, (d) IV16384, (e) AA1000, (f) A1

   *c.* With your cell pointer in cell A1:
   TYPE: **PERSONAL FINANCIAL PLANNER**
   PRESS: ENTER

   *d.* Enter the following text labels:

| *Move to Cell* | *Type* |
|---|---|
| C3 | **Budget** |
| D3 | **Actual** |
| A6 | **VISA** |
| A7 | **Chevron** |
| A8 | **AMEX** |
| A9 | **M/C** |

*e.* Enter the following numbers:

| *Move to Cell* | *Type* |
|---|---|
| C6 | **1200** |
| C7 | **500** |
| C8 | **200** |
| C9 | **75** |
| D6 | **1200** |
| D7 | **450** |
| D8 | **215** |
| D9 | **135** |

*f.* Change the label in cell A6 from "VISA" to "Discover" by typing over the existing entry.

*g.* Change the label in cell A8 from "AMEX" to "AMEX Gold" using the mouse to edit the text in the cell.

*h.* Change the label in cell A9 from "M/C" to "Mastercard."

*i.* Change the budgeted value for Chevron in cell C7 to 400.

*j.* Reverse the change in the last step using the Undo button ( ).

*k.* Change the Actual value for AMEX Gold in cell D8 to 210.

*l.* Reverse the change in the last step by pressing CTRL + **z**.

2. This exercise uses the same worksheet to practice entering formulas.

*a.* Move to cell A11.

*b.* TYPE: **Total Balances**

*c.* Move to cell C11. Enter a formula that adds the Budget values in column C by typing the formula.

*d.* Move to cell D11. Enter a formula that adds the Actual values in column D by pointing to the cell references using the mouse.

*e.* Move to cell E3.

*f.* TYPE: **Variance**

*g.* In cell E6, enter a formula to subtract the actual Discover card balance from the budgeted value.

*h.* In cell E7, enter a formula to subtract the actual Chevron balance from the budgeted value.

*i.* Enter formulas to calculate the variance for the remaining cards.

*j.* Enter a formula to calculate the variance for the Total Balances.

*k.* Save the workbook as "My Financial Plan" onto the Advantage Diskette. Your worksheet should now appear similar to Figure 1.15.

*l.* Exit Excel.

**FIGURE 1.15** "MY FINANCIAL PLAN" WORKBOOK

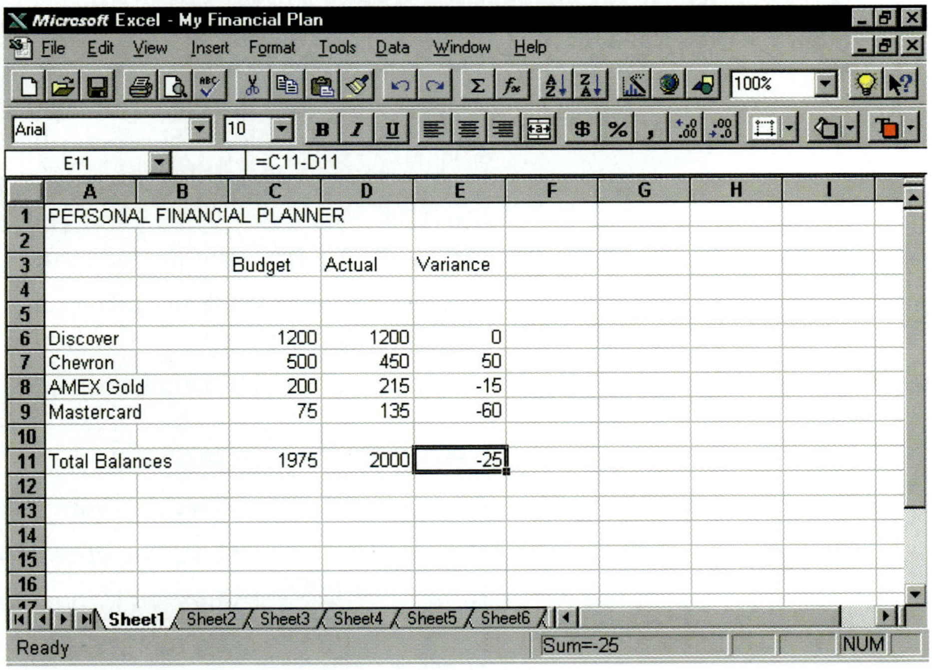


## CASE PROBLEMS THE BONDABLE GROUP

(*Note:* In the following case problems, assume the role of the primary characters and perform the same steps that they identify. You may want to re-read the session opening.)

1. Realizing that Pancho and Mackenzie need some help getting started on their spreadsheet, Jennifer calls a meeting for that afternoon. At 3:00 P.M. precisely, the three friends congregate in the boardroom around a small oval table. "Okay, let's review what our objectives are," Jennifer says, opening the meeting with her usual sentence. "First, we want to develop a spreadsheet that we can show to clients on the screen to help them better understand financial planning concepts. Second, we want to develop a single template that we can re-use for all of our clients. Is everyone with me so far?" The two gentlemen nod in agreement as Jennifer writes down the points on a flip chart. "Great, now let's brainstorm

about what information we want to include." After more than an hour, the three partners emerge from the boardroom with a list of features that they want to appear in the spreadsheet.

The following list is a summary of the points written on the flip chart during the partners' afternoon meeting. Your job is to implement these points in an Excel spreadsheet.

- Enter the title of the worksheet "Your Guide to Financial Planning Success," in the top left-hand corner (cell A1).
- Enter the company's name, "The Bondable Group," immediately below the title of the worksheet.
- Leaving two blank lines after the company's name, enter the text label "Five Principles of Successful Investing:" in column A.
- Below this title, enter each of the five principles on a separate row: (1) Establish your goals. (2) Start early. (3) Make saving part of your regular routine. (4) Invest for the long term. (5) Diversify your portfolio.
- Leaving two more blank lines, enter the text label "Scoring Your Investment Objectives:"
- Below this title, enter the following information in columns A and B:

| POINTS | QUESTION |
|---|---|
| | What is your age? |
| | What is your income? |
| | When will you need the money? |
| | How much risk can you take? |
| | TOTAL SCORE |

- Save the worksheet as "Bondable Plan" onto the Advantage Diskette.

2. On Friday morning, Pancho and Mackenzie receive their new notebook computers and immediately launch Microsoft Excel. They are very pleased with their new toys and don't even try to suppress their grins as they click away at the keyboards. "Hey Pancho, I've got a client meeting with Garrett Buggey before lunch. I'll try out the "Bondable Plan" workbook and let you know how it works." Pancho thanks Mackenzie and scurries from the office to make his own appointments.

   Mackenzie arrives early at Garrett's office and is led to a small meeting room. While waiting for his client, Mackenzie opens the notebook computer and loads the "Bondable Plan" workbook. "Hiya Mac!" Garrett calls as he enters the room. "Hey, that's a nice system you've got there. When did you get it?" Mackenzie explains that the computer had arrived that morning and that he wants to show Garrett a new spreadsheet. Based on his personal information and a point-scoring system developed by Jennifer, Mackenzie enters the following information into the spreadsheet:

| POINTS | QUESTION |
|---|---|
| 5500 | What is your age? |
| 4320 | What is your income? |
| 1745 | When will you need the money? |
| 7500 | How much risk can you take? |
| | TOTAL SCORE |

After he enters the numbers into the spreadsheet, Mackenzie realizes that they forgot to create a formula for the TOTAL SCORE line. This is the most important figure in the entire spreadsheet! Fortunately, Mackenzie remembers how to total a column of numbers using an addition formula. With the total score displaying in the worksheet, Garrett changes his mind on how much risk he is prepared to take in his investments. Mackenzie changes the point score from 7500 to 6275, and they both watch as the TOTAL SCORE line changes instantaneously.

Perform the same steps Mackenzie did after loading the "Bondable Plan" workbook. Save the new worksheet as "Garrett Buggey" onto the Advantage Diskette.

3. Mackenzie returns to the office after a successful meeting with Garrett. After telling Pancho about the forgotten formula, they decide to review and revise the entire "Bondable Plan" workbook. Refer to the following list and implement the changes in your worksheet:

    - Edit the title "Your Guide to Financial Planning Success" to read "The Personal Guide to Financial Planning Success."
    - Add a sixth principle to the "Successful Investing" list called "(6) Make adjustments over time." Make sure that you edit this area's title, as well.
    - Edit the question about risk in the "Scoring Your Investment Objectives" area to read "How much risk do you want to take?"
    - Add a new area titled "Determining Your Asset Mix" to the spreadsheet, two lines below the "Scoring Your Investment Objectives" area. Enter the following information, in three columns, below this area's title.

| ANSWER | RESULT | QUESTION |
|---|---|---|
| | | What is your monthly salary? |
| | | (a) % of monthly salary for Investment |
| | | (b) % of investment for Savings |
| | | (c) % of investment for Income Funds |
| | | (d) % of investment for Growth Funds |

- Given that Pancho and Mackenzie will enter a client's information into the ANSWER column create formulas for the RESULT column that will provide calculation results similar to the following example. Ensure that items (b), (c), and (d) in the ANSWER column add up to 100%, and that the same items in the RESULT column add up to the RESULT for (a) (in this example, 500).

| ANSWER | RESULT | QUESTION |
|---|---|---|
| $5,000 | | What is your monthly salary? |
| 10% | 500 | (a) % of monthly salary for investment |
| 30% | 150 | (b) % of investment for Savings |
| 30% | 150 | (c) % of investment for Income Funds |
| 40% | 200 | (d) % of investment for Growth Funds |

- Practice using the new table by inputting several combinations of figures into the ANSWER column. Manually check that the calculations in the RESULTS column are correct.

Save the revised "Bondable Plan" workbook, updating the existing version that appears on the Advantage Diskette.

Microsoft Excel 7.0 for Windows 95

# *Working with Spreadsheets*

## SESSION OUTLINE



## INTRODUCTION

Spreadsheets may look complicated, but even a new user can begin to construct one in a short period of time. With Microsoft's new IntelliSense® technology, Excel now provides several "Auto" features that correct your spelling mistakes, format worksheet cells, and calculate formulas automatically. This session shows you how to set up a new spreadsheet, enter data efficiently, and use AutoCalculate, AutoComplete, AutoCorrect, and AutoFormat. Once your spreadsheet is created, you can easily modify it and use it over and over.

## CASE STUDY MADRID CLOTHING COMPANY

Suriya Amin opened the first mall location for the Madrid Clothing Company in 1988. Since then the company has expanded into six locations across the Pacific Northwest, from the Alderwood Mall near Seattle to the Pacific Center in Vancouver, British Columbia. The Madrid Clothing Company supplies European casual wear for a middle- to upper-class clientele.

Suriya's younger brother Khalid, who is also one of her store managers, wants to expand the operation into California. Realizing that Suriya would never accept a serious proposal from her younger brother, Khalid decides to create and submit an anonymous "what-if" spreadsheet that compares the worst-case and best-case scenarios for such an expansion. To ensure that she takes the proposal seriously, Khalid must strive to give the report a very professional appearance. To this end, he must learn how to format a worksheet in Microsoft Excel and how to print the report with headers and footers.

In this session, you and Khalid will improve your efficiency working with Excel. You will create, proof, customize, enhance, save, and then print a workbook. By the end of this session, you will know how to apply these skills to any workbook you create.

## CREATING A NEW WORKBOOK

When you first load Excel, an empty workbook called *Book1* appears in the document window. To create a new workbook, you simply enter information into the worksheets labeled from *Sheet1* to *Sheet16* and then save the workbook under a new filename. (*Note:* In Session 4, you learn how to add and delete sheets in a workbook.) If you've already entered information into *Book1* and want to create a new workbook, choose the File, New command or click the New Workbook button (▯) on the Standard toolbar. Because each workbook that you open consumes memory, you should save your work and close all unnecessary documents before creating a new workbook.

In the next two sections, you will create the worksheet shown in Figure 2.1. You will use this worksheet throughout the session to practice several spreadsheet procedures.

**FIGURE 2.1** THE SALES PROJECTIONS WORKSHEET

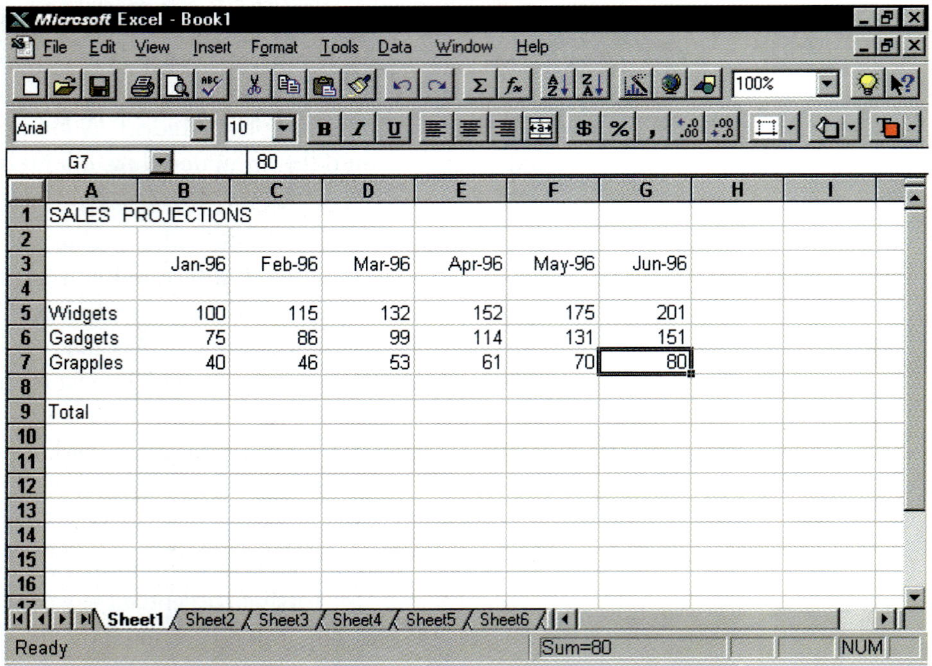


Perform the following steps.

1. Make sure that you've loaded Microsoft Excel and that a new worksheet appears in the document window. Enter the following text labels for headings on the worksheet:

| *Move to Cell* | *Type* |
|---|---|
| A1 | **SALES PROJECTIONS** |
| A5 | **Widgets** |
| A6 | **Gadgets** |
| A7 | **Grapples** |
| A9 | **Total** |

2. Enter the following dates as column headings:

| *Move to Cell* | *Type* |
|---|---|
| B3 | **Jan-96** |
| C3 | **Feb-96** |
| D3 | **Mar-96** |
| E3 | **Apr-96** |
| F3 | **May-96** |
| G3 | **Jun-96** |

Before entering the numeric values for the spreadsheet, proceed to the next section to learn about cell ranges.

## INTRODUCING CELL RANGES

In most Windows programs, you select objects and then perform commands to act on the objects, such as a copy or format operation. To enhance an Excel worksheet, for example, you select a cell or group of cells—called a **cell range**—and then choose a formatting command. After executing the command, Excel leaves the selected range highlighted for you to choose additional commands. You can use either the keyboard or the mouse to select a cell range in a worksheet.

A cell range is a single cell or a rectangular block of worksheet cells. Each cell range has a beginning and an ending cell address. The top left-hand cell is the beginning cell in a range and the bottom right-hand cell is the ending cell in a range. To specify a cell range in a worksheet formula, you enter the two cell addresses separated by a colon (for example, B4:C6). Figure 2.2 illustrates some cell ranges.

**FIGURE 2.2** CELL RANGES

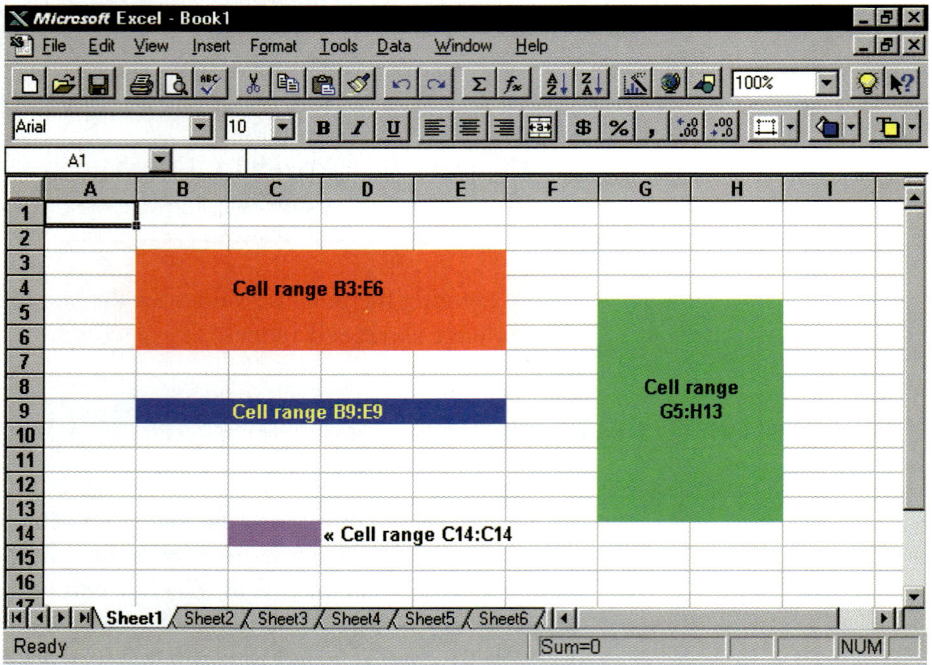


Perform the following steps to practice selecting cell ranges.

1. Move to cell B3.
2. To select the range of cells from B3 to G3 using the keyboard:
   PRESS: SHIFT and hold it down
   PRESS: → five times
   If the highlight does not extend from cell B3 to G3, make sure that you are holding down the SHIFT key as you press →.
3. When the range is highlighted, release the SHIFT key.
4. To remove the range selection, you can press any arrow key:
   PRESS: ←
   (*Note:* You can also click on any cell to remove the highlighting from the cell range.)
5. To select the range of cells from B5 to G7 using a mouse:
   CLICK: cell B5 and hold down the left mouse button
   DRAG: the mouse pointer down and to the right until you reach G7
6. When the range is highlighted, release the left mouse button. A selected range is highlighted in reverse (white text on a black background) from the rest of the worksheet. The exception to this rule is the active cell with the cell pointer, in this case cell B5 in the range B5:G7.

7. You can make your job of entering data easier and more accurate by using cell ranges. As you type information into a highlighted cell range, the cell pointer is automatically moved to the next cell in the range when you press ENTER. For example, do the following while the cell range remains selected:
   TYPE: **100**
   PRESS: ENTER
   Notice that the cell pointer moves down to cell B6. When the cell pointer reaches the last cell at the bottom of the selected column, it will move to the top of the next column in the range.

8. With the cell range still highlighted, complete the data entry as follows:

| | B | C | D | E | F | G |
|---|---|---|---|---|---|---|
| 5 | 100 | 115 | 132 | 152 | 175 | 201 |
| 6 | 75 | 86 | 99 | 114 | 131 | 151 |
| 7 | 40 | 46 | 53 | 61 | 70 | 80 |

9. With the cell range still highlighted, practice moving from cell to cell:
   PRESS: ENTER to move down one cell at a time; when you reach the bottom cell, the cell pointer moves to the top of the next column
   PRESS: SHIFT + ENTER to move up one cell at a time; when you reach the top cell, the cell pointer moves to the previous column
   PRESS: TAB to move right one cell; when you reach the rightmost cell in a row, the cell pointer moves to the next row
   PRESS: SHIFT + TAB to move left one cell; when you reach the left-most cell, the cell pointer moves to the previous row

10. To remove the highlighting and return to cell A1:
   PRESS: CTRL + HOME

**QUICK REFERENCE**
Selecting a Range of Cells Using the Mouse

1. **Click once on the cell in the top left-hand corner of the range.**
2. **While holding down the left mouse button, drag the mouse pointer and extend the highlight to the bottom right-hand corner of the range.**
3. **Release the mouse button.**

**QUICK REFERENCE**
Selecting a Range of Cells Using the Keyboard

1. **Position the cell pointer in the top left-hand corner of the cell range.**
2. **PRESS: SHIFT key and hold it down**
3. **Extend the highlight over the desired group of cells using the arrow keys (←, →, ↑, and ↓).**
4. **Release the SHIFT key.**

## SPELL-CHECKING A WORKSHEET

This section introduces the Spell Checker for correcting typographical errors and misspellings. You can perform a spelling check on a particular cell range, a single sheet, several sheets, or the entire workbook. When a spelling check is requested, Excel begins scanning the cells with textual information. Each word is compared to entries in Excel's main dictionary, which contains well over 100,000 words. If a word cannot be found, the Spell Checker attempts to find a match in a custom dictionary that you may have created. Custom dictionaries usually contain proper names, abbreviations, and technical terms.

New in Excel 7.0, the **AutoCorrect** utility is duly named for its ability to automatically correct your typographical and capitalization errors as you type. You will find this feature extremely handy if you habitually misspell or mistype particular words. For example, people commonly type "thier" instead of "their"—knowing perfectly well how to spell the word but making a simple typing mistake. Excel's AutoCorrect utility provides corrections for this word and hundreds of other commonly misspelled words. It also lets you easily insert complex symbols like © and ™ into your worksheet cells.

To start a spelling check, click the Spelling button (ABC✓) on the Standard toolbar. When the Spell Checker cannot identify a word and believes it to be misspelled, a dialog box appears allowing you to correct or ignore the entry, or to add the word to the custom dictionary or AutoCorrect list. The Spell Checker also flags errors relating to repeated words (for example, "the ball was was red") and mixed case (for example, "the baLL was rEd"). An added benefit for users of Microsoft Office is that the terms you add to the custom dictionary and to AutoCorrect are shared among all the applications.

To practice spell-checking a worksheet, perform the following steps.

1. Move to cell A2.
2. Enter a misspelled word:
   TYPE: **Summury**
   PRESS: ENTER
3. PRESS: CTRL + HOME to move to the top of the worksheet
4. To begin the spelling check:
   CLICK: Spelling button (ABC✓)
   (*Note:* You can also choose the Tools, Spelling command on the Menu bar to start a spelling check.) When Excel finds the first misspelled word, it displays the dialog box shown in Figure 2.3 and waits for further instructions.

FIGURE 2.3 SPELLING DIALOG BOX

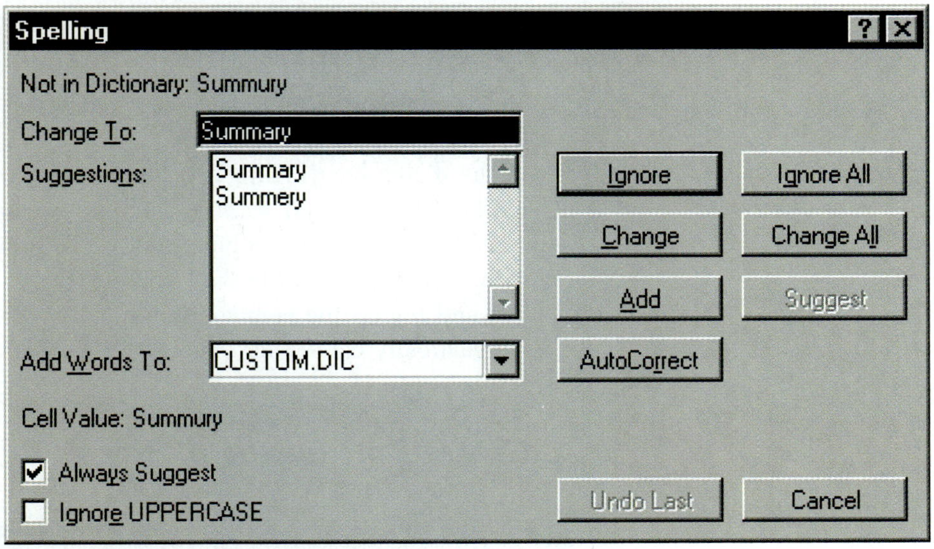


5. You have several options when the Spell Checker cannot find a word:
   - Select the correctly spelled word in the *Suggestions* list box and then click the Change command button.
   - Type the correct spelling of the word in the *Change To* text box and then click the Change command button.
   - If the word is spelled correctly and not frequently used, click the Ignore or Ignore All buttons to proceed to the next word.
   - If the word is spelled correctly and frequently used, click the Add button to add it to the custom dictionary.
   - If the word is one that you frequently mistype and the correct spelling appears in the *Change To* text box, click the AutoCorrect command button to have Excel correct this mistake automatically in the future.

   To correct the spelling of Summary and proceed:
   CLICK: Change command button
6. Continue the spelling check for the remainder of the worksheet. A message box will appear notifying you when the spelling check is finished. To proceed:
   PRESS: ENTER or CLICK: OK
7. To demonstrate using AutoCorrect:
   CLICK: cell F1
   TYPE: **(c)**
   PRESS: Space bar
   AutoCorrect replaces "(c)" with the proper copyright symbol "©" automatically when you press the Space bar.

8. To complete the cell entry:
   TYPE: ***your name***
   PRESS: ENTER
   (*Hint:* Do not take the above instruction literally. Enter your own name and not the text "your name.")
9. To review some of the other entries available in AutoCorrect:
   CHOOSE: Tools, AutoCorrect
   In the dialog box (Figure 2.4) that appears, notice the two columns in the list box: *Replace* and *With.* What you type into a worksheet cell is presented in the *Replace* column and what AutoCorrect replaces your typing with is presented in the *With* column. On your own, scroll through the list box and review the commonly misspelled words that AutoCorrect will automatically correct for you.

**FIGURE 2.4** AUTOCORRECT DIALOG BOX

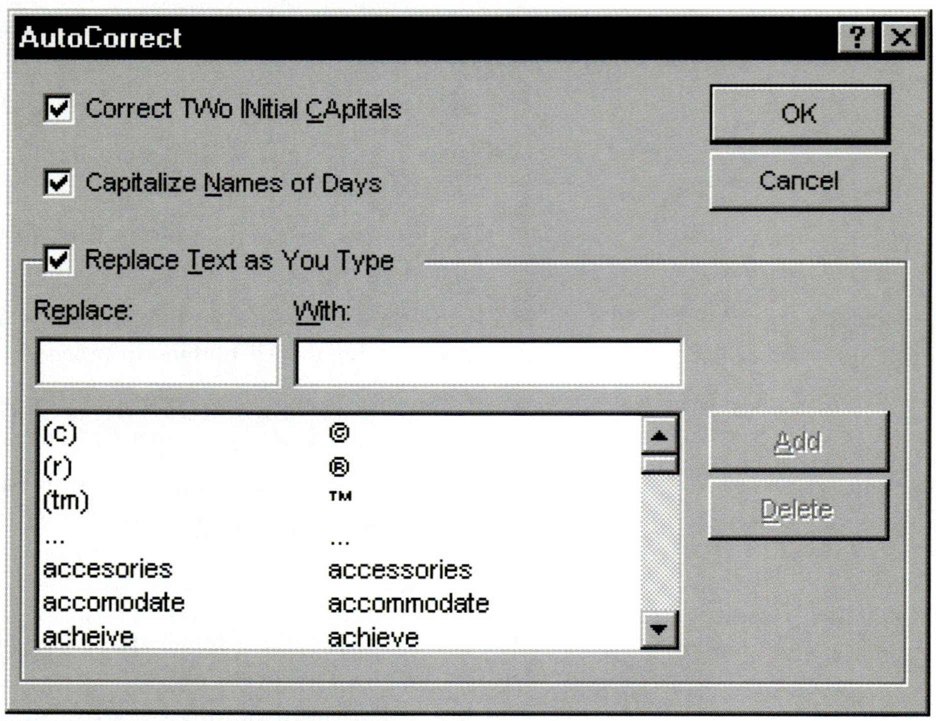


10. To proceed, ensure that all the check boxes are selected (as shown in Figure 2.4) and then do the following:
    CLICK: Cancel command button
11. PRESS: CTRL + HOME to move to the top of the worksheet
12. Save the workbook as "Sales Projections" onto the Advantage Diskette and then close the workbook.

**QUICK REFERENCE**
Spell-Checking a Worksheet

1. **CLICK: Spelling button (), or**
   **CHOOSE: Tools, Spelling**
2. **When a misspelled word is located, Excel suggests alternative spellings. Select a suggestion and then click a command button to change the entry, add it to the dictionary, add it to AutoCorrect, or ignore the word for the remainder of the spelling check.**

## DATA ENTRY USING AUTOCOMPLETE

Have you ever experienced a conversation with a person who insisted on finishing your sentences for you? Perhaps it was a friend, a business associate, or even your spouse. Although tremendously annoying in a social situation, this type of imposition proves to be an exceptional software feature—and it's called AutoComplete!

Newly introduced with Excel 7.0, **AutoComplete** second-guesses what you are about to type into a worksheet cell by reviewing your past entries in that cell's column. Similar to the AutoCorrect feature, AutoComplete watches your keystrokes and then jumps in when it thinks it can help. While AutoCorrect at least lets you finish typing a word before correcting a mistake, AutoComplete lets only a few letters go by before completing a matching entry.

To illustrate AutoComplete, perform the following steps.

1. Open the workbook called "Problem Report" stored on the Advantage Diskette. This workbook contains a single worksheet that is used to record problems in a computer lab. Notice that there are repeating entries beneath the columns labeled Shift, Supervisor, and Machine.
2. Let's add two new items to the worksheet. First, enter a date:
   CLICK: cell A15
   TYPE: **4/1/96**
   PRESS: →
3. To add "Blue" in the Shift column:
   TYPE: **b**
   AutoComplete scans the existing entries in the column and then fills in the remaining letters in the word "blue". (*Note:* If "blue" does not appear, press ESC and then choose the Tools, Options command. Click the Edit tab in the dialog box and then ensure that the *Enable AutoComplete for Cell Values* check box is selected. Click the OK command button to complete the dialog box.)

4. To move to cell C15 and accept the AutoComplete entry:
   PRESS: ➔
   Notice that the "b" is now capitalized in "Blue" so as to conform to the existing entries in the column.

5. Watch closely as you type each letter to add a new Supervisor to column C:
   TYPE: **Brandon**
   Notice that AutoComplete fills in "Bradley" as you type the "Bra" portion of the name. When you type the "n," AutoComplete realizes that you are entering a new Supervisor's name and removes the letters it had previously inserted for "Bradley."

6. To move to cell D15:
   PRESS: ➔

7. An additional feature of AutoComplete is its ability to generate an up-to-date list of the unique entries from a column. To illustrate:
   RIGHT-CLICK: cell D15

8. On the shortcut menu that appears:
   CHOOSE: Pick from list
   AutoComplete generates a list of items contained in the column and then displays its results in a pop-up list box. Your screen should now appear similar to Figure 2.5.

**FIGURE 2.5** ENTERING DATA USING A PICK LIST OF EXISTING ENTRIES

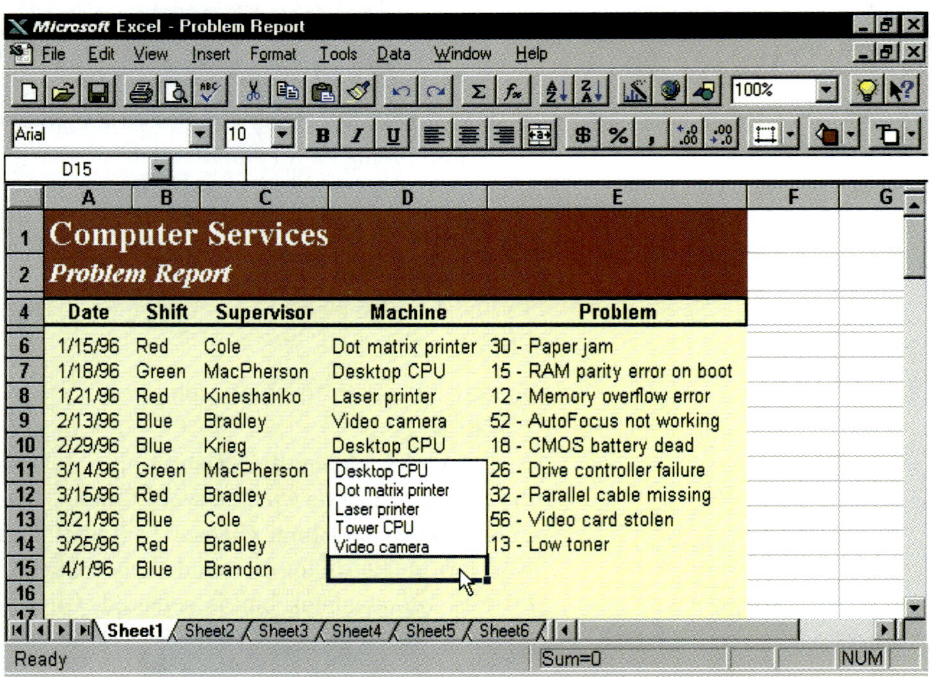

9. SELECT: "Tower CPU" from the Pick List
10. To finish the line item
    RIGHT-CLICK: cell E15
    SELECT: "15 - RAM parity error on boot" from the Pick List
11. Practice using the typing method and the Pick List to enter the following item to the Problem Report:

| *Move to Cell* | *Entry* |
|---|---|
| A16 | **5/15/96** |
| B16 | **Green** |
| C16 | **Kineshanko** |
| D16 | **Laser printer** |
| E16 | **13 - Low toner** |

12. Save the workbook as "Problem Report" back to the Advantage Diskette and then close the workbook.

## CALCULATING TOTALS

Adding together a few numbers on your worksheet is easy using a simple addition formula. Imagine the time it would take, however, to sum a column of 100 numbers with a formula such as =A1+A2+A3...+A99. Fortunately, Excel has anticipated many of these repetitive operations and provides a library of electronic shortcuts called **functions,** organized into the following categories:

- Database
- Date & Time
- Financial
- Information
- Logical
- Lookup & Reference
- Math & Trig
- Statistical
- Text

The mathematical and statistical functions are the most commonly used, enabling you to sum or average a range of numbers, count cell entries, and extract maximum and minimum results from a cell range. This section introduces the **SUM function** which is used as a replacement for long addition formulas. To enter the SUM function into a cell, you can type the expression or click the AutoSum button (Σ) on the Standard toolbar. Thanks to Excel's new

**AutoCalculate** utility, you can view the sum of a selected cell range in the Status bar without even entering the SUM function!

## THE SUM FUNCTION

The first step in using the SUM function is to move to the cell where you want the result to appear. Functions, like formulas, begin with an equal sign to inform Excel to expect a function name as opposed to a text label. The syntax for the SUM command is "=SUM(cell range)," where the cell range is the block of cells to be summed. You can enter the cell range by typing the cell addresses or by highlighting the block of cells using the mouse.

The objective of the following exercise is to demonstrate these two methods for entering the SUM function. Normally, you would not use a different method to sum each column. However, this example provides an opportunity to practice some important skills. Perform the following steps.

1. Ensure that there are no open workbooks in the document area of the Excel application window.
2. Open the "Sales Projections" workbook stored on the Advantage Diskette.
3. Move to cell B9.
4. To calculate the total sales for the month of January, enter the SUM function by typing the cell addresses:
   TYPE: **=sum(b5:b7)**
   PRESS: →
   The value 215 appears in the cell. (*Note:* You can enter the function name and cell range using uppercase or lowercase letters.)
5. To calculate the total sales for February, enter the SUM function into cell C9 by pointing to the cell range using the keyboard:
   TYPE: **=sum(**
   PRESS: ↑ four times to move to cell C5
   PRESS: SHIFT and hold down
   PRESS: ↓ twice to extend the range to cell C7
   TYPE: **)** and release the SHIFT key
   PRESS: →
   The number 247 appears in cell C9.
6. To calculate the total sales for March, enter the SUM function into cell D9 by pointing to the cell range using the mouse:
   TYPE: **=sum(**
   CLICK: cell D5 and hold down the left mouse button
   DRAG: mouse pointer to cell D7 and then release the mouse button
   TYPE: **)**
   PRESS: →
   The number 284 appears in cell D9.

7. SELECT: cell range from E9 to G9
8. To calculate the total sales for April through June, enter the SUM function once and copy the formula to the remaining cells in the range using a keyboard shortcut:
   TYPE: **=sum(e5:e7)**
   PRESS: CTRL + ENTER
   When you press CTRL + ENTER, Excel copies the entry in the active cell to the remaining cells in the highlighted range; in this case, F9 and G9.
9. To demonstrate using AutoCalculate:
   CLICK: cell B9 and hold down the left mouse button
   Notice that the Status bar displays "Sum=215."
10. DRAG: mouse pointer to C9 and keep the mouse button depressed
    The Status bar now displays "Sum=462", the sum of the selected cell range B9:C9. AutoCalculate provides an immediate summation of the selected cells without entering a formula or using a function.
11. DRAG: mouse pointer to G9 slowly, watching the Status bar as you move the cell pointer from D9 through to G9
    The Status bar should now display "Sum=1881", the sum of the selected cell range B9:G9.
12. On your own, select other cell ranges on the worksheet and watch the "Sum=" portion of the Status bar change to reflect the results.

## THE AUTOSUM BUTTON

Rather than entering an addition formula or the SUM function manually, you can use the AutoSum button (Σ) to automatically sum a cell range. To AutoSum a cell range, you position the cell pointer where you want the result to appear and click the AutoSum button (Σ) once. Excel enters the SUM function with its best guess of the desired cell range. If the range is correct, press ENTER to complete the entry. You can also bypass the need to press ENTER by double-clicking the AutoSum button (Σ) with the cell pointer in the desired cell.

Let's complete the "Sales Projections" worksheet by calculating the total sales for each product.

1. Move to cell H3.
2. TYPE: **Total**
3. Move to cell H9.
4. To calculate the total sales for all products:
   CLICK: AutoSum button (Σ)
   Verify that the cell range appearing in the cell and in the Formula bar is correct before proceeding to the next step.

5. To proceed:
   CLICK: ✓ in the Formula bar
   (*Note:* You can also press **ENTER** or click the AutoSum button (Σ) a second time to accept the cell range.)
6. To calculate the total sales for each individual product, select the cell range from H5 to H7. Ensure that the entire range is highlighted.
7. CLICK: AutoSum button (Σ)
   Because more than one cell is highlighted, the SUM function is automatically entered for all three cells. Your worksheet should now appear similar to Figure 2.6.

**FIGURE 2.6** ENTERING THE SUM FUNCTION AND USING AUTOSUM

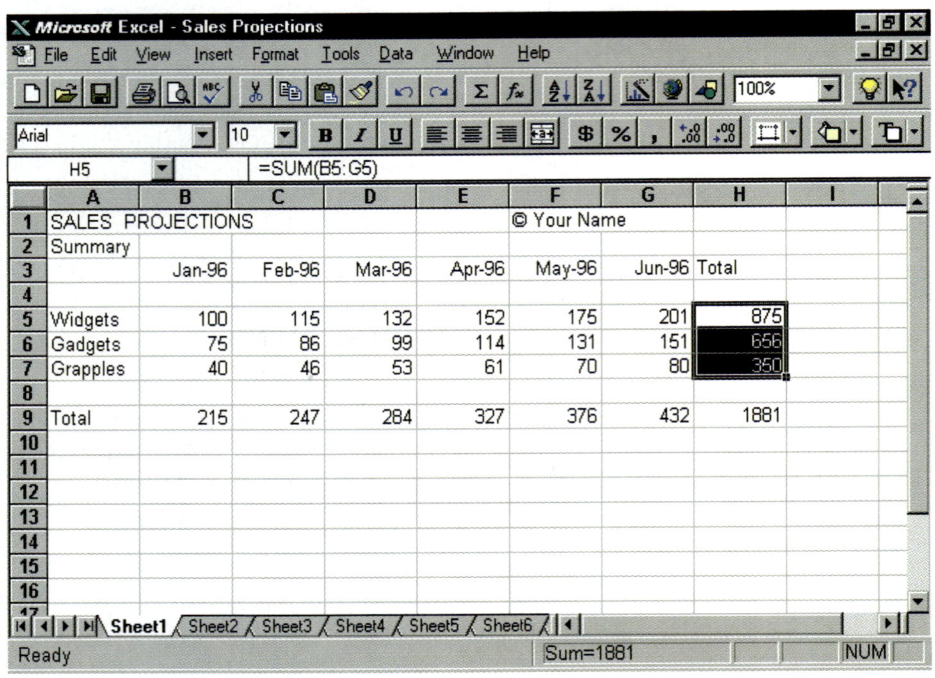


8. Using the mouse, click each of the cells H5, H6, and H7 and read the cell references in the Formula bar. Ensure that each SUM function sums the correct cell range.
9. Save the "Sales Projections" workbook to the Advantage Diskette.

**QUICK REFERENCE**
AutoSum Button

1. **Move the cell pointer to where you want the result to appear.**
2. **CLICK: AutoSum button (Σ)**

## CHANGING COLUMN WIDTHS

You can increase the **column width** of your worksheet columns to allow for long text labels, numbers, and date formats. To change a column's width from the default or standard width, move the cell pointer to any cell in the desired column and then choose the Format, Column, Width command from the Menu bar. The dialog box in Figure 2.7 appears:

**FIGURE 2.7** COLUMN WIDTH DIALOG BOX

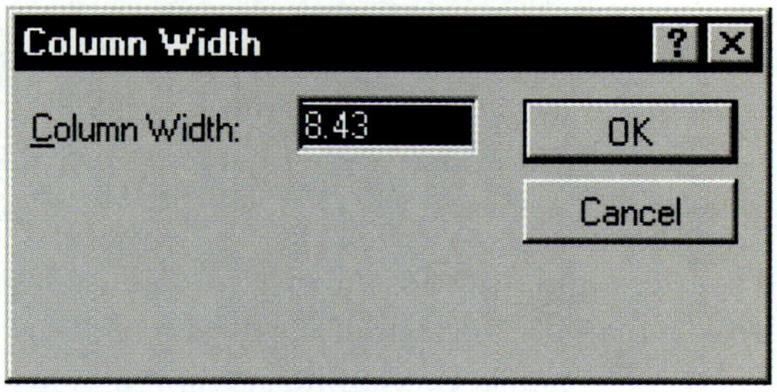


In the *Column Width* text box, you type the desired width (up to 255) and press ENTER or click on OK. To change the width of more than one column at a time, you highlight cells within the columns (on any row) before you issue the command. You can also choose the Format, Column, AutoFit Selection command to have Excel calculate the best width for the column based on its entries. As with most procedures, there are keyboard and mouse methods for changing a column's width. Using a mouse, you can modify a column's width by dragging the column borders within the frame area.

Perform the following steps.

1. Move to cell A1.
2. To change the width of column A to 10 characters:
   CHOOSE: Format, Column, Width
3. In the *Column Width* text box, enter the number of characters:
   TYPE: **10**
   PRESS: ENTER or CLICK: OK
   The column's width is changed and you are returned to the worksheet.
4. To change the width of column B to 12 characters using the mouse, first move the mouse pointer into the column frame area where the column letters (A, B, and so on) appear.

5. Position the mouse pointer over the borderline between column B and column C. The mouse pointer changes shape from a cross to a black vertical line split by a horizontal double-headed arrow.
6. CLICK: the borderline and hold down the mouse button
   DRAG: the mouse pointer to the right to increase the width to 12
   (*Hint:* The width is displayed in the Name box of the Formula bar.)
7. Release the mouse button.
8. To concurrently change multiple columns to the same width, you must first select the columns by dragging the mouse pointer over the column letters in the frame area. For this step, select columns B through H using the mouse by clicking on the letter B and then dragging the mouse pointer to column H.
9. To have Excel select the best width for each of the columns:
   CHOOSE: Format, Column, AutoFit Selection
   Although the columns are adjusted to best fit their cell entries, most appear too narrow.
10. With the columns still selected, drag any border in the highlighted frame area to increase the width of all columns to 8 characters. When you release the mouse button, all of the columns are sized to 8 characters wide.

**QUICK REFERENCE**
Changing a Column's Width

1. **Select a cell in the column that you want to format.**
2. **CHOOSE: Format, Column, Width**
3. **Type the desired column width in the text box.**
4. **PRESS: ENTER or CLICK: OK**

## CHANGING ROW HEIGHTS

You can change the **row height** of any worksheet row to customize borders and line spacing. To change a row's height, move the cell pointer to any cell in the desired row and then choose Format, Row, Height from the Menu bar. The dialog box in Figure 2.8 appears:

**FIGURE 2.8** ROW HEIGHT DIALOG BOX

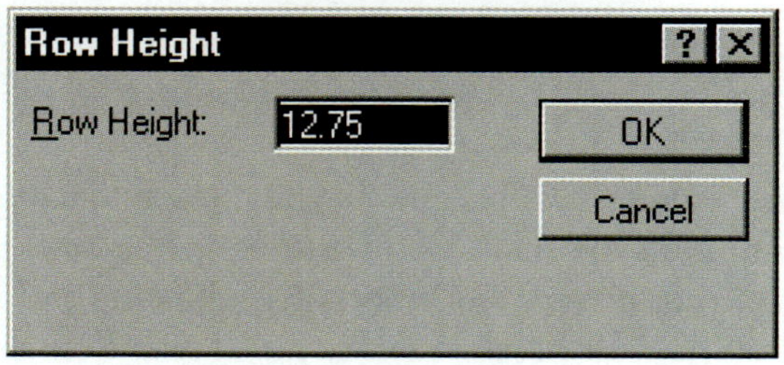


In the *Row Height* text box, you type the desired height in points (up to 409, where 72 points is equal to one inch) and press ENTER or click on OK. To change the height of more than one row at a time, you highlight the rows in the frame area before you issue the command. Similarly to changing a column's width, you can use a mouse to drag the row borders within the frame area to increase or decrease a row's height.

Perform the following steps.

1. Move to cell A1.
2. To change the height of Row 1 to 25 points (approximately 3/8 inch), issue the formatting command:
   CHOOSE: Format, Row, Height
3. In the *Row Height* text box, enter a number for the height in points:
   TYPE: **25**
   PRESS: ENTER or CLICK: OK
   The row's height is changed, and you are returned to the worksheet.
4. To change the height of Row 3 to 21 points using a mouse, first move the mouse pointer into the frame area where the row numbers appear.
5. Position the mouse pointer over the borderline between Row 3 and Row 4. The mouse pointer changes shape from a cross to a black horizontal line split by a vertical double-headed arrow.
6. CLICK: the borderline and hold down the mouse button
   DRAG: the mouse pointer down to increase the row height to 21
   (*Hint:* The height is displayed in the Name box of the Formula bar.)
7. Release the mouse button.
8. To change multiple rows to the same height, you must first select the rows by dragging the mouse in the frame area. For this step, select the range from row 5 to row 9 by clicking on the number 5 and then dragging the mouse pointer to row 9.

9. To change the row height to 16 points:
   CHOOSE: Format, Row, Height
   TYPE: **16**
   PRESS: ENTER or CLICK: OK
10. Save the "Sales Projections" workbook to the Advantage Diskette.

Unlike column widths, row heights are automatically adjusted to their best fit according to the font size of entries in the row. However, you can still modify the spacing in your worksheets by adjusting row heights manually. If you want to reset the row height back to the standard or default setting, choose the Format, Row, AutoFit command from the menu.

**QUICK REFERENCE**
Changing a Row's Height

1. **Select a cell in the row to format.**
2. **CHOOSE: Format, Row, Height**
3. **Type the desired row height in the text box.**
4. **PRESS: ENTER or CLICK: OK**

## FORMATTING YOUR WORKSHEET

With Excel's spreadsheet publishing capabilities, you can enhance your worksheets with a variety of fonts, borders, and shading. You can also format numbers to display currency and percentage symbols and to specify the number of decimal places. The combination of these features enables you to produce professional-looking reports and presentations using Excel.

### SELECTING CELL RANGES

To format your worksheet, select the cells that you want to enhance and then issue a formatting command. To this point in the guide, you've learned how to select a single cell and a block of cells called a range. There are several additional methods for selecting cells in a worksheet that will improve your productivity. For example, you can select multiple cell ranges in different areas of a worksheet and then apply a single command to format them all. Some common selection methods are provided below.

- To apply formatting changes to an entire worksheet, select the worksheet by pressing CTRL+**a** or by clicking once on the Select All button (▢), located in the top left-hand corner of the frame area.
- To select multiple cell ranges, select the first cell range as usual and then hold down the CTRL key as you select the additional cell ranges using the mouse.

- To select a cell range that spans several pages of the worksheet (for example, A1:M300), select the first cell (top left-hand corner of the range) and then scroll to the last cell (bottom right-hand corner of the range) using the scroll bars. When the last cell is visible, press and hold down the SHIFT key and click the cell once. All the cells in between the first and last are highlighted.

Because a cell range remains highlighted after issuing a command, you can choose additional formatting commands without having to re-select cells. To remove the highlighting from a cell range, press an arrow key or click on any cell in the worksheet using the mouse.

## USING FONTS

One of the most effective means of enhancing a worksheet is to vary the **fonts**—that is, the **typefaces** and point sizes—that are used in titles, column headings, row labels, and other worksheet cells. Although fonts are effective at drawing the reader's attention to specific topics, don't feel that you must use every font in each worksheet. Remember, a worksheet must be easy to read and understand—too many fonts are distracting.

To enhance your worksheet, select the cell or range of cells to format and then issue the Format, Cells command from the menu. (*Hint:* You can also select the Format Cells command from a shortcut menu.) For fonts and styles, select the *Font* tab by clicking on it using the mouse. After making the desired selections from the dialog box, press ENTER or click the OK command button.

Rather than accessing the Format Cells dialog box (Figure 2.9) from the menu, you can click buttons on the Formatting toolbar: Font (Arial), Font Size (10), Bold (B), Italic (I), and Underline (U). These buttons provide single-step access to the most popular features found in the Format Cells dialog box.

**FIGURE 2.9** FORMAT CELLS DIALOG BOX: FONT TAB

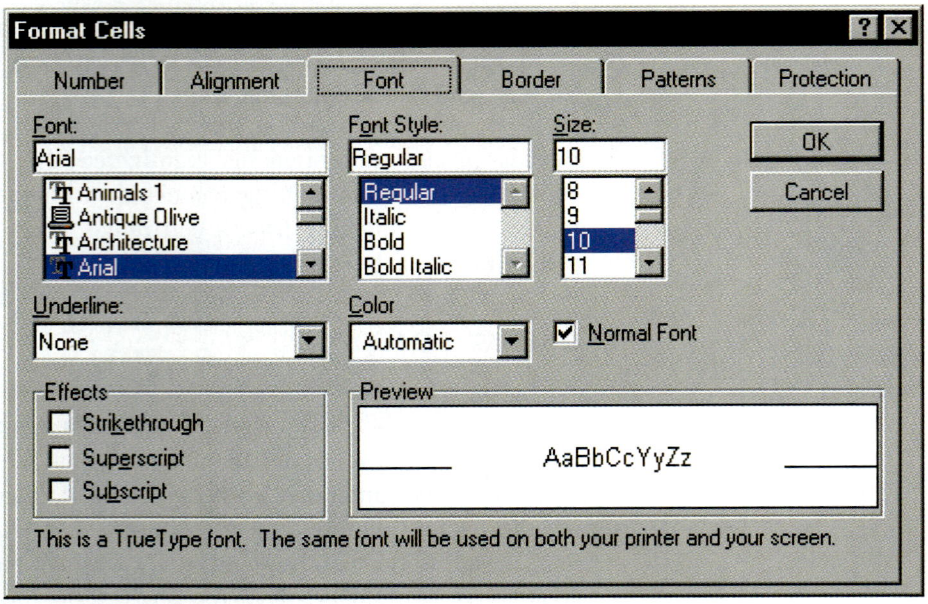


Perform the following steps to change fonts and styles in the worksheet.

1. SELECT: cell range from B3 to H3
2. To emphasize the column headings, make the dates bold:
   CLICK: Bold button (B)
3. SELECT: cell range from A5 to A9
4. To italicize the product names:
   CLICK: Italic button (I)
5. RIGHT-CLICK: cell A1
   A shortcut menu appears.
6. To enhance the title:
   CHOOSE: Format Cells
   CLICK: Font tab
7. SELECT: Times New Roman from the *Font* list box
   SELECT: Bold Italic from the *Font Style* list box
   SELECT: 18 from the *Size* list box
   PRESS: ENTER or CLICK: OK
8. SELECT: cell A2

9. To enhance the sub-title using the Formatting toolbar:
   SELECT: Times New Roman from the Font drop-down list box (Arial)
   SELECT: 14 from the Font Size drop-down list box (10)
   (*Hint:* To display the options in a drop-down list, click the down arrow beside the drop-down list on the toolbar.) Your screen should now appear similar to Figure 2.10.

**FIGURE 2.10** APPLYING FONTS TO THE WORKSHEET

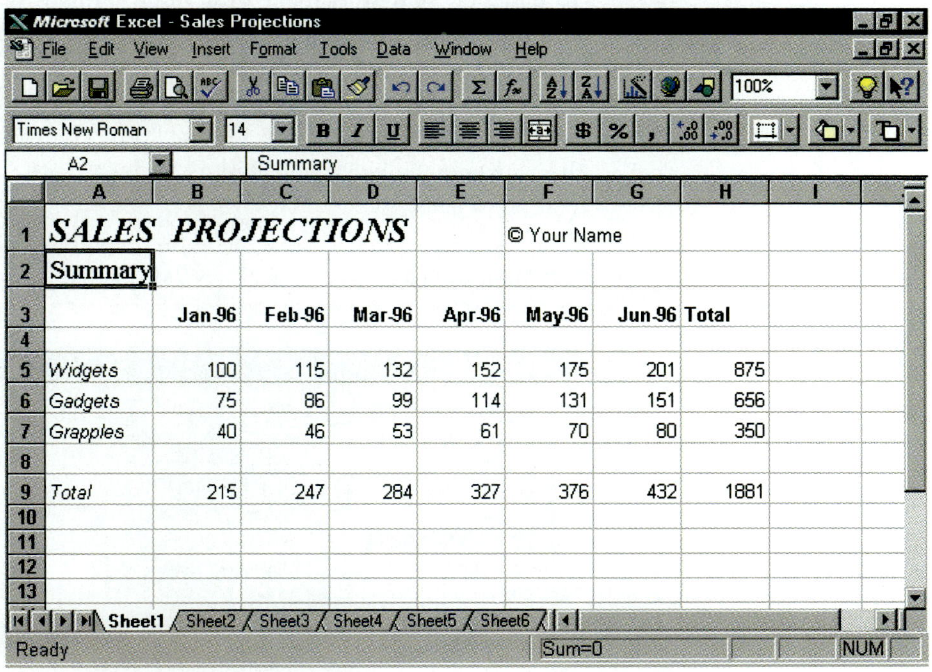


**QUICK REFERENCE**
Using Fonts

1. **SELECT: the cell or cell range that you want to format**
2. **CHOOSE: Format, Cells**
3. **CLICK: Font tab**
4. **SELECT: a Font, Font Style, Size, Color, and Effects**
5. **PRESS: ENTER or CLICK: OK**

## FORMATTING VALUES

Numeric formats improve the appearance and readability of numbers in a worksheet by inserting dollar signs, commas, percentage symbols, and decimal places. Although the number appears differently on the worksheet when formatting is applied, the value in the Formula bar does not change—only the appearance of the number changes. In addition to dollar figures and percentages, Excel stores date and time entries as values and allows you to customize their display in the worksheet.

To enhance your worksheet with value formatting, select the desired cell range and then issue the Format, Cells command. (*Hint:* You can also select the Format Cells command from a shortcut menu.) When the dialog box appears, click the Number tab to display a variety of numeric formatting options. Figure 2.11 provides an example of the Format Cells dialog box with the Number tab and the Currency category selected.

**FIGURE 2.11** FORMAT CELLS DIALOG BOX: *NUMBER* TAB

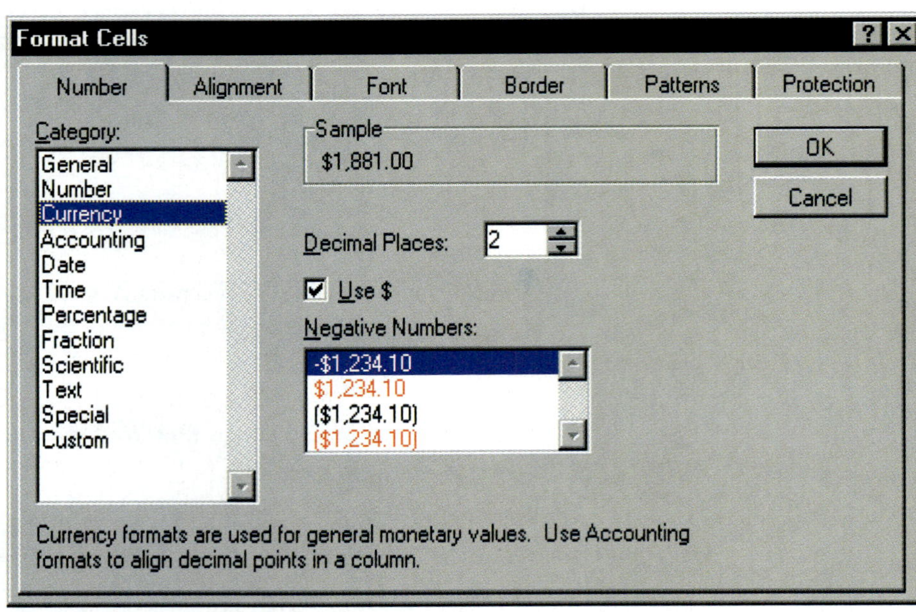


To format the values in your worksheet, select an option in the *Category* list box and then make selections from that category's formatting options. When completed, you press ENTER or click on OK. You can also format values by clicking the following buttons on the Formatting toolbar: Currency Style ($), Percent Style (%), Comma Style (,), Increase Decimal ( ), and Decrease Decimal ( ). These buttons provide single-step access to the most popular features found in the Format Cells dialog box.

Perform the following steps.

1. SELECT: cell range from B9 to H9
2. To display the dialog box of numeric formatting options:
   RIGHT-CLICK: any cell in the highlighted cell range
   CHOOSE: Format Cells
   CLICK: Number tab
3. To view the currency formatting options:
   SELECT: Currency in the *Category* list box
4. To select a currency format with a dollar sign, commas, and two decimal places:
   SELECT: 2 in the *Decimal Places* spin box
   SELECT: *Use $* check box so that a "✓" appears
   SELECT: ($1,234.00) in the *Negative Numbers* list box (either the red or black option)
   PRESS: ENTER or CLICK: OK
5. To increase the width of column H only to 10 characters:
   CLICK: cell H9
   CHOOSE: Format, Column, Width
   TYPE: **10**
   PRESS: ENTER or CLICK: OK
6. SELECT: cell range from B5 to H7
7. To select a number format with commas:
   CLICK: Comma Style button ( , )
8. If there are no decimals displaying for the Comma style:
   CLICK: Increase Decimal button (.00) twice
   Otherwise, proceed to the next section.

Upon selecting a numeric or date formatting option, a cell may display a series of pound signs (########). This is Excel's way of informing you that the cell is not wide enough to display the value using the selected format. Your options are either to increase the column's width or select a different numeric format.

**QUICK REFERENCE**
Formatting Numbers and Dates

1. **SELECT: the cell or cell range that you want to format**
2. **CHOOSE: Format, Cells**
3. **CLICK: Number tab**
4. **SELECT: a format from the Category list box**
5. **SELECT: formatting options for the selected category**
6. **PRESS: ENTER or CLICK: OK**

## ALIGNING A CELL'S CONTENTS

Excel automatically aligns text against the left edge of a cell and values against the right edge. However, you can easily change the **cell alignment** for any type of information in the worksheet. Using the menu, choose the Format, Cells command and then make selections from the Alignment tab in the dialog box (Figure 2.12). Using the Formatting toolbar, click the Align Left (), Center (), Align Right (), and Center Across Columns () buttons to align cell information.

**FIGURE 2.12** FORMAT CELLS DIALOG BOX: *ALIGNMENT* TAB

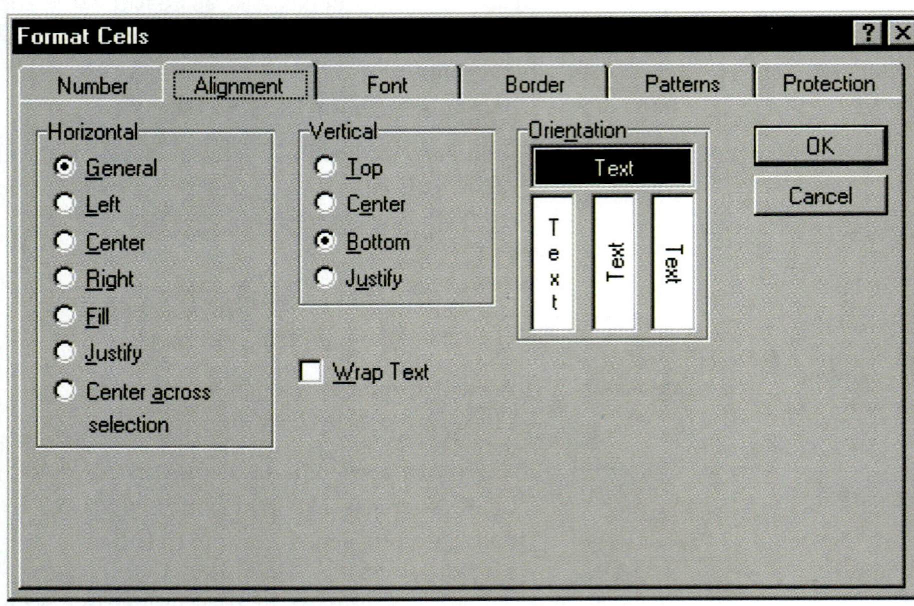


Perform the following steps.

1. SELECT: cell range from B3 to H3
2. To center the date column headings:
   CLICK: Center button ()
3. SELECT: cell range from A5 to A9
4. To right-align the product or row headings:
   CLICK: Align Right button ()
5. To center the sub-title in A2 across the width of the worksheet:
   SELECT: cell range from A2 to H2
6. CLICK: Center Across Selection button ()

7. Move to cell A2. Notice that the sub-title appears in the Formula bar, even though the worksheet displays the sub-title between columns A and H. Your screen should now appear similar to Figure 2.13.
8. Save the "Sales Projections" workbook to the Advantage Diskette.

**FIGURE 2.13** ALIGNING CELL INFORMATION

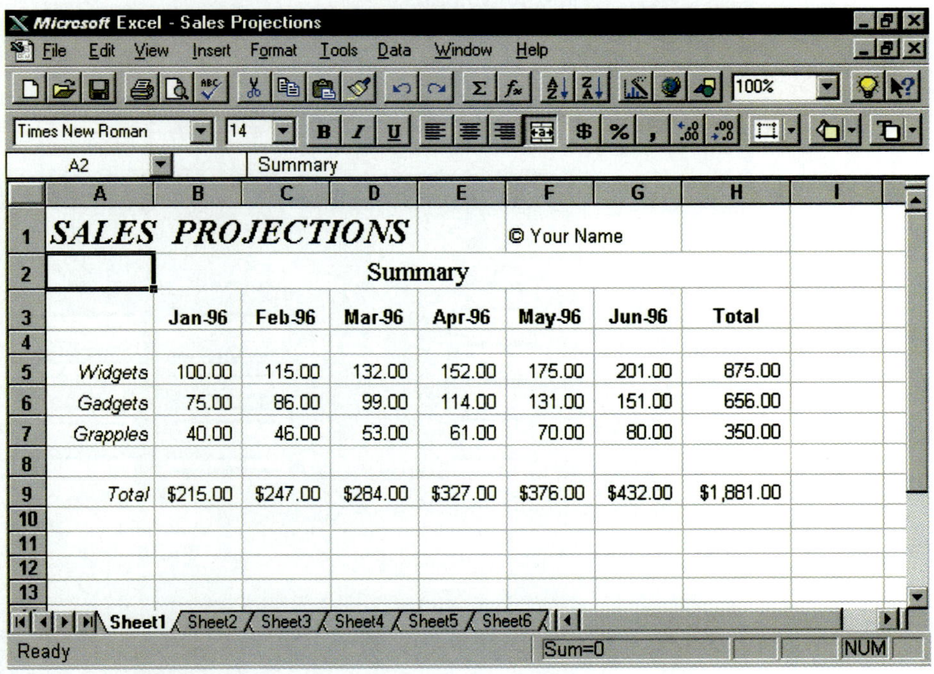


**QUICK REFERENCE**
Changing a Cell's Alignment

1. **SELECT: the cell or cell range that you want to format**
2. **CLICK: an alignment button on the Formatting toolbar, such as Align Left ( ), Center ( ), Align Right ( ), or Center Across Selection ( ) buttons**

## ADDING BORDERS AND SHADING CELLS

The gridlines that appear in the document window are nonprinting lines, provided only to help you line up information in the worksheet. To enhance the readability of your printed worksheets, you can add borders, underlines, and shading to cells. Borders are used to separate data into logical sections and to emphasize titles. These features also allow you to create professional-looking invoice forms, memos, and tables.

To add borders and shaded patterns to your worksheet, select the desired cell or cell range and issue the Format, Cells command. In the dialog box that appears, select the Border tab to display the dialog box in Figure 2.14 or the Patterns tab to display the dialog box page shown in Figure 2.15. When you are finished making selections from the two pages, you press ENTER or click on the OK command button. You can also click the Borders drop-down list () on the Formatting toolbar to quickly apply borders to a selection or use the Color button () and the Font Color button () to change the background and font colors.

**FIGURE 2.14** FORMAT CELLS DIALOG BOX: BORDER TAB

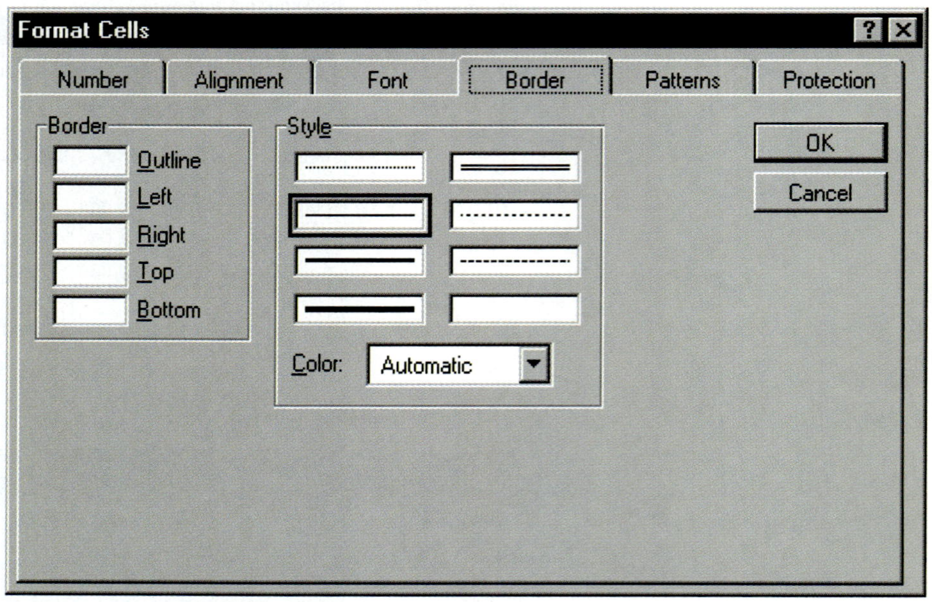

**FIGURE 2.15** FORMAT CELL DIALOG BOX: PATTERNS TAB

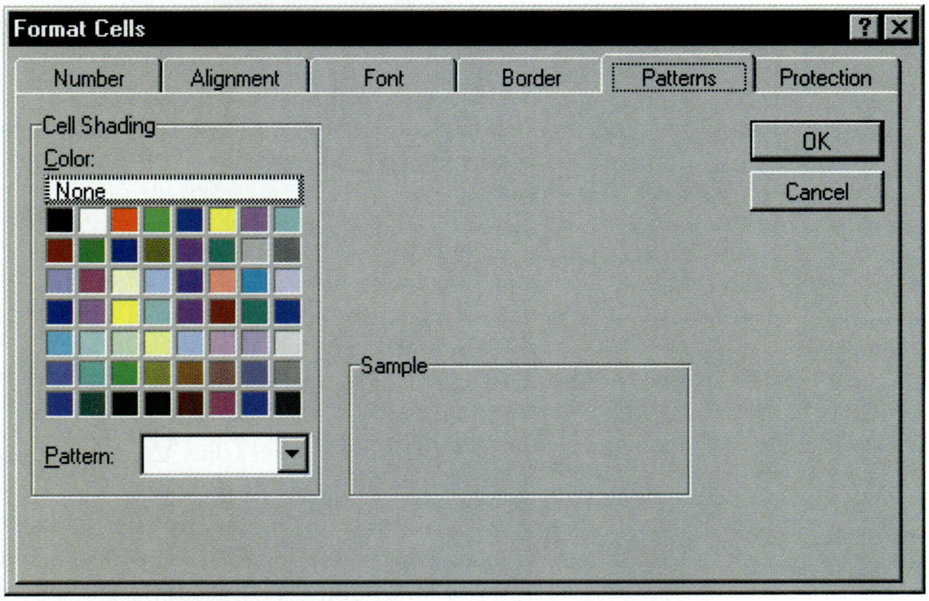


Perform the following steps to practice creating borders and shading cells.

1. SELECT: cell range from B3 to H3
2. To add a border to the worksheet:
   CLICK: down arrow beside the Borders drop-down list ( )
   You should see a list of sample border formats appear.
   (*CAUTION:* Make sure that you click the down arrow and not the button itself.)
3. SELECT: a thick outline border (in the bottom right-hand corner)
   The formatting is immediately applied to the selection.
4. To apply a color to the cells' background:
   CLICK: down arrow beside the Color drop-down list ( )
   SELECT: a pale yellow color
5. To change the text color:
   CLICK: down arrow beside the Font Color drop-down list ( )
   SELECT: a dark blue color
6. SELECT: cell range from B9 to H9

7. To add two different borders to this range:
   CHOOSE: Format, Cells
   CLICK: Border tab
   SELECT: Top in the *Border* group
   SELECT: a single line (second from the top) in the *Style* group
   SELECT: Bottom in the *Border* group
   SELECT: a double line (top of the second column) in the *Style* group
   PRESS: ENTER or CLICK: OK

8. In order to get a full appreciation of fonts and borders, Excel lets you temporarily remove the **gridlines** from the worksheet. This provides a more accurate view of how the worksheet will look when printed. To temporarily remove the gridlines from your worksheet:
   CLICK: cell A12
   CHOOSE: Tools, Options
   CLICK: View tab
   SELECT: *Gridlines* check box to remove the "✓"
   PRESS: ENTER or CLICK: OK
   (*Note:* Although this option provides a cleaner view of your worksheet on the screen, it does not affect how the worksheet will print. The print options for gridlines and headings are specified in the Page Setup dialog box, described later in this session.)
   Your worksheet should now appear similar to Figure 2.16.

**FIGURE 2.16** APPLYING BORDERS AND COLORS, AND REMOVING THE GRIDLINES

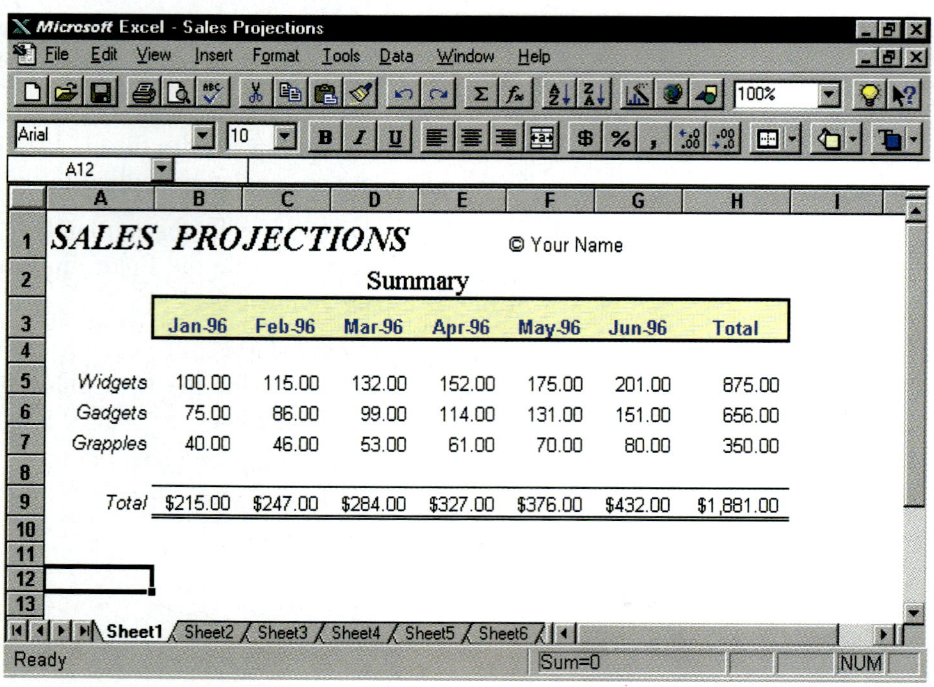

9. To return the display to normal:
   CHOOSE: Tools, Options
   CLICK: View tab (if it is not already selected)
   SELECT: *Gridlines* check box so that a "✓" appears
   PRESS: ENTER or CLICK: OK
10. Save the "Sales Projections" workbook to the Advantage Diskette.

**QUICK REFERENCE**
Adding Borders, Colors, and Patterns

1. **SELECT: the cell or cell range that you want to format**
2. **CHOOSE: Format, Cells**
3. **CLICK: Border tab to specify border lines**
4. **CLICK: Patterns tab to specify a shading level or color**
5. **PRESS: ENTER or CLICK: OK**

## COPYING FORMATTING OPTIONS

Excel's Format Painter button (🖌) lets you copy the formatting styles from one area in your worksheet to another. To copy a cell's formatting, select the cell and click the Format Painter button (🖌). To apply the formatting, you drag the paintbrush mouse pointer across the cell range that you want to format. When you release the mouse button, the formatting styles are copied from the original selection to your new selection. Not only does this feature speed formatting operations, it ensures consistency among the cell formatting in your worksheet.

Let's practice—perform the following steps.

1. To practice copying styles, let's format a cell with new options:
   SELECT: cell B5
   CLICK: Decrease Decimal button (.00→.0) twice
   The entry in cell B5 will now appear as 100.
2. To copy this formatting change to the rest of the values:
   CLICK: Format Painter button (🖌)
3. Move the mouse pointer into the document window. Notice that the mouse pointer is now a cross with a paintbrush.
4. SELECT: the cell range from B5 to H9
5. Release the mouse button. Notice that all the values in the range are now formatted with the same features as cell B5.
6. To undo the last operation:
   CLICK: Undo button (↶)
   PRESS: ESC to remove the dashed marquee from around cell B5

7. To re-format cell B5:
   CLICK: cell B6
   CLICK: Format Painter button (button)
   CLICK: cell B5
   The cell appears with its original formatting (two decimals).
8. PRESS: CTRL + HOME to move to cell A1

**QUICK REFERENCE**
Copying a Cell's Formatting

1. **SELECT: the cell whose formatting you want to copy**
2. **CLICK: Format Painter button (button) on the Standard toolbar**
3. **SELECT: the cell range that you want to format**
4. **Release the mouse button to complete the operation.**

## REMOVING FORMATTING OPTIONS

If you want to remove the formatting features applied to an area on your worksheet, select the cell or range of cells and then choose the Edit, Clear command from the menu. On the cascading menu that appears, select the Formats command. This command removes the formatting options only, not the contents of the cell or range of cells.

To demonstrate, perform the following steps.

1. SELECT: cell A1
2. To remove the formatting for this cell:
   CHOOSE: Edit, Clear, Formats
   Notice that the cell's formatting is stripped while its contents are left intact.
3. To undo the last command:
   CLICK: Undo button (button)

**QUICK REFERENCE**
Removing a Cell's Formatting

1. **SELECT: a cell or cell range**
2. **CHOOSE: Edit, Clear, Formats**

## USING THE AUTOFORMAT COMMAND

The **AutoFormat** command lets you apply a predefined table format, complete with numeric formats, alignments, borders, shading, and colors, to a group of cells on your worksheet. This feature assumes that your data is organized in the worksheet as a table, with labels running down the left column and across the top row. To automatically format your worksheet, select a cell range and then choose the Format, AutoFormat command from the menu. In the dialog box that appears, you can view a sample of each format by clicking on its name in the *Table Format* list box. When you find a table format that you like, press ENTER or click on OK.

Let's apply a few different formats to our worksheet. Perform the following steps.

1. SELECT: cell range from A3 to H9
2. To display the AutoFormat dialog box:
   CHOOSE: Format, AutoFormat
3. In the *Table Format* list box:
   SELECT: Colorful 2
   PRESS: ENTER or CLICK: OK
4. To remove the highlighting from the range:
   SELECT: cell A12
   Your screen should now appear similar to Figure 2.17.

**FIGURE 2.17** APPLYING THE AUTOFORMAT COMMAND

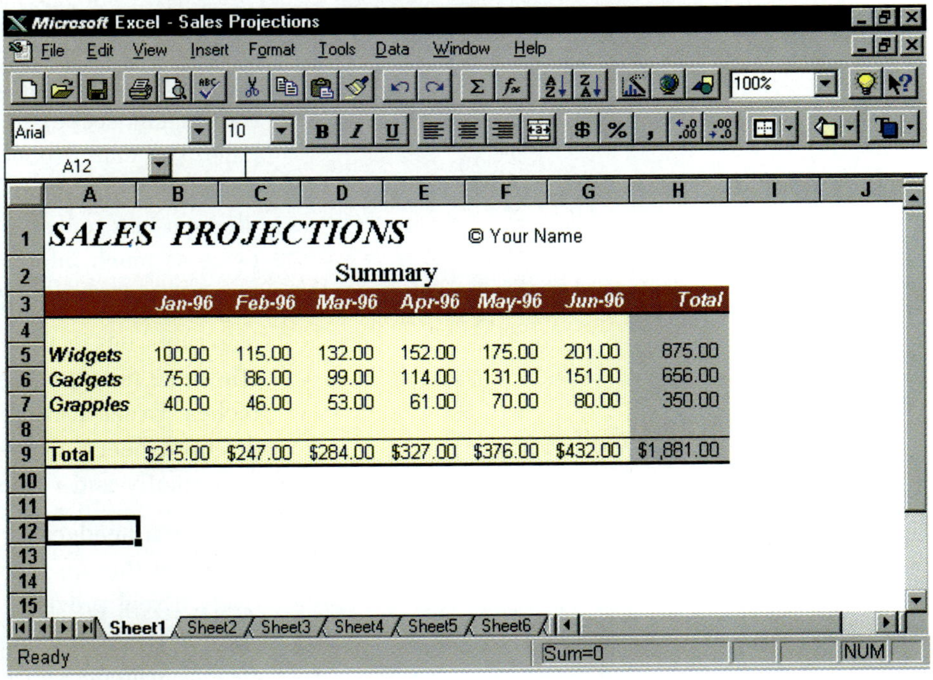


5. Practice choosing some of the other table format options from the AutoFormat dialog box. Before proceeding, re-select the Colorful 2 option in the *Table Format* list box.
6. Save the "Sales Projections" workbook to the Advantage Diskette.

**QUICK REFERENCE**
Using AutoFormat

1. **SELECT: the cell or cell range that you want to format**
2. **CHOOSE: Format, AutoFormat**
3. **SELECT: an option from the *Table Format* list box**
4. **PRESS: ENTER or CLICK: OK**

## PRINTING THE WORKBOOK

This section introduces the commands for printing a workbook, including options for setting up the page and previewing the output.

### DEFINING THE PAGE LAYOUT

You define the page layout settings for printing a workbook using the File, Page Setup command. In the dialog box that appears, you specify **margins, headers, footers,** and whether gridlines or row and column headings should appear on the final printed document. To make the process more manageable, Excel organizes the page layout settings under four tabs in the Page Setup dialog box:

- Page tab — The Page tab lets you specify the paper size and the workbook's print orientation (for example, portrait or landscape). To print more information on a page, you can also adjust or scale the print size to be smaller than normal using this tab. For example, you can reduce the print size to 50% to fit twice as much information on each page.
- Margins tab — You specify the top, bottom, left, and right margins using this tab in the Page Setup dialog box. Unless otherwise noted, you enter all measurements in inches. Excel also provides options for centering the worksheet range on the printed page, both horizontally and vertically.
- Header/Footer tab — You use a header and footer to print static information at the top and bottom of each page, respectively. Excel provides several predefined headers and footers or you can customize your own using special symbols and formatting styles.
- Sheet tab — You can specify what you want printed using the *Sheet* tab. Besides specifying the actual print area, you tell Excel whether to print the gridlines or row and column headings. Excel also lets you use print titles that repeat at the top of each page. Print titles are dynamic and relate directly to the print area, unlike headers which are static text.

In this section, you define the page layout specifications for the "Sales Projections" worksheet. Perform the following steps.

1. Before changing options in the Page Setup dialog box, you need to specify the desired print area of the worksheet:
   SELECT: cell range from A1 to H9
   CHOOSE: File, Print Area, Set Print Area
   PRESS: CTRL + HOME
   Notice that the print area on the worksheet is now surrounded by dashed lines.

2. To specify the page layout settings:
   CHOOSE: File, Page Setup
   CLICK: Page tab
   The Page Setup dialog box appears as shown in Figure 2.18.

**FIGURE 2.18** PAGE SETUP DIALOG BOX: *PAGE* TAB

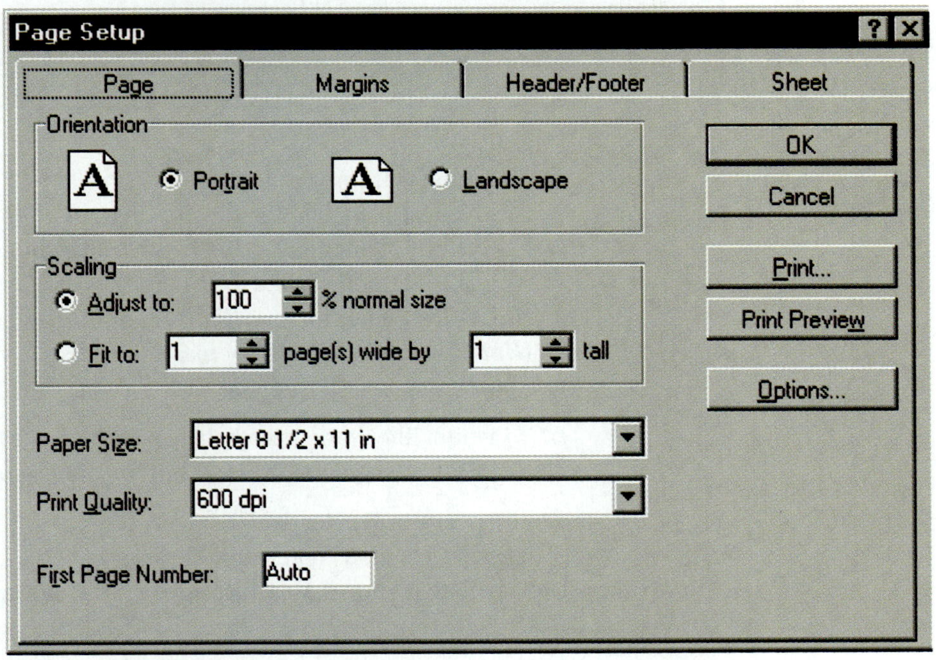


3. Make the following selections:
   SELECT: Portrait in the *Orientation* group
   SELECT: Adjust to 100% normal size in the *Scaling* group
   SELECT: "Letter 8½ x 11 in" in the *Paper Size* drop-down list box

4. To specify the margins:
   CLICK: Margins tab
   The Page Setup dialog box appears as shown in Figure 2.19.

**FIGURE 2.19** PAGE SETUP DIALOG BOX: MARGINS TAB

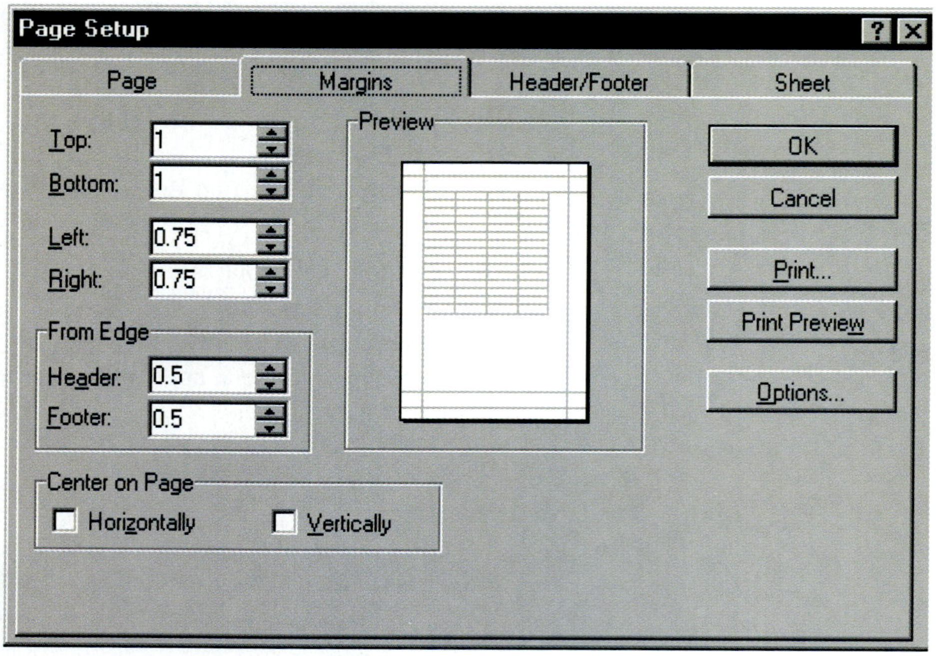


5. Make the following selections:
   SELECT: 1.5 inches for the *Top* margin
   SELECT: 1.5 inches for the *Bottom* margin
   SELECT: 1 inch for the *Left* margin
   SELECT: 1 inch for the *Right* margin
   (*Hint:* To increase and decrease the margin values, you click the up and down triangles that appear to the right of each spin box.)
6. To center the worksheet between the left and right margins:
   SELECT: *Horizontally* check box in the *Center on Page* group
7. To specify a header and a footer:
   CLICK: Header/Footer tab
   The Page Setup dialog box appears as shown in Figure 2.20.

FIGURE 2.20 PAGE SETUP DIALOG BOX: HEADER/FOOTER TAB

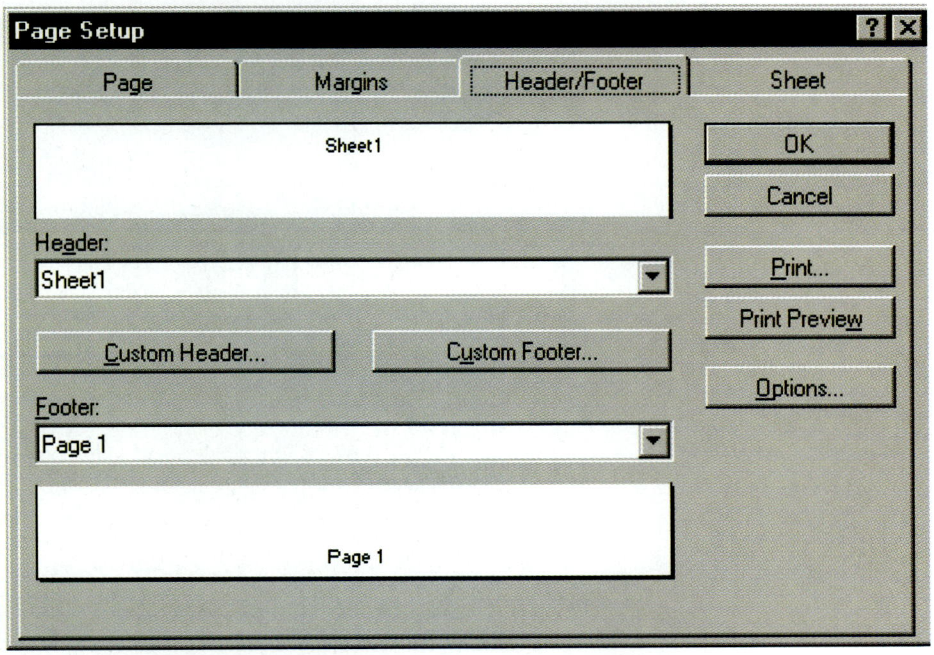


8. To create a custom header:
   SELECT: "(none)" at the top of the *Header* drop-down list box
   CLICK: Custom Header command button
   Figure 2.21 shows the Header dialog box and labels the buttons used for inserting information into the different sections.

**FIGURE 2.21** CUSTOM HEADER DIALOG BOX

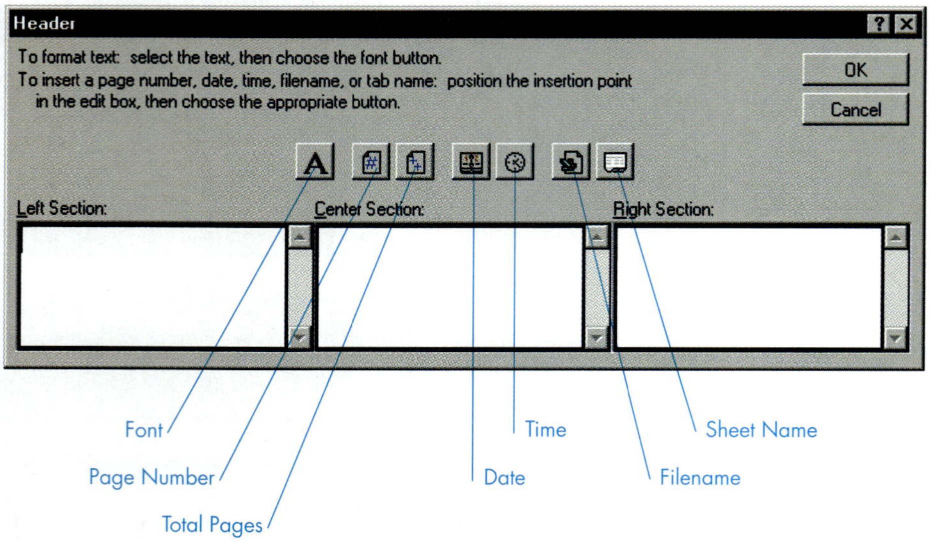


9. To create a header that prints the current date against the right margin:
   CLICK: the mouse pointer in the *Right Section* once
   TYPE: **`Printed on:`**
   PRESS: Space bar once
   CLICK: Date button (as labeled in Figure 2.21)
   CLICK: OK command button
   You will see the custom header appear in the Page Setup dialog box.
10. To select a predefined footer:
    SELECT: "Sales Projections, Page 1" from the *Footer* drop-down list box
11. To specify whether to print gridlines on the printed worksheet:
    CLICK: Sheet tab
    The Page Setup dialog box appears as shown in Figure 2.22.

**FIGURE 2.22** PAGE SETUP DIALOG BOX: SHEET TAB

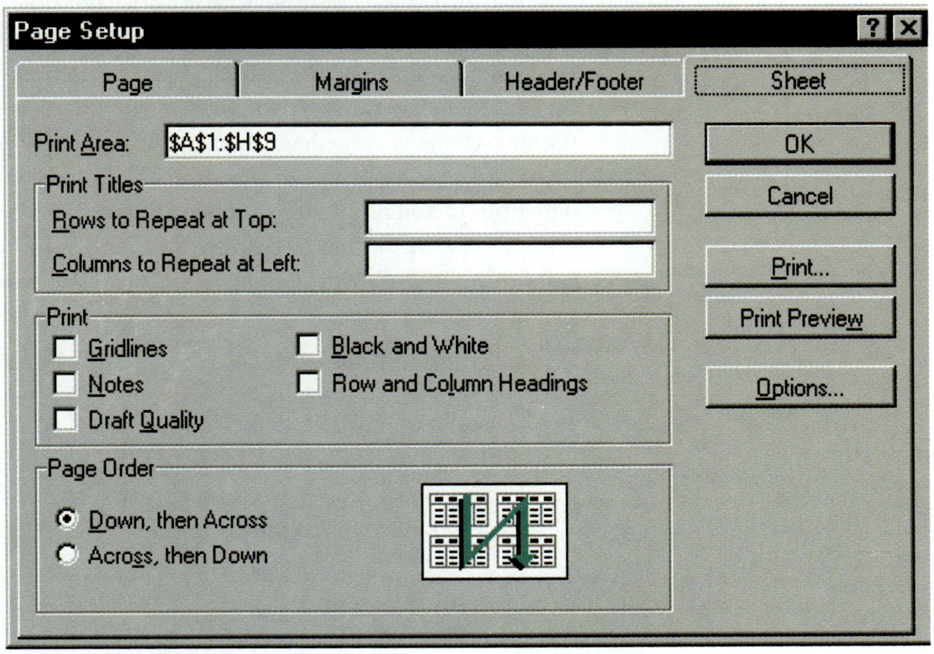


12. Confirm that the cell range from A1 to H9 appears in the *Print Area* text box.

13. For this example, we do not want to print gridlines or row and column headings along with the worksheet. Therefore, make sure that there are no check boxes selected in the *Print* group before proceeding. (*Note:* By default, Excel does not print gridlines on your worksheet.)

14. To complete the Page Setup dialog box and return to the worksheet:
PRESS: ENTER or CLICK: OK

**QUICK REFERENCE**
Preparing to Print

1. **SELECT: the cell range that you want to print**
2. **CHOOSE: File, Print Area, Set Print Area**
3. **CHOOSE: File, Page Setup**
4. **In the Page Setup dialog box, specify options for page layout settings, margins, headers and footers, and whether to print gridlines or column and row headings.**
5. **PRESS: ENTER or CLICK: OK**

## PREVIEWING THE OUTPUT

You can preview a workbook in a full-page display by choosing the File, Print Preview command or clicking the Print Preview button ( ). Once the preview is displayed, use the Next and Previous command buttons near the top of the screen to move through the document page by page. Notice that the mouse pointer changes to a magnifying glass over the page display area to allow you to zoom in on a portion of the page. You click once to zoom in and click a second time to zoom out. If you need to modify some page layout options, you can click the Setup button to display the Page Setup dialog box or the Margins button to drag margin lines right in the Preview window.

Perform the following steps.

1. To preview how the "Sales Projections" workbook will print:
   CLICK: Print Preview button ( )
   A full-page Preview window appears. (*Note:* You can also choose the File, Print Preview command to preview a worksheet.)
2. To zoom in on the page:
   CLICK: Zoom command button
3. To zoom out, move the mouse pointer over the preview page and then click the left mouse button once.
4. When you are finished previewing the worksheet:
   PRESS: ESC or CLICK: Close

**QUICK REFERENCE**
Previewing Your Worksheet

1. **CLICK: Print Preview button ( )**
2. **CLICK: Zoom command button to zoom in and out on a page**
3. **CLICK: Page Setup command button to modify the page layout**
4. **CLICK: Margins command button to modify the margin settings**
5. **PRESS: ESC or CLICK: Close**

## PRINTING THE SELECTED RANGE

When you are satisfied with your worksheet in the Preview mode, choose the File, Print command or click the Print button ( ) to send it to the printer. A dialog box appears with some final print options, as shown in Figure 2.23. You use this dialog box to specify what to print (a cell range or the entire workbook, for example) and how many copies.

**FIGURE 2.23** PRINT DIALOG BOX

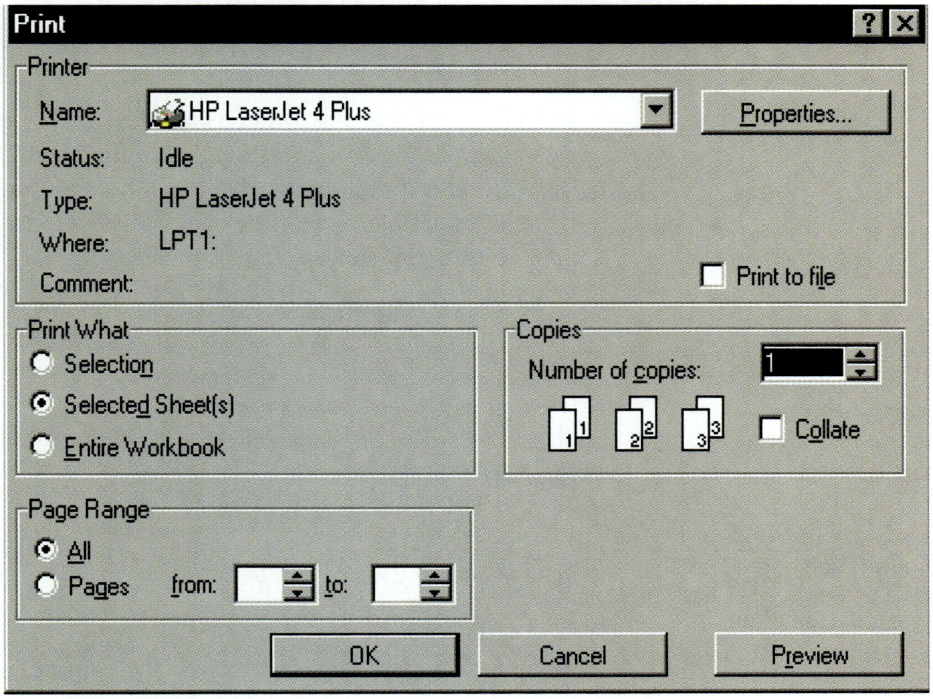


Perform the following steps to print your worksheet.

1. To send the worksheet to the printer and bypass displaying the Print dialog box:
   CLICK: Print button (🖨)
   The document is printed using the default settings. This produces the same result as choosing the File, Print command and then clicking the OK command button, without changing any settings in the dialog box.
2. Save the worksheet as "Sales Projections" to the Advantage Diskette.
3. Exit Excel.

**QUICK REFERENCE**
Printing a Worksheet

1. **CLICK: Print button (🖨)**
2. **SELECT: additional print options, as desired**
3. **PRESS: ENTER or CLICK: OK**

# SUMMARY

This session introduced you to the everyday procedures required to effectively work with Microsoft Excel. To try out these procedures, you created a workbook and practiced entering formulas and the SUM function. You also learned to use some of Excel's "Auto" features, including AutoCalculate, AutoComplete, AutoCorrect, and AutoFormat. The majority of the session, however, dealt with Excel's formatting capabilities for producing presentation quality output. Column widths, row heights, fonts, numeric formats, cell alignments, borders, colors, and shading were all modified in customizing the sample workbook. Toward the end of the session, you concentrated on setting up and previewing a workbook for printing.

Many of the commands introduced in the session are provided in Table 2.1, the Command Summary.

**TABLE 2.1**

Command Summary

| *Command* | *Description* |
|---|---|
| Tools, Spelling (icon) | Spell-checks a cell range, worksheet, or workbook. |
| Format, Column, Width | Changes the column width. |
| Format, Column, AutoFit Selection | Changes the column width to the best fit. |
| Format, Row, Height | Changes the row height. |
| Format, Cells | Font tab: Applies fonts, styles, and point sizes to cells.<br>Number tab: Changes the appearance of values.<br>Alignment tab: Changes the alignment of a cell.<br>Borders tab: Applies borders to cells.<br>Patterns tab: Applies shading to cells. |
| Format, AutoFormat | Formats the selected range using predefined styles. |
| Tools, Options | Removes gridlines from the screen display. |
| Edit, Clear, Formats | Removes formatting from the selected cell range. |
| File, Page Setup | Sets the print area, margins, headers, and footers. |
| File, Print Preview (icon) | Previews the workbook before printing. |
| File, Print (icon) | Prints the workbook. |

## KEY TERMS

**AutoCalculate**

In Excel, a software feature that sums the selected range of cells and displays the result in the Status bar.

**AutoComplete**

In Excel, a software feature that assists you in entering data into a worksheet by filling in letters from existing entries in the column as you type.

**AutoCorrect**

In Excel, a software feature that corrects common typing and spelling mistakes automatically as you type. It also enables you to enter complex symbols quickly and easily.

**AutoFormat**

In Excel, a software feature that applies professionally designed formatting styles to your worksheet tables.

**cell alignment**

In spreadsheets, the positioning of data entered into a cell in relation to the cell borders.

**cell range**

One or more cells in a spreadsheet that together form a rectangle.

**column width**

The width of a worksheet column measured in characters. Because the actual width of a group of characters changes depending on the font size, it is often used only as a relative measure.

**font**

All the characters of one size in a particular *typeface;* includes numbers, punctuation marks, and upper- and lowercase letters.

**footers**

Descriptive information (such as page number and date) that appears at the bottom of each page of a document.

**functions**

Shortcuts that can be used in formulas to perform calculations.

**gridlines**

The lines on an Excel worksheet that assist the user in lining up the cell pointer with a particular column letter or row number.

**headers**

Descriptive information (such as page number and date) that appears at the top of each page of a document.

**margins**
Space between the edge of the paper and the top, bottom, left, and right edges of printed text.

**row height**
The height of a worksheet row measured in points. Points are the measurement unit for type—there are 72 points to the inch.

**SUM function**
Function used to add values stored in a range of spreadsheet cells.

**typeface**
The shape and appearance of characters. There are two categories of typefaces: serif and sans serif. Serif type (for example, Times Roman) is more decorative and, some say, easier to read than sans serif type (for example, Arial).

## EXERCISES

### SHORT ANSWERS

1. What is the purpose of the SUM function?
2. What is meant by a "best fit" column width?
3. How do you apply formatting changes to an entire worksheet?
4. How do you select multiple cell ranges?
5. What does "#########" in a cell indicate?
6. Does turning the gridlines off for the screen display affect the way the document prints? Explain.
7. How does AutoCorrect differ from AutoComplete?
8. Define the acronym WYSIWYG.
9. Name the tabs in the Page Setup dialog box.
10. What unit of measure is used to specify the height of a row?

### HANDS-ON

(*Note:* In the following exercises, save your workbooks onto and retrieve files from the Advantage Diskette.)

1. This exercise retrieves an existing workbook from the Advantage Diskette, edits the information, and saves the workbook under a new filename. You also send a copy of the updated file to the printer.

   *a.* Open the "Expenses - Qtr 1" workbook that is stored on the Advantage Diskette.

*b.* Modify the worksheet to reflect the second quarter's expenses by editing the cells listed below.

| *Move to Cell* | *Type* |
|---|---|
| D1 | **your name** |
| B2 | **Apr-96** |
| C2 | **May-96** |
| D2 | **Jun-96** |
| B6 | **43.44** |
| C4 | **39.65** |
| C7 | **119** |
| D6 | **83.91** |
| D8 | **98.60** |

*c.* Save this workbook to the Advantage Diskette under the name "Expenses - Qtr 2". (*Hint:* Use the File, Save As command.)

*d.* Specify a header that prints the current date in the top left-hand corner of the page.

*e.* Specify a footer that prints the page number in the bottom right-hand corner of the page.

*f.* Review the worksheet in Print Preview mode.

*g.* Print the workbook.

*h.* Save the workbook again to the Advantage Diskette and replace the old version of the file.

2. This exercise uses the formatting commands covered in this session to enhance the "Expenses - Qtr 2" workbook.

   *a.* If the workbook is not already loaded into memory, open the "Expenses - Qtr 2" workbook located on the Advantage Diskette.

   *b.* Make the following changes to column widths:

| *Column* | *Width* |
|---|---|
| A | **15** |
| B | **10** |
| C | **10** |
| D | **10** |
| E | **12** |

*c.* Make the following changes to row heights:

| *Row* | *Height* |
|---|---|
| 1 | **25** |
| 2 | **20** |
| 3 | **6** |
| 9 | **6** |
| 10 | **18** |

*d.* Make the headings from cell B2 to E2 bold and italic.

*e.* Center the headings over their appropriate columns.

*f.* Make the Expense items (the row labels) from A4 to A10 bold.

*g.* Right-align the Expense items.

*h.* Increase the size of the font for the title (in cell A1) to 18 points.

*i.* Select the cells from B2 to E2.

*j.* Place an outline border around these cells and then shade the interior a light gray color.

*k.* Change the screen display by removing the column and row headings and the gridlines.

*l.* Delete the word "Type" in cell A2.

*m.* Save the workbook as "Expenses - Formatted" to the Advantage Diskette.

*n.* Print the workbook.

*o.* Close the workbook.

3. This exercise provides a step-by-step approach to using the formatting commands covered in this session to create a memo or fax form.

*a.* Open a new workbook.

*b.* Move to cell A1.

*c.* TYPE: **Memorandum**

*d.* Center the title between columns A and E using the appropriate toolbar button.

*e.* Choose an interesting font with boldface and a point size of 24 for the title.

*f.* Make columns A through E at least 12 characters wide.

*g.* Enter the following information:

| *Move to cell* | *Type* |
|---|---|
| A3 | **DATE:** |
| A5 | **TO:** |
| A7 | **FROM:** |
| A9 | **SUBJECT:** |
| C7 | ***your name*** |

*h.* Right-align, italicize, and make bold each of the row headings in column A.

*i.* Color the cell range from A1 to E1.

*j.* Color the cell range from A11 to E11.

*k.* Save this workbook as "Memorandum" to the Advantage Diskette. Your worksheet should appear similar to Figure 2.24.

*l.* Print the workbook.

*m.* Close the workbook

*n.* Exit Excel.

**FIGURE 2.24** "MEMORANDUM" WORKSHEET

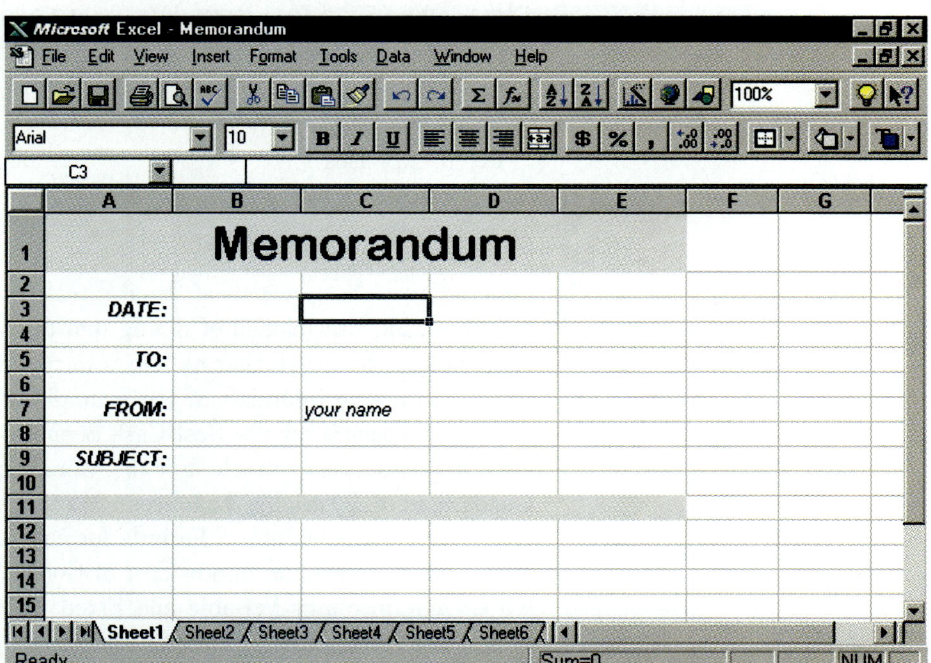

## CASE PROBLEMS — MADRID CLOTHING COMPANY

(*Note:* In the following case problems, assume the role of the primary characters and perform the same steps that they identify. You may want to re-read the session opening.)

1. It's 10 o'clock on a Sunday morning and Khalid's one day off will be spent in front of his computer. He must create, format, and print the spreadsheet for his expansion proposal today. He will venture to the company's main office tomorrow and place the proposal strategically on Suriya's desk before anyone else arrives. With the caffeine from a fourth cup of coffee tingling through his veins, Khalid opens his folder of handwritten notes. His first task is to create the basic spreadsheet layout.

   From the following table that Khalid has drawn by hand, create a spreadsheet called "Lucky 7" and then save it onto the Advantage Diskette.

| *California Expansion* | *Q1/97* | *Q2/97* | *Q3/97* | *Q4/97* |
|---|---|---|---|---|
| Best-Case Scenario: | | | | |
| Sales Revenue | 22,500 | 38,000 | 52,800 | 85,700 |
| Cost of Goods Sold | | | | |
| Gross Margin | | | | |
| Variable Expenses | | | | |
| Fixed Expenses | 6,000 | 6,000 | 6,000 | 6,000 |
| Net Profit | | | | |
| Worst-Case Scenario: | | | | |
| Sales Revenue | 15,800 | 18,900 | 26,500 | 36,000 |
| Cost of Goods Sold | | | | |
| Gross Margin | | | | |
| Variable Expenses | | | | |
| Fixed Expenses | 7,500 | 7,500 | 7,500 | 7,500 |
| Net Profit | | | | |

2. Looking over the spreadsheet, Khalid realizes how much work is still ahead of him. But instead of diving into the spreadsheet haphazardly, he contemplates the steps that he needs to perform. First of all, he must complete the missing information. For example, the Cost of Goods Sold and Variable Expenses for the Best-Case Scenario are 55% and 10% of the Sales Revenue, respectively. For the Worst-Case Scenario, the Cost of Goods Sold and Variable Expenses are 60% and 15% of the Sales Revenue. He must also enter a formula for each quarter to calculate the Gross Margin (Sales Revenue minus Cost of Goods Sold) and the Net Profit (Gross Margin minus Variable and Fixed Expenses). Lastly, Khalid decides to add a column called YTD that totals the figures from the four quarters.

Complete the "Lucky 7" spreadsheet following the steps that Khalid has outlined and then save the file to the Advantage Diskette.

3. Knowing that the presentation of facts and figures is sometimes as important as the information itself, Khalid must now format the "Lucky 7" worksheet to give it a professional appearance. Having worked through the examples in this session, Khalid applies fonts, styles, and numeric formats to the worksheet, aligns the cell contents of the column headings, and changes the column widths. When satisfied with its appearance, Khalid checks the spelling in the spreadsheet and then prints it with the current date and page number appearing in the footer of the page.

   Following Khalid's lead, format, spell-check, and print the workbook, and then save the file to the Advantage Diskette. Make sure that you test the accuracy of the spreadsheet's formulas using the AutoCalculate feature and by inserting new values for the Sales Revenue and watching the Net Profit change. You should check at least one of the columns manually using a calculator.

# *Increasing Your Productivity*

SESSION

3

## SESSION OUTLINE



## INTRODUCTION

Electronic spreadsheets are timesavers compared to the old pencil-and-paper spreadsheets. Now let us demonstrate some timesavers for the timesaver. Instead of building a worksheet from scratch, Excel can help you get started immediately using professionally designed spreadsheet templates. You will also learn to use some command shortcuts that work with cell ranges and how to enter built-in functions for performing complex calculations.

## CASE STUDY RIVERSIDE FORD, INC.

Riverside Ford is one of New Jersey's largest car dealerships. Located near the Meadowlands Arena, Riverside has always maintained a high profile in the community and has easily met Ford's contractual obligations for selling new product. One of Zachary Rempel's duties as a business manager with Riverside is to generate the month-end summary report that must be submitted to Ford's regional office.

Just last week, the owner, Jackson L. Davies, purchased a new computer for Zachary and made him personally responsible for generating all of the dealership's reports. With an increased workload, Zachary knew that he would have to streamline operations and find a more efficient method for summarizing the data he received. Fortunately, the computer came with Microsoft Excel installed and, after only a few days, Zachary is now creating, formatting, and printing worksheets. However, Zachary has also become a little frustrated with Excel. He doesn't like entering long and complex formulas to perform standard calculations, like finding the average value for a column of numbers, picking the highest salesperson's commission in the month, or showing the monthly payment for a financed vehicle. And though he knows that there must be a better way, he doesn't have time to figure out these other methods on his own.

In this session, you and Zachary learn to improve your productivity in creating and editing worksheets. In addition to learning how to copy and move information and how to insert and delete columns and rows, you are introduced to Excel's built-in functions for performing standard calculations. Combined with a brief discussion on Excel's professionally designed templates, this session provides you with some of the most powerful tools that Excel has to offer.

## USING TEMPLATES

Templates help you to do your work quicker and more efficiently. Whether you need to submit an expense report or calculate a loan payment, a **template** can help get you started and headed in the right direction. It's not necessary to understand all the ins and outs of templates and how they are created; but it is important to know that there are several professionally designed spreadsheets already available and easily accessible. During the installation process, you choose which templates to load onto your hard disk. After a complete installation, you will be able to select from the spreadsheet solutions appearing in Table 1.1. You can also create and store your own custom-designed templates for repeated use.

**TABLE 3.1**

Spreadsheet Templates

| *Name* | *Description* |
|---|---|
| Business Planner | Analyzes your current financial situation and provides an income statement, balance sheet, and cash flow forecast. |
| Car Lease | Determines the optimal leasing program and provides a payment schedule showing the lessor's profit and your effective interest rate for up to four options. |
| Change Request | Lets you track, record, and report problems with a product, service, or process. |
| Expense Statement | Lets you track, record, and submit items for typical work-related expenses. |
| Invoice | Provides a professional-looking invoice form that you can fill in and print out instantly. |
| Loan Manager | Calculates a loan payment and provides an amortization schedule and graph showing the repayment breakdown of principal and interest. |
| Personal Budgeter | Lets you budget your monthly income against several expenditures including utilities, insurance, living expenses, entertainment, and credit cards. |
| Purchase Order | Lets you track, record, and print a vendor purchase order. |
| Sales Quote | Lets you track, record, and print a customer sales quote. |
| Timecard | Lets you track, record, and print an employee's timecard record for specific projects and periods. |

Templates contain the boilerplate text, formulas, formatting, and macros (discussed in Session 4) that you need to get up and running quickly. Once displayed, you can customize a template and then save it like any other workbook. For additional help in customizing a template, position your mouse pointer over cells appearing with a red dot in the upper right-hand corner. A pop-up window appears with a helpful note, called a CellTip, describing the type of information to enter into the cell. CellTips provide the same type of context-sensitive help for worksheet cells that ToolTips provide for toolbar buttons. You can create your own CellTips by selecting a cell and then issuing the Insert, Note command from the menu.

Perform the following steps to access Excel's spreadsheet templates.

1. Make sure that you've loaded Microsoft Excel and that a new worksheet appears in the document window. Place the Advantage Diskette into drive A: or drive B:.

2. To open a spreadsheet template:
   CHOOSE: File, New
   CLICK: Spreadsheet Solutions tab in the New dialog box
   (*Note:* If you haven't installed any spreadsheet templates, you will not be able to perform the steps in this section.) Your screen should appear similar to Figure 3.1.

**FIGURE 3.1** NEW DIALOG BOX: SPREADSHEET SOLUTIONS TAB

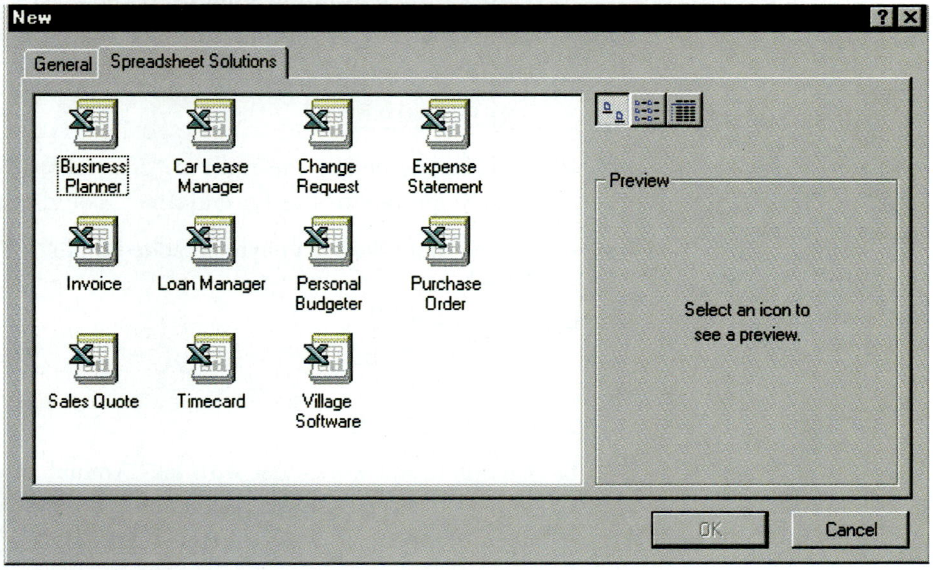


3. To demonstrate using a template to create a new workbook:
   DOUBLE-CLICK: Loan Manager template icon ( )
   A new workbook, complete with text labels, formulas, and its own toolbar (shown below), appears in the document area.

4. To find out a little more about the Loan Manager template:
   CLICK: Template Help button ( ) in the Loan toolbar
   Notice that this template is licensed to Microsoft by Village Software®, as are all of the templates listed in Table 1.1.
5. After reading the contents of the secondary Help window:
   CLICK: Close button ( ) on the Help window

6. To better view the information in the worksheet:
   CLICK: down arrow beside the Zoom Control (100%) drop-down list box on the Standard toolbar
   SELECT: 100%

7. Using the scroll arrows on the vertical and horizontal scroll bars, position the worksheet so that you can see the Customize command button in the top right-hand corner and the Basic Loan and Payment information in the worksheet.

8. Let's enter some basic loan data for this worksheet:
   CLICK: the cell to the right of "Lender Name"
   The Name box in the Formula bar should now read "data1".

9. TYPE: **Bank of America**
   PRESS: ENTER

10. CLICK: the cell to the right of "Amount"
    The Name box in the Formula bar should read "data2".

11. To calculate the loan payment schedule for a $15,000 car loan, starting on March 1st:
    TYPE: **15000**
    PRESS: ENTER
    TYPE: **Mar-1**
    PRESS: ENTER

12. Complete the worksheet with an "Annual Interest Rate" of 9.00% and a four-year term, with 12 payments per year. The "Calculated Payment" should appear as $373.28 (see Figure 3.2).

**FIGURE 3.2** ENTERING DATA IN THE LOAN MANAGER TEMPLATE

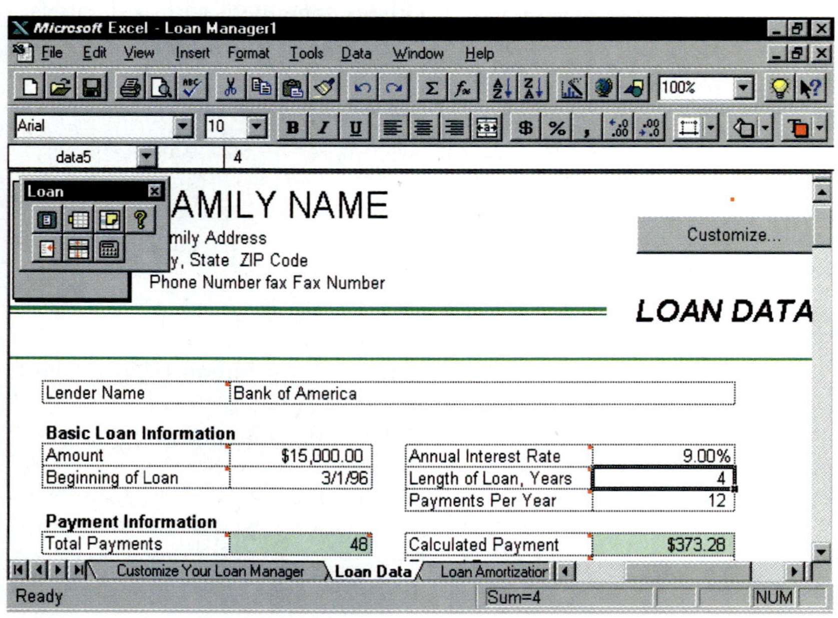

13. To personalize the worksheet template with your name:
CLICK: Customize command button

14. At the top of the "Customize Your Loan Manager" sheet, position the mouse pointer over the red dot appearing in the center of the worksheet. You should see a CellTip appear describing the purpose of this worksheet. (*Note:* You can hover the mouse pointer over any red dot in the workbook template to display a pop-up window with help information and instructions.)

15. In the "Type Personal Information here" portion of the worksheet, enter your name, address, and phone number.

16. Near the bottom of the worksheet window:
RIGHT-CLICK: any one of the Tab Scroll arrows ( )
CHOOSE: Loan Amortization Table from the shortcut menu

17. To print the amortization table for your records:
CHOOSE: File, Print
SELECT: *Selected Sheet(s)* option button in the *Print What* group
CLICK: OK command button

18. To view the graph:
RIGHT-CLICK: any one of the Tab Scroll arrows ( )
CHOOSE: Summary Graph from the shortcut menu

19. CLICK: down arrow beside the Zoom Control (100%) drop-down list box on the Standard toolbar
SELECT: 50%
On your own, use the scroll bars and Zoom Control to view the graph.

20. Save the workbook as "My Loan Table" onto the Advantage Diskette and then close the workbook.

**QUICK REFERENCE**
Using Templates

1. **CHOOSE: File, New**
2. **CLICK: *Spreadsheet Solutions* tab**
3. **DOUBLE-CLICK: a template icon ( ) in the New dialog box**
4. **Customize and then save the workbook.**

## ABSOLUTE AND RELATIVE CELL ADDRESSES

This section adds a new twist to referencing cells in formulas. In previous sessions, you typed the cell address or clicked on the cell that you wanted to include in a formula. You should be aware, however, that there are two types of cell addresses that can be entered into formulas: relative and absolute. The differences between the two become important when you start copying and moving information in your worksheet.

When a formula is copied from one location to another, Excel analyzes both the original cell containing the formula and the destination cell. Excel automatically adjusts the cell references in the copied formula to reflect their new location in the worksheet. This adjustment spares you from having to type many similar formulas into the worksheet and thus saves a tremendous amount of time. A cell reference that adjusts when it is copied is referred to as a **relative cell address.** On the other hand, there are times when you don't want a cell reference to automatically adjust when it is copied. A cell reference that refers to an exact location on the worksheet and does not adjust is called an **absolute cell address.**

In Excel, formulas are entered using relative cell references unless you specify otherwise. To use an absolute cell reference, you must precede the column letter and the row number of the cell address with a dollar sign. For example, to make cell B5 an absolute cell reference in a formula, you would type dollar signs before the B and before the 5, such as $B$5. If you wanted to have the cell reference automatically adjust the row number when it was copied but not the column letter, then you would type a dollar sign before the column letter only, such as $B5.

You will practice using these types of cell references in the next section on copying and moving worksheet information.

## COPYING AND MOVING INFORMATION

To efficiently construct a worksheet, you need tools that reduce the number of repetitive entries you are required to make. For example, once you have created a formula that adds figures in one column, why not copy that formula to sum the adjacent column as well? Two of the most common editing activities in a worksheet are copying and moving data.

There are several different methods for copying and moving information in a worksheet. Similar to most Windows applications, Excel provides the **Clipboard** for sharing information within a workbook, among workbooks, and among applications. For quick "from-here-to-there" copy and move operations, Excel provides the **drag and drop** method where you use the mouse to drag cell information in a worksheet. This section provides examples using both methods for copying and moving information.

### USING THE CLIPBOARD

If the drag and drop method is quicker and easier, why use the Clipboard to copy and move information? The Clipboard provides greater flexibility, allows you to copy information to multiple locations in a worksheet, and allows you to copy and move information to and from other applications. The general process for copying and moving information using the Clipboard is summarized in the following steps:

*a.* Select the cell or cell range that you want to copy or move.

*b.* Cut or copy the selection to the Clipboard.

*c.* Move the cell pointer to where you want to place the information.

*d.* Paste the information from the Clipboard into the worksheet.

*e.* Repeat Steps *c* and *d,* as desired.

The Clipboard tools for cutting, copying, and pasting appear in Table 3.2.

**TABLE 3.2**
Copying and Moving Information Using the Clipboard

| *Task Description* | *Menu Command* | *Toolbar Button* | *Keyboard Shortcut* |
|---|---|---|---|
| Moves the selected cell range from the worksheet to the Clipboard | Edit, Cut | | CTRL + X |
| Copies the selected cell range to the Clipboard | Edit, Copy | | CTRL + C |
| Inserts the contents of the Clipboard at the cell pointer | Edit, Paste | | CTRL + V |

To practice using the Clipboard to copy information, you will retrieve the "Sales Reps" workbook (Figure 3.3). This workbook provides an incomplete summary for three sales representatives.

**FIGURE 3.3** "SALES REPS" WORKBOOK

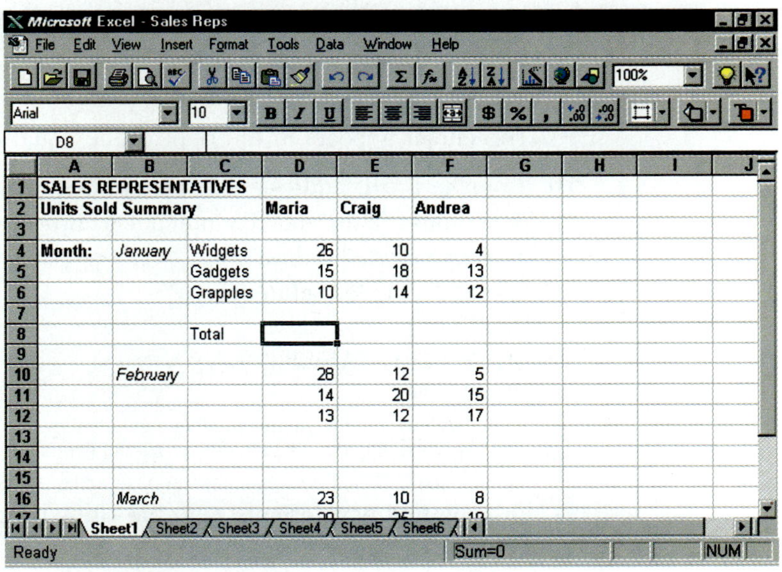

Perform the following steps to copy information using the Clipboard.

1. Open the "Sales Reps" workbook, located on the Advantage Diskette.
2. The first step in completing this worksheet is to sum the January data for each salesperson. Do the following:
   CLICK: cell D8
3. For the remainder of this session, let's cancel Excel's option for moving the cell pointer down one row each time you press ENTER:
   CHOOSE: Tools, Options
   CLICK: Edit tab
   SELECT: *Move Selection after Enter* check box so that no "✓" appears
   PRESS: ENTER or CLICK: OK
4. TYPE: =**d4**+**d5**+**d6**
   PRESS: ENTER
   The cell should now include the sum of the figures in column D (51).
5. To copy this formula onto the Clipboard:
   CLICK: Copy button (📋)
   A dashed marquee now surrounds the cell range.
6. CLICK: cell E8
7. To place a copy of the Clipboard's contents into the cell and remove the marquee around cell D8:
   PRESS: ENTER
   Notice that the result of the formula is the sum of the figures in column E (42). Because the formula uses relative cell addresses, the formula's cell references automatically adjusted to the new column in which they were placed. Look in the Formula bar to see the new formula.
8. To see the effect of using absolute cell references, you are now going to edit the formula in cell E8:
   DOUBLE-CLICK: cell E8
   You will see the formula appear in the cell ready for editing.
9. PRESS: HOME
   PRESS: ➔ once
   The cursor appears to the right of the equal sign.
10. To make a cell address absolute, you could type a dollar sign in front of the column letter and row number. However, there is a shortcut method, as demonstrated below:
    PRESS: F4 (Absolute key)
    PRESS: ➔
    PRESS: F4 (Absolute key)
    PRESS: ➔
    PRESS: F4 (Absolute key)
    PRESS: ENTER
11. To copy this new formula onto the Clipboard:
    PRESS: CTRL +**c**

12. CLICK: cell F8

13. To place a copy of the Clipboard's contents into the cell:
    PRESS: ENTER
    Notice that the result of the formula is still the sum of the figures in column E. The formula did not automatically adjust because it uses absolute cell references.

14. To clean up the Total line, you are going to enter a new formula and copy it to columns E and F. To begin:
    CLICK: cell D8

15. PRESS: DELETE

16. DOUBLE-CLICK: AutoSum button (Σ)

17. CLICK: Copy button ( )

18. To paste the information:
    SELECT: cell range from E8 to F8
    PRESS: ENTER

**QUICK REFERENCE**

Copying and Moving Cell Information

1. **Select the source cell or cell range.**
2. **To copy or move information:**
   **CLICK: Copy button ( )**
   **CLICK: Cut button ( )**
3. **Select the destination cell or cell range.**
4. **PRESS: ENTER or CLICK: Paste button ( )**

## USING DRAG AND DROP

One of Excel's most popular features is drag and drop. This method uses the mouse to drag selected cells around the worksheet without using the Clipboard. The drag and drop method is the easiest way to copy and move information short distances. The Clipboard is not used during a drag and drop operation; therefore, you can copy or move information only from one location to another. In other words, you cannot use drag and drop to perform multiple pastes. However, you can use drag and drop to copy information between sheets in a workbook by holding down the ALT key and dragging the selection over a sheet tab.

Perform the following steps to practice using drag and drop.

1. To demonstrate how you can move cells using drag and drop:
   SELECT: cell range from D2 to F2

2. Position the mouse pointer over a border of the selected cell range until a white arrow appears.

3. CLICK: left mouse button and hold it down
   DRAG: mouse pointer downward one row until a shaded outline appears around cells D3 to F3
4. Release the left mouse button. The contents are moved to the newly highlighted cell range.
5. To undo the last move operation:
   CLICK: Undo button (↶)
6. To copy cells using drag and drop:
   SELECT: cell range from C4 to C8
7. Position the mouse pointer over a border of the selected cell range until a white arrow appears.
8. PRESS: CTRL and hold it down
   CLICK: left mouse button and hold it down
   DRAG: mouse pointer downward until a shaded outline appears around cells C10 to C14
   (*Note:* When you hold down the CTRL key and click on the selected range's border, a plus sign appears at the tip of the mouse pointer to inform you that dragging and dropping the selection will result in a copy operation.)
9. Release the left mouse button. Using the same process, copy the cell range from C10 to C14 to the cell range C16 to C20. Your screen should appear similar to Figure 3.4.

**FIGURE 3.4** "SALES REPS" WORKBOOK AFTER COPYING AND MOVING CELL INFORMATION

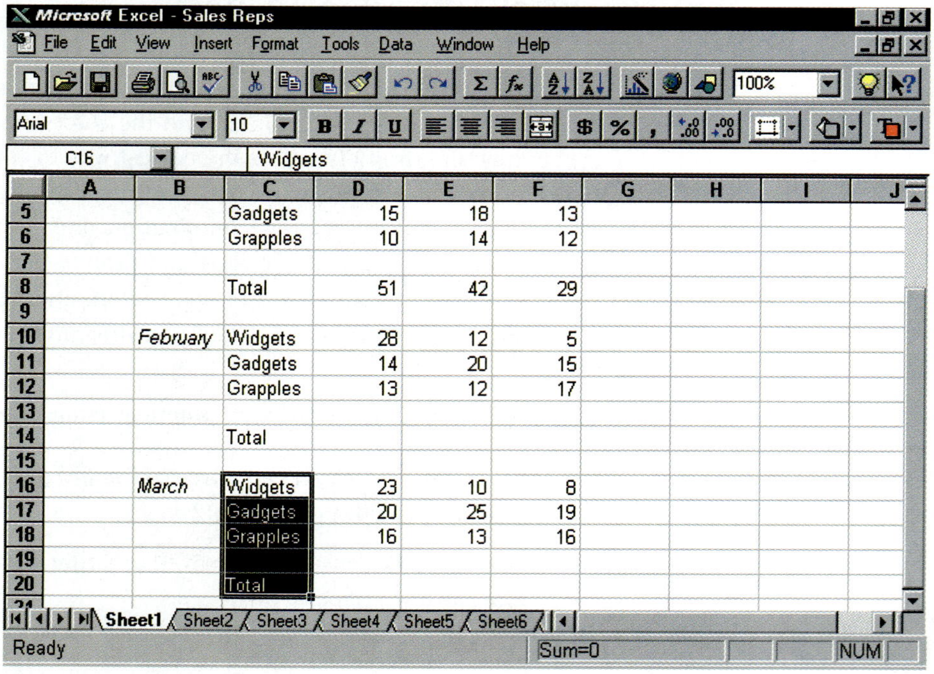

**QUICK REFERENCE**
Move and Copy Cells Using Drag and Drop

1. **Select the cell or cell range to copy or move.**
2. **Position the mouse pointer (a white arrow) over any border of the selected cells.**
3. **If copying the cells, press and hold down the CTRL key.**
4. **If copying or moving the selection between sheets in a workbook, press and hold down the ALT key.**
5. **Drag the selected cells to their destination.**
6. **Release the mouse button and, if necessary, CTRL and/or ALT.**

## USING FILL RIGHT AND FILL DOWN

Excel provides two commands specially designed for copying formulas: Edit, Fill, Right and Edit, Fill, Down. These commands are used when you have entered a single formula or function that needs to be extended across a row (Fill Right) or down a column (Fill Down). Rather than choosing the menu commands, you can select the cell range and press the keyboard shortcuts CTRL + **r** for Fill Right or CTRL + **d** for Fill Down.

To demonstrate, perform the following steps.

1. Using the drag and drop method, copy the formula from D8 to D14.
2. To copy the formula in D14 to the cell range from E14 to F14:
   SELECT: cell range from D14 to F14
   Notice that the cell with the formula appears in the top left-hand corner of the selected range.
3. To perform the copy:
   CHOOSE: Edit, Fill, Right
   The formula in cell D14 is immediately copied to the adjacent columns. (*Note:* The shortcut key for this command is CTRL + **r**.)
4. CLICK: cell D14
5. To copy the formula in cell D14 to D20:
   PRESS: CTRL + **c**
   CLICK: cell D20
   PRESS: ENTER
6. To practice using the Edit, Fill, Right command:
   SELECT: cell range from D20 to F20
7. To execute the keyboard shortcut for the Fill Right command:
   PRESS: CTRL + **r**
8. Save the "Sales Reps" workbook onto the Advantage Diskette.

**QUICK REFERENCE**
Using Fill Right and Fill Down

1. **Select the cell that contains the information to copy.**
2. **Extend the cell range downward or to the right, depending on where you want to place the copies. The cell to copy always appears in the top left-hand corner of the cell range.**
3. **CHOOSE: Edit, Fill, Right (CTRL + r) or Edit, Fill, Down (CTRL + d), depending on where you want to place the copies.**

## CREATING A SERIES WITH AUTOFILL

With Excel's AutoFill feature, you can quickly enter a series into a worksheet. A **series** is simply a sequence of data that follows a pattern, typically mathematical (1, 2, 3, ...) or date (Jan, Feb, Mar, ...). From the menu, you enter a series using the Edit, Fill, Series command. If you prefer using the mouse, you can drag a cell's **fill handle,** which is the black square that appears in the lower right-hand corner of a cell or cell range. You can also use the fill handle to copy a cell's contents to its adjacent cells, similar to the Fill Right and Fill Down commands.

Perform the following steps to practice using AutoFill.

1. In this exercise, we move to a blank area of the worksheet to demonstrate some uses for the fill handle. To begin, do the following:
   CLICK: Name box in the Formula bar
   TYPE: **a50**
   PRESS: ENTER or CLICK: OK
2. To enter a series of dates, move the cell pointer to cell B45 to start.
3. TYPE: **Jan**
   PRESS: ENTER
   Notice that you have to type in at least one cell entry as the starting point for a series. Make sure that your cell pointer remains on cell B45.
4. Position the mouse over the small black square in the bottom right-hand corner of cell B45. The mouse pointer will change to a cross hair.
5. CLICK: left mouse button and hold it down
   DRAG: the cell range outline to cell G45
6. Release the mouse button to complete the AutoFill operation. Since Jan was the starting entry for the series, Excel increments the series by one month for each column.
7. Move to cell B46.
8. TYPE: **Qtr1**
   PRESS: ENTER

9. DRAG: fill handle for B46 to cover the range from B46 to G46
10. Release the mouse button. Notice that Excel understands that the word "Qtr" refers to one in four. After Qtr4, Excel begins again with Qtr1.
11. Move to cell B47.
12. To create a custom data series:
    TYPE: **Jan-96**
    PRESS: ➡
    TYPE: **Apr-96**
    PRESS: ENTER
    You must enter values into the first two cells so that Excel can extrapolate the value needed to increment the series further.
13. SELECT: cell range from B47 to C47
    Make sure that both cells are selected before proceeding. Notice that there is only one fill handle for the range even though two cells are selected.
14. DRAG: fill handle to cover the cell range from B47 to G47
15. Release the mouse button. Your worksheet should now appear similar to Figure 3.5.
16. Save the "Sales Reps" workbook onto the Advantage Diskette.

FIGURE 3.5 USING AUTOFILL TO FILL IN A SERIES

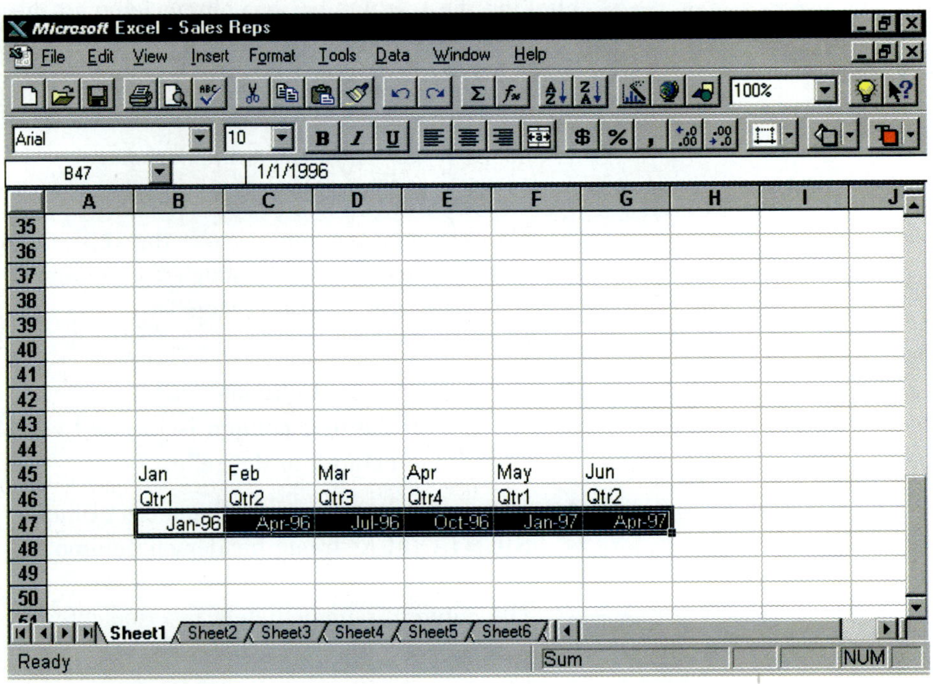

**QUICK REFERENCE**
Using AutoFill

1. **Select the cell that contains the data to continue in a series.**
2. **Position the mouse on the cell's fill handle, a small black square in the bottom right-hand corner of the cell, until it changes to a cross hair mouse pointer.**
3. **Drag the fill handle to extend the series.**
4. **Release the mouse button to complete the operation.**

## INSERTING AND DELETING ROWS AND COLUMNS

One way that you can quickly modify the layout of a worksheet is to add or delete rows and columns. As we mentioned in Session 1, people often create worksheets or design a report without fully understanding the problem that they are trying to solve. Therefore, worksheets must evolve as needs change and as the initial objectives become better defined. The ability to reorganize a worksheet by inserting and deleting rows and columns is an important part of this evolution.

To add a row or column to the worksheet, you choose the Insert, Rows or Insert, Columns command. To delete a row or column, you select a row or column and then choose the Edit, Delete command. The easiest method for selecting a row or column is to click its row number or column letter in the frame area. And the easiest method for choosing the Insert or Delete command is by right-clicking the row number or column letter in the frame area.

Perform the following steps to practice modifying a worksheet.

1. To view the top of the worksheet page:
   PRESS: CTRL + HOME
2. To add a blank column, move the cell pointer to where you want the column inserted. (*Note:* Although the column location is important, you may select any row.) For this step:
   CLICK: cell E1
3. CHOOSE: Insert, Columns
   Notice that the new column is inserted and the original information is moved one column to the right.
4. To insert a column using the shortcut menu:
   RIGHT-CLICK: frame header on column G
   CHOOSE: Insert
   The column is immediately inserted into the worksheet.
5. To delete a column:
   RIGHT-CLICK: frame header on column B
   CHOOSE: Delete

6. To undo the last command issued:
   CLICK: Undo button (↶)

7. To delete a row between the product figures and the total monthly sales lines, do the following:
   RIGHT-CLICK: 7 in the row frame
   CHOOSE: Delete
   RIGHT-CLICK: 12 in the row frame
   CHOOSE: Delete
   RIGHT-CLICK: 17 in the row frame
   CHOOSE: Delete

8. Close the "Sales Reps" workbook without saving the changes.

**QUICK REFERENCE**
Inserting and Deleting Rows and Columns

1. **RIGHT-CLICK: column letter or row number in the frame area**
2. **CHOOSE: Insert to insert a row or column**
   **CHOOSE: Delete to delete a row or column**

## FUNCTIONS

This section introduces you to some very useful functions that can save you a tremendous amount of time in creating worksheets. And don't let the word *function* conjure up visions of your last algebra or calculus class; Excel functions are substitutes for lengthy formulas and are best described as *electronic shortcuts.*

Excel provides a library of over 300 built-in functions to make entering complicated formulas as easy as possible. With the help of Excel's functions, anyone can calculate a mortgage payment, car loan, or an investment's return without ever having to take a finance course. Excel's functions are grouped together into categories: Database, Date & Time, Financial, Information, Logical, Lookup & Reference, Math & Trig, Statistical, and Text.

For step-by-step assistance, you can enter functions with the help of the Function Wizard. You simply click the Function Wizard button (*fx*) on the Standard toolbar and answer the on-screen prompts. You can also enter a function like any other formula. First, type an equal sign followed by the function name. Then, depending on the type of function, you enter numbers, cell references, or range names within parentheses after the function name. Since you already have experienced selecting cell ranges in a worksheet, the next section introduces you to naming a cell range.

## CREATING RANGE NAMES

A **range name** is a label that you give to a group of cells on the worksheet. This label or name can be used in formulas and functions to refer to a cell or cell range. For example, with named ranges, you can enter a self-explanatory function like "=SUM(widgets)" rather than "=SUM(B3:B7)." Not only do named ranges make it easier to construct a worksheet, they make a worksheet easier to understand.

To create a range name, select the cell range and then click once in the Name box in the Formula bar. When the existing information appears highlighted in the Name box, type a new name and press ENTER. To display a drop-down list of all the named ranges in a workbook, you can click the down arrow beside the Name box. This list is useful for entering range names into formulas and for moving quickly to a particular range.

**QUICK REFERENCE**
Naming a Cell Range

1. **Select a cell or cell range to name.**
2. **CLICK: Name box in the Formula bar**
3. **Type a name for the selected range.**
4. **PRESS: ENTER or CLICK: OK**

The following sections use range names in discussing some of the more commonly used mathematical, statistical, financial, and miscellaneous functions.

## USING MATH AND STATISTICAL FUNCTIONS

Mathematical and statistical functions are among the most commonly used categories of functions in spreadsheets. They are also the easiest functions to learn how to use. As described in Table 3.3, the SUM, AVERAGE, MAX, and MIN functions provide a great deal of flexibility and power for the typical application.

**TABLE 3.3**
Math and Statistical Functions

| *Function* | *Syntax* | *Description* |
|---|---|---|
| SUM | =SUM(range) | Adds together a range of cells. |
| AVERAGE | =AVERAGE(range) | Determines the average value in a range of cells. |
| MAX | =MAX(range) | Determines the maximum value in a range of cells. |
| MIN | =MIN(range) | Determines the minimum value in a range of cells. |

Perform the following steps to practice using statistical functions.

1. Open the "Functions" workbook, located on the Advantage Diskette. This workbook file uses tabs to separate the exercises for Statistical, Financial, and Miscellaneous functions.
2. CLICK: Statistical sheet tab
   (*Hint:* Using the mouse, click the worksheet tab named Statistical, located at the bottom of the document window.)
3. Before entering the functions appearing in Table 3.3, your first step is to assign a name to the range of cells containing the student grades. To begin:
   SELECT: cell range from B3 to B12
4. CLICK: Name box in the Formula bar
   (*Note:* When selected properly, the "B3" appears highlighted.)
5. TYPE: **grades**
   PRESS: ENTER
   You can now reference these cells using the name GRADES.
6. CLICK: cell F4
7. To sum the column of results, use the SUM function:
   TYPE: =**sum(grades)**
   CLICK: cell F6
   The answer 756 appears in cell F4. (*Note:* You can enter the expression using lower- or uppercase letters.)
8. To average the column of results, use the AVERAGE function:
   TYPE: =**average(grades)**
   CLICK: cell F8
   The answer 75.6 appears in cell F6.
9. To enter the MAX function using the Function Wizard:
   TYPE: =**max**
   CLICK: Function Wizard button (*fx*) in the Formula bar
   TYPE: **grades**
   Your screen should now appear similar to Figure 3.6. Notice that you bypassed Step 1 of the Function Wizard by typing in the function's name "max". You are now on Step 2 of 2 in the dialog box.

**FIGURE 3.6** FUNCTION WIZARD: MAX FUNCTION

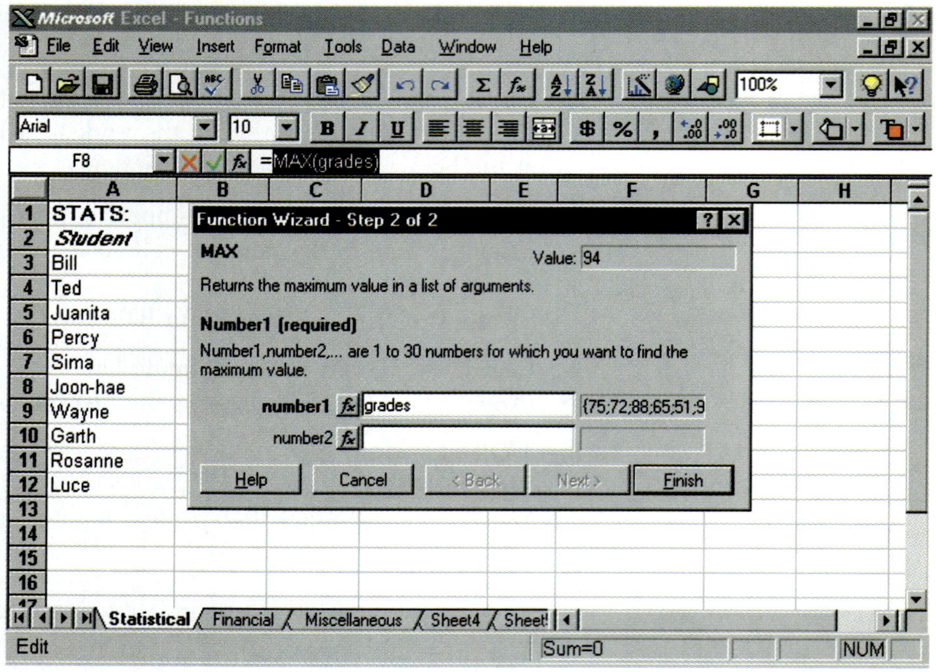


10. CLICK: Finish
    CLICK: ✓ in the Formula bar
    The answer 94 appears in cell F8.

11. CLICK: cell F10

12. To find the minimum value in the column:
    CLICK: Function Wizard button (fx) in the Standard toolbar
    SELECT: Statistical in the *Function Category* list box
    SELECT: MIN in the *Function Name* list box
    The Function Wizard dialog box should now appear similar to Figure 3.7.

**FIGURE 3.7** FUNCTION WIZARD - STEP 1 OF 2

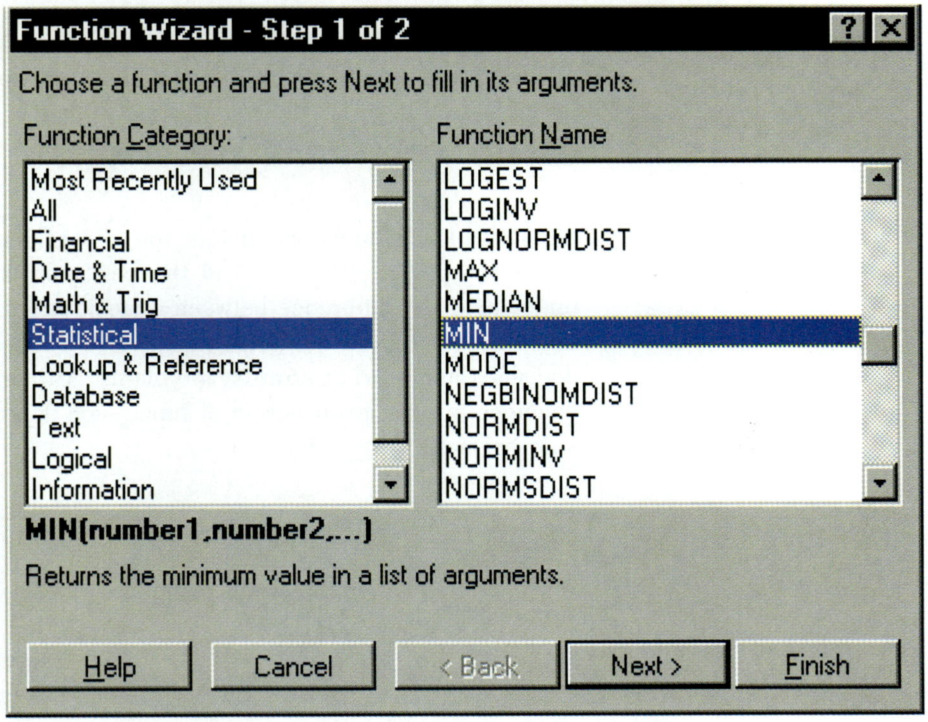


13. To proceed to Step 2 of 2 in the Function Wizard:
    CLICK: Next >
    TYPE: **grades**
    CLICK: Finish
14. Let's use AutoCalculate to find some statistical results. As you may remember from Session 2, you selected a cell range and AutoCalculate displayed the sum of the range in the Status bar. You can also display a count of the values in a selected range, or the average, minimum, and maximum values. To demonstrate:
    SELECT: cell range from B3 to B12
    Notice that "Sum = 756" appears in the Status bar.
15. To display a count of the values in the selected range:
    RIGHT-CLICK: on the AutoCalculate display area of the Status bar
    CHOOSE: Count
    The answer "Count = 10" appears in the Status bar.
16. To display the minimum value in the range using AutoCalculate:
    RIGHT-CLICK: on the AutoCalculate display area of the Status bar
    CHOOSE: Min
    The answer "Min = 51" appears in the Status bar.

17. Let's reset the AutoCalculate display area:
    RIGHT-CLICK: on the AutoCalculate display area of the Status bar
    CHOOSE: Sum
18. On your own, change some of the numbers in the grades column (column B) to see the effects on the statistical functions in column F.

## USING FINANCIAL FUNCTIONS

Excel's financial functions enable you to confidently use complex financial formulas in your worksheets. And the best part is that you don't even need to understand the difference between a stock and a bond! Some of the more popular financial functions, listed in Table 3.4, are devoted to making investment decisions and solving **annuity** problems. An annuity is a series of equal cash payments over a given period of time, such as an investment contribution or a loan payment.

**TABLE 3.4**

Financial Functions

| *Function* | *Syntax* | *Description* |
|---|---|---|
| =PV | =PV(rate,periods,payment) | Calculates the **present value** (the principal) of a series of equal cash payments made at even periods in the future and at a constant interest rate. |
| =FV | =FV(rate,periods,payment) | Calculates the **future value** of a series of equal cash payments made at even periods in the future and at a constant interest rate. |
| =NPV | =NPV(rate,cell range) | Calculates the **net present value** of a series of investments and returns (cash flows) appearing in a cell range, given a constant discount or interest rate. |
| =IRR | =IRR(cell range,guess) | Calculates the **internal rate of return** for a series of periodic investments and returns (cash flows) appearing in a cell range. |
| =PMT | =PMT(rate,periods,pv) | Calculates the payment amount for a loan or mortgage, given a constant interest rate and number of periods. |

Perform the following steps to practice using financial functions. The worksheet that you will use includes a loan payment calculation, an annuity, and an investment scenario.

1. CLICK: Financial tab in the "Functions" workbook
2. CLICK: cell F3
3. As an example of a payment calculation, you will now calculate the monthly payments for a $20,000 car loan. The payments are made over three years (36 periods) at an annual interest rate of 8.5%. In other words, the Present Value or PV for the calculation is 20000; the periods are 36 (3 years × 12 months); and the rate is 8.5%/12. The rate is divided by 12 months in order to change the annual interest rate to a monthly rate. Let's use the Function Wizard to help us enter this equation:
   TYPE: **=pmt**
   CLICK: Function Wizard button (*fx*) in the Formula bar
   The Function Wizard dialog box appears for the PMT function. (*Note:* You can also click the Function Wizard button on the Standard toolbar.)
4. By dragging its Title bar using the mouse, move the Function Wizard dialog box away from the figures in column B.
5. With the insertion point in the *rate* text box:
   CLICK: cell B4 to place the cell address in the dialog box
6. To ensure that the rate is calculated on a monthly basis:
   TYPE: **/12**
7. SELECT: *nper* text box
   CLICK: cell B5
   SELECT: *pv* text box
   CLICK: cell B3
   Notice that the worksheet values that correspond to the cell references appear in the dialog box along with the function's result in the top right-hand corner. Your screen should appear similar to Figure 3.8.

**FIGURE 3.8** FUNCTION WIZARD: PMT FUNCTION

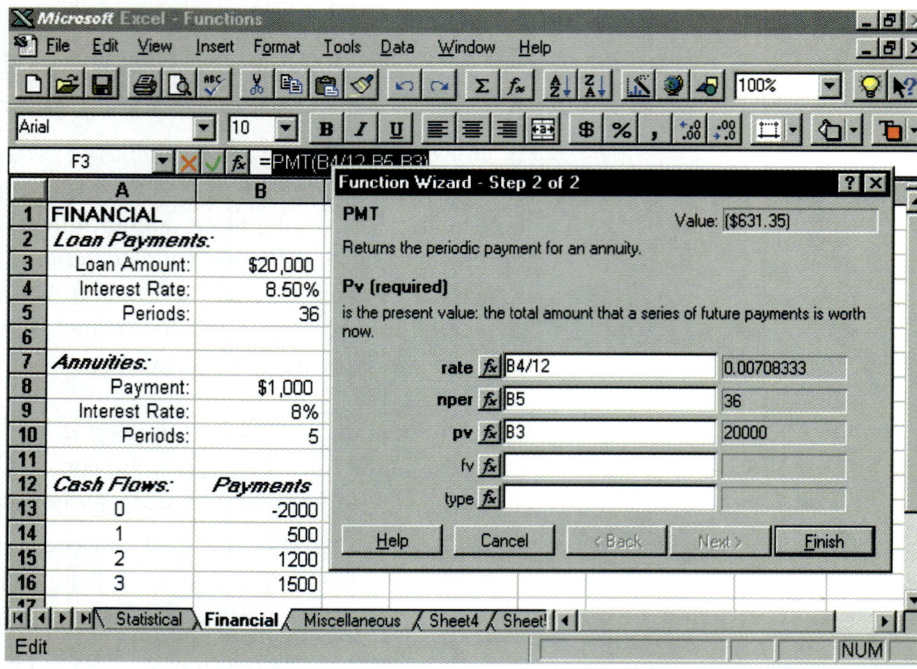


8. To complete using the Function Wizard:
   CLICK: **Finish**
9. To enter the function into the cell:
   CLICK: ✓ in the Formula bar
   The answer ($631.35) appears in cell F3. The payment appears in parentheses to indicate it is a negative number, since it is a cash outflow from yourself to the bank.
10. CLICK: cell F8
11. In this scenario, someone offered you a choice between receiving a flat $6,000 at the end of five years or an annuity of $1,000 per year for the next five years. With an interest rate of 8% per year, which would be the better offer? This problem requires that you enter a future value calculation using the following syntax: FV(rate,periods,payment). Do the following:
    TYPE: =**fv(b9,b10,b8)**
    PRESS: **ENTER**
    The better offer is $6,000 at the end of five years, since the future value of the annuity is only $5,866.60. With the majority of these calculations, you are concerned with the **absolute** or positive **value** for the number. Therefore, you can ignore the negative sign or parentheses.

12. CLICK: cell F9
13. Picture this happening: someone offers you a choice between receiving $4,000 today or an annuity of $1,000 per year for the next five years. With an interest rate of 8% per year, which would be the better offer? This problem requires that you enter a present value calculation using the following syntax: PV(rate,periods,payment). Do the following:
    TYPE: =**pv(b9,b10,b8)**
    PRESS: ENTER
    The better offer is $4,000 today, compared to receiving $3,992.71 in today's dollars over the next five years.
14. CLICK: cell F13
15. Some friends have just asked you to invest in a wonderful opportunity. The deal is simple. You give them $2,000 now and they will pay you $500 at the end of the first year, $1,200 in the second year, and $1,500 in the third year. In total, you are receiving $3,200 for your $2,000 investment. Is this a good investment? The net present value and internal rates of return are two profitability measures for such investments. To calculate the internal rate of return, you need to enter an estimate of the expected rate of return. For this example, we use 20% in the function:
    TYPE: =**irr(b13:b16,20%)**
    PRESS: ENTER
    Not a bad deal at all! This calculation shows that you would make a 23.16% return on your investment.
16. CLICK: cell F14
17. Another test for the profitability of an investment is the net present value. We will use 10% as the expected interest rate:
    TYPE: =**npv(10%,b13:b16)**
    PRESS: ENTER
    This calculation confirms that it is a wise investment opportunity. An investment is profitable if the net present value result is a positive number. Your worksheet should now appear similar to Figure 3.9.

**FIGURE 3.9** "FUNCTIONS" WORKBOOK: FINANCIAL TAB

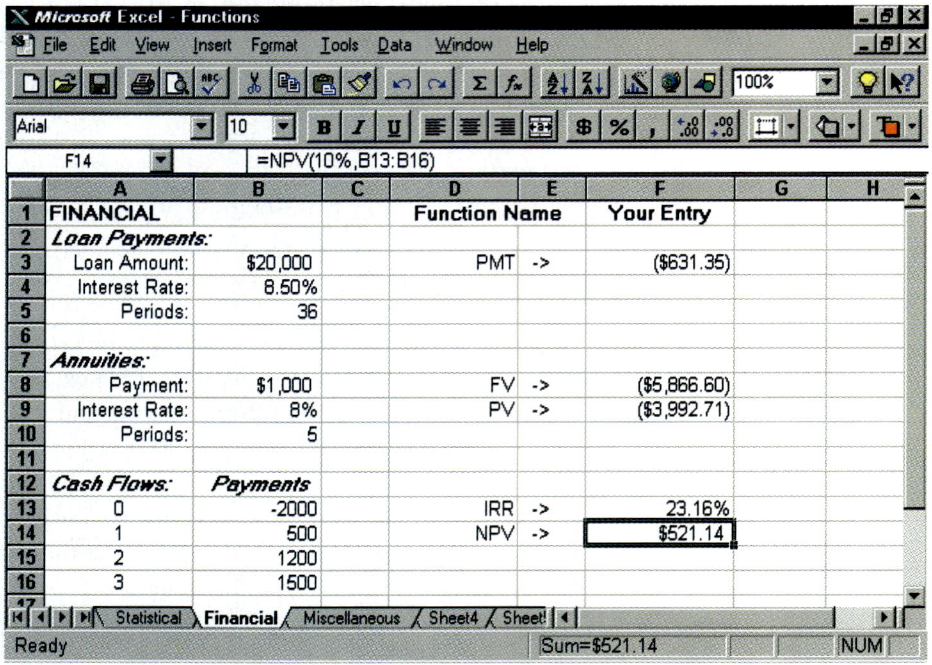


18. Change some numbers in the loan payments, savings account, and cash flow sections to see their effects on the functions that you entered. For example, what would the monthly payment be for a $15,000 car loan over four years? What if your friends needed $2,500 for their startup capital in Step 15? Would it still be a wise investment?

## USING MISCELLANEOUS FUNCTIONS

This section describes some miscellaneous functions taken randomly from their formal categories. Although often considered an intermediate-to-advanced topic, the IF function is one of the most useful functions available. Using the IF function, you can have Excel evaluate a cell's value and then make a decision to perform a calculation based on its contents. The miscellaneous functions covered in this section are described in Table 3.5.

**TABLE 3.5**

Miscellaneous Functions

| *Function* | *Syntax* | *Description* |
|---|---|---|
| =NOW | =NOW( ) | Provides the current date and time. |
| =ABS | =ABS(cell) | Provides the **absolute value** of a cell. |
| =ROUND | =ROUND(cell,digits) | Provides the **rounded value** of a cell to the number of digits specified. |
| =IF | =IF(condition,true,false) | Performs a calculation based on the condition being met. |

Perform the following steps.

1. CLICK: Miscellaneous tab in the "Functions" workbook
2. CLICK: cell E3
3. TYPE: =**now()**
   PRESS: **ENTER**
   (*Note:* You can format the date using the Format, Cells command.)
4. CLICK: cell E4
5. In this scenario, you want cell E4 to display a commission rate that is based on a salesperson's unit sales. If sales are less than 10,000 units, the commission is 5%; otherwise, the commission is 6%. To enter this function, you use the following syntax: IF(condition,true,false). Do the following:
   TYPE: =**if(b4<10000,5%,6%)**
   PRESS: **ENTER**
6. To copy this expression to the next two cells:
   SELECT: cell range from E4 to E6
   CHOOSE: Edit, Fill, Down
7. CLICK: cell E11
8. Let's enter the ROUND function:
   TYPE: =**round(a11,2)**
   PRESS: **ENTER**
   (*Note:* Make sure that you type a11 and not the word "all.")
9. CLICK: cell E13
10. To get the absolute or positive value for the number in cell A13:
    TYPE: =**abs(a13)**
    PRESS: **ENTER**
    Your worksheet should appear similar to Figure 3.10.

**FIGURE 3.10** "FUNCTIONS" WORKBOOK: MISCELLANEOUS TAB

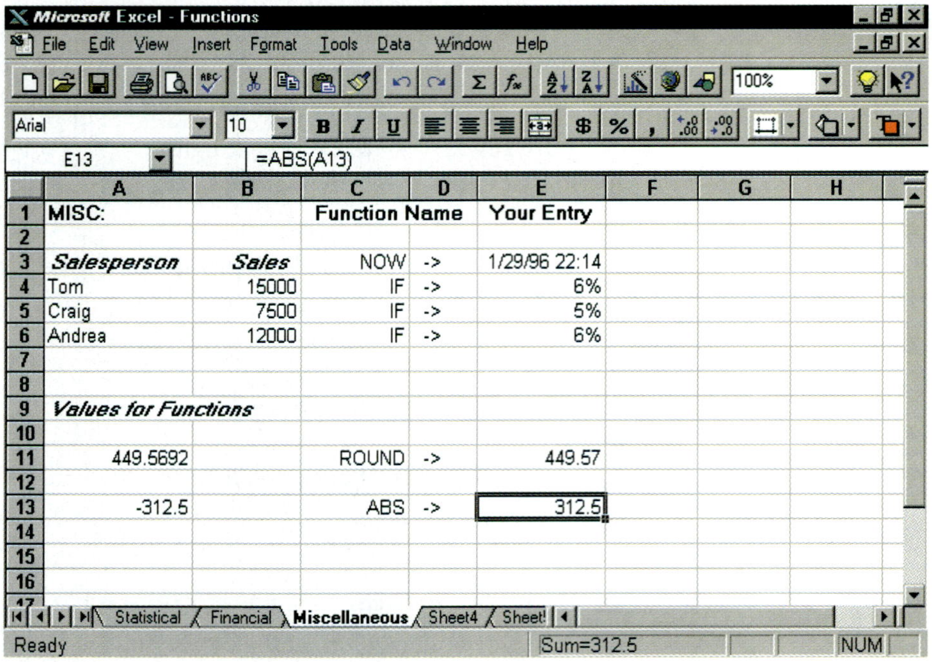


11. Change some numbers in the worksheet to see the effects on the functions that you entered.
12. Save the workbook as "Functions" onto the Advantage Diskette, replacing the original file.

## USING GOAL SEEK

The Goal Seek command is a powerful "what-if" tool that lets you find questions for answers—similar to playing Jeopardy on television. For example, you can state exactly what you need as a bottom-line profit and Goal Seek automatically calculates the sales required to meet this goal. How does Goal Seek work? Since profit is dependent on sales (sales less expenses equals profit), Goal Seek quickly substitutes values into the sales variable until the desired profit is achieved.

To use Goal Seek, you choose the Tools, Goal Seek command from the menu. In the dialog box that appears, you enter the cell that contains the formula for calculating the target value (for example, profit) and then enter the target value itself. You also need to tell Goal Seek what variable it is allowed to change in order to achieve this target value (for example, sales). Once completed, you press **ENTER** or click on OK.

Perform the following steps.

1. CLICK: Financial tab in the "Functions" workbook
2. If you changed any of the original values on this page, ensure that the Loan Amount is $20,000 (in cell B3), the Interest Rate is 8.50% (in cell B4), and the Periods is 36 (in cell B5) before proceeding.
3. Let's use Goal Seek to calculate the maximum loan amount that we can afford with monthly payments of $500. To start Goal Seek:
   CLICK: cell F3
   CHOOSE: Tools, Goal Seek
4. In the *Set cell* text box, make sure that the cell address is $F$3.
5. To enter the monthly payment that we can afford:
   SELECT: *To value* text box
   TYPE: **−500**
   Notice that we enter −500, since it is a cash outflow to the bank.
6. To specify the loan amount as the variable to change in this calculation:
   SELECT: *By changing cell* text box
   TYPE: **b3**
   Your screen should now appear similar to Figure 3.11.

**FIGURE 3.11** ENTERING VALUES INTO THE GOAL SEEK DIALOG BOX

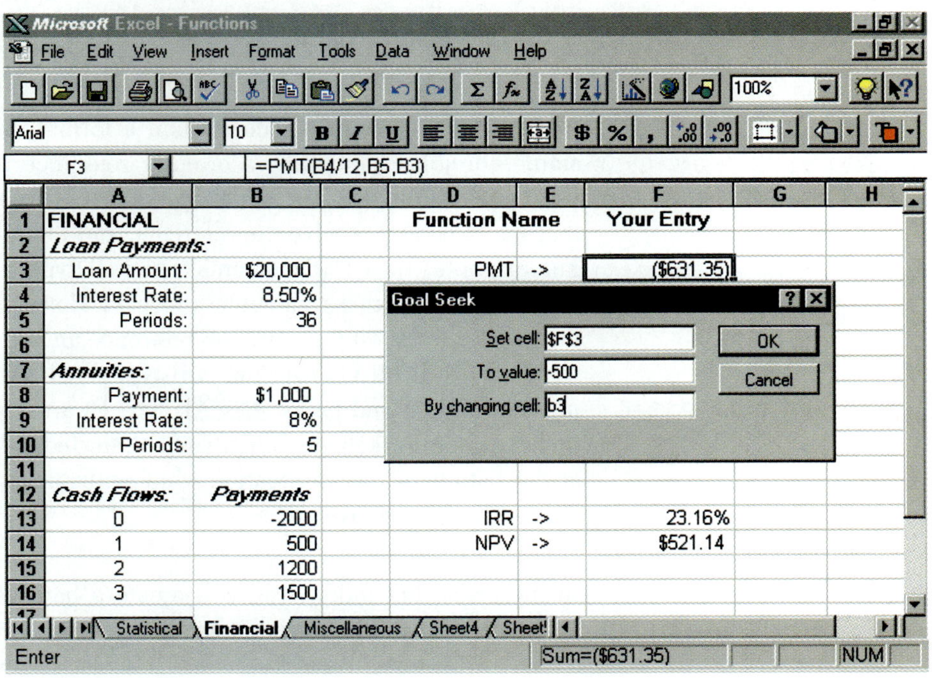

7. To solve the equation:
   CLICK: OK to accept the Goal Seek dialog box
   CLICK: OK to bypass the Goal Seek Status
   When you return to the worksheet, the Loan Amount has been changed to $15,839 in cell B3 and the payment in cell F3 is now $500.

8. Save the workbook as "Functions" onto the Advantage Diskette and then close the workbook.

**QUICK REFERENCE**
Using Goal Seek

1. **CHOOSE: Tools, Goal Seek**
2. **Specify the formula or expression which contains the target value.**
3. **Enter the desired target value.**
4. **Specify the variable to change.**
5. **PRESS: ENTER or CLICK: OK**

**IN ADDITION**

SOLVING MORE COMPLEX "WHAT-IF" SCENARIOS

For more complex problems, Excel provides the **Solver** tool which allows you to specify more than one variable to change in order to meet multiple goals and constraints. Using Solver is not covered in this learning guide as it is a more advanced topic.

## CIRCULAR REFERENCES: AVOIDING THEM

A **circular reference** occurs when a formula references itself in an expression. Formulas containing a circular reference produce erroneous results that can ripple throughout the entire worksheet. The problem with these formulas is that Excel cannot resolve the reference and therefore displays a zero in the cell. For example, in a few moments you will type a formula into cell A4 that is intended to add three amounts above it. However, you are going to type it in incorrectly, including a circular reference in the formula. The correct formula would be =SUM(A1:A3). You will type =SUM(A1:A4). When you finish typing the formula and press ENTER, Excel warns you that there is a circular reference in the worksheet. When you acknowledge Excel's warning, the Status bar at the bottom of the application window displays the cell in which the circular reference was discovered.

In the steps that follow, you will create a new workbook with a circular reference. Perform the following steps.

1. To start a new worksheet:
   CLICK: New button ()

2. Enter the following information into the worksheet:

| *Move to cell* | *Type* |
|---|---|
| A1 | 10 |
| A2 | 12 |
| A3 | 20 |

3. CLICK: cell A4
4. In this cell, you will enter an incorrect SUM function:
   TYPE: **=sum(a1:a4)**
   PRESS: ENTER
5. A dialog box appears containing a warning message that your formula contains a circular reference. To accept the warning:
   PRESS: ENTER or CLICK: OK
   Because Excel could not resolve the circular reference, the answer is displayed as 0. Notice that the Status bar at the bottom of the application window directs you to the cell that contains the circular reference. To eliminate the circular reference, you edit the cell that contains the formula with the circular reference. In this case, you would edit cell A4 to contain =SUM(A1:A3).
6. Close the workbook and do not save the changes to the worksheet when you are prompted.
7. Exit Microsoft Excel.

## SUMMARY

This section explored several new commands for increasing your productivity. After a discussion on using templates, you were introduced to the commands and shortcut keys for copying and moving information around your worksheet. Some final formatting commands were also introduced for inserting and deleting columns and rows in your worksheet.

The latter half of the session introduced several of Excel's built-in functions. The Statistical and Financial categories were emphasized with the SUM, AVERAGE, MAX, MIN, PV, FV, IRR, NPV, and PMT functions. Several miscellaneous functions were also introduced, including the IF function for calculating an expression based on a set of conditions.

Many of the commands used in the session are provided in Table 3.6, the Command Summary. See Tables 3.3 to 3.5 for the Function summaries.

**TABLE 3.6**

Command Summary

| *Command* | *Description* |
|---|---|
| Edit, Copy or () | Places a copy of a cell or cell range onto the Clipboard. |
| Edit, Cut or () | Moves a cell or cell range from the worksheet to the Clipboard. |
| Edit, Paste or () | Pastes the contents of the Clipboard into the active cell or selected cell range. |
| Edit, Fill, Right | Copies a cell to adjacent cells across the worksheet. |
| Edit, Fill, Down | Copies a cell to adjacent cells down the worksheet. |
| Insert, Column/Row | Inserts a column or row in the worksheet. |
| Edit, Delete | Deletes a column or row from the worksheet. |
| Tools, Goal Seek | Launches the Goal Seek tool for performing "what-if" analysis. |

## KEY TERMS

**absolute cell address**

Cell reference in an electronic spreadsheet program that does not adjust when copied to other cells.

**absolute value**

The value of a real number, disregarding its sign. For example, the absolute value of the number −5 is 5.

**annuity**

A series of equal cash payments over a given period of time.

**circular reference**

The situation created when a formula references its own cell address in an expression.

**Clipboard**

In Windows, the Clipboard is a program that allows you to copy and move information within an application or among applications. The Clipboard temporarily stores the information in memory before you paste the data in a new location.

**drag and drop**

A feature of Windows that allows you to copy and move information by dragging cell information from one location to another using the mouse.

**fill handle**

The small black square that is located in the bottom right-hand corner of a cell or cell range. You use the fill handle to create a series or to copy cell information (similarly to the Edit, Fill, Right and Edit, Fill, Down commands).

**future value**
The value in future dollars of a series of equal cash payments.

**internal rate of return**
The rate of return at which the net present value is 0.

**net present value**
A calculation used to determine whether an investment provides a positive or negative return, based on a series of cash outflows and inflows.

**present value**
The value in present-day dollars of a series of equal cash payments made sometime in the future.

**range name**
A name that is given to a range of cells in the worksheet. This name can then be used in formulas and functions to refer to the cell range.

**relative cell address**
Cell reference in an electronic spreadsheet program that automatically adjusts when copied to other cells.

**series**
A sequence of numbers or dates that follows a mathematical or date pattern.

**Solver**
An Excel tool that facilitates "what-if" analysis. Although similar to Goal Seek, Solver enables you to specify more than one variable to modify and more than one goal to attain.

**template**
A special type of workbook in Excel that typically contains text, formulas, and macros. You use a workbook template as an example or boilerplate for creating your own workbook.

## EXERCISES

### SHORT ANSWER

1. What is the difference between an absolute cell address and a relative cell address?
2. What is the primary difference between using the Edit, Copy command and the drag and drop method to copy information?

3. Explain the fastest way to put monthly headings at the top of your worksheet (i.e., January, February, March, ...).
4. Why would you want to name a range of cells?
5. List the function categories in Excel.
6. Describe four statistical functions.
7. Describe five financial functions.
8. What is the purpose of the NOW function?
9. What is the purpose of the IF function?
10. What is a circular reference? How would you locate the cell that contains a circular reference?

## HANDS-ON

(*Note:* In the following exercises, save your workbooks onto and retrieve files from the Advantage Diskette.)

1. The objective of this exercise is to create a new workbook, reorganize its layout, construct formulas, and then practice copying and moving information.

   *a.* Ensure that Microsoft Excel is loaded and that a blank worksheet appears on the screen.

   *b.* Type the text and numbers as displayed in Figure 3.12 into the appropriate cells. Make sure that you type your name into cell C1. Once completed, perform a spell-check of the worksheet. (*Note:* Don't worry about the text labels spilling over into the next column, as you will increase the column widths in Step *d.*)

**FIGURE 3.12** "INCOME STATEMENT" WORKSHEET

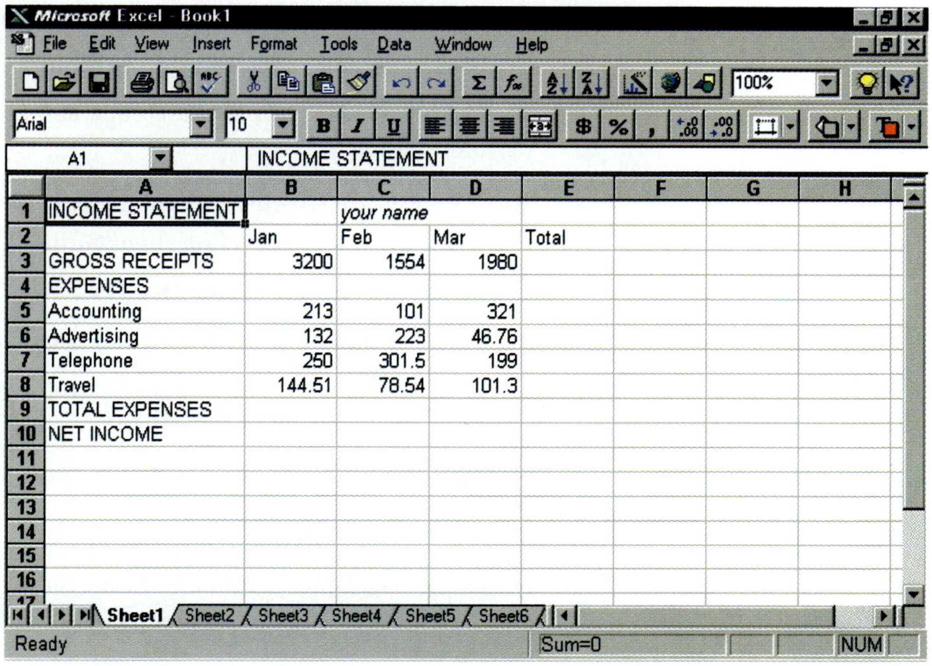


| | A | B | C | D | E |
|---|---|---|---|---|---|
| 1 | INCOME STATEMENT | | your name | | |
| 2 | | Jan | Feb | Mar | Total |
| 3 | GROSS RECEIPTS | 3200 | 1554 | 1980 | |
| 4 | EXPENSES | | | | |
| 5 | Accounting | 213 | 101 | 321 | |
| 6 | Advertising | 132 | 223 | 46.76 | |
| 7 | Telephone | 250 | 301.5 | 199 | |
| 8 | Travel | 144.51 | 78.54 | 101.3 | |
| 9 | TOTAL EXPENSES | | | | |
| 10 | NET INCOME | | | | |

*c.* Insert one row between each of the following:

- the INCOME STATEMENT line and the month headings
- the month headings and the GROSS RECEIPTS line
- the GROSS RECEIPTS line and the EXPENSES line
- the TOTAL EXPENSES line and the NET INCOME line

*d.* Set column A's width to 20 characters.

*e.* Set columns B through E to 10 characters wide.

*f.* Center the month headings, cells B3 to E3, and then make them bold and italic.

*g.* Center the row headings in cells A5 to A14.

*h.* Italicize the row headings.

*i.* Make the title in cell A1 bold and assign a font of 14 points in size.

*j.* Enter the SUM function in cell E5 to sum the GROSS RECEIPTS.

*k.* Copy the function in cell E5 to cells E8 through E12 using the Clipboard and the toolbar buttons.

*l.* Use the AutoSum button to sum the expenses for each month.

*m.* Enter a formula into cell B14 that subtracts the TOTAL EXPENSES for January from the GROSS RECEIPTS.

*n.* Copy the formula from cell B14 to the cell range C14 to E14.

*o.* Select the cell range from B5 to E14.

*p.* Apply a numeric format to insert commas and two decimal places.

*q.* Select the cell range from B3 to E3.

*r.* Place a border around these cells and apply a background color to the interior.

*s.* Select the cell range from B12 to E12

*t.* Add top and bottom borderlines to this range.

*u.* Select the cell range from B14 to E14.

*v.* Place a single line for the top border and a double line for the bottom border.

*w.* Print the workbook.

*x.* Save the workbook as "Income Statement" onto the Advantage Diskette.

2. This exercise takes the "Income Statement" workbook, now saved on the Advantage Diskette, modifies the worksheet, applies names to cell ranges, and then inserts some of the statistical functions.

*a.* If it's not already displayed, open the "Income Statement" workbook located on the Advantage Diskette.

*b.* Insert a row between the Travel Expense item and the TOTAL EXPENSES line.

*c.* Select the cell range from B5 to D5.

*d.* Name this cell range "Receipts" using the Name box.

*e.* Name the following cell ranges:

| *Select the Range* | *Name the Range* |
|---|---|
| B8 to D8 | **Accounting** |
| B9 to D9 | **Advertising** |
| B10 to D10 | **Telephone** |
| B11 to D11 | **Travel** |
| B13 to D13 | **Expenses** |

*f.* Move to cell F3.

*g.* TYPE: **Average**

*h.* Set the column F's width to 10 characters.

*i.* Move to cell F5.

*j.* To average the GROSS RECEIPTS:
TYPE: =**average(receipts)**
PRESS: ENTER

*k.* Complete the column as follows:

| *Move to cell* | *Type* |
|---|---|
| F8 | =**average(accounting)** |
| F9 | =**average(advertising)** |
| F10 | =**average(telephone)** |
| F11 | =**average(travel)** |
| F13 | =**average(expenses)** |

*l.* Copy cell E15 to F15 using drag and drop.

*m.* To copy the formatting characteristics of the cells in column E:
SELECT: cell range from E3 to E15
CLICK: Format Painter button ( )
CLICK: cell F3 with paintbrush mouse pointer
The formatting is automatically applied to the same rectangular shape of the cells that you copied. Your worksheet should now look similar to Figure 3.13.

**FIGURE 3.13** FORMATTING THE "INCOME STATEMENT" WORKSHEET

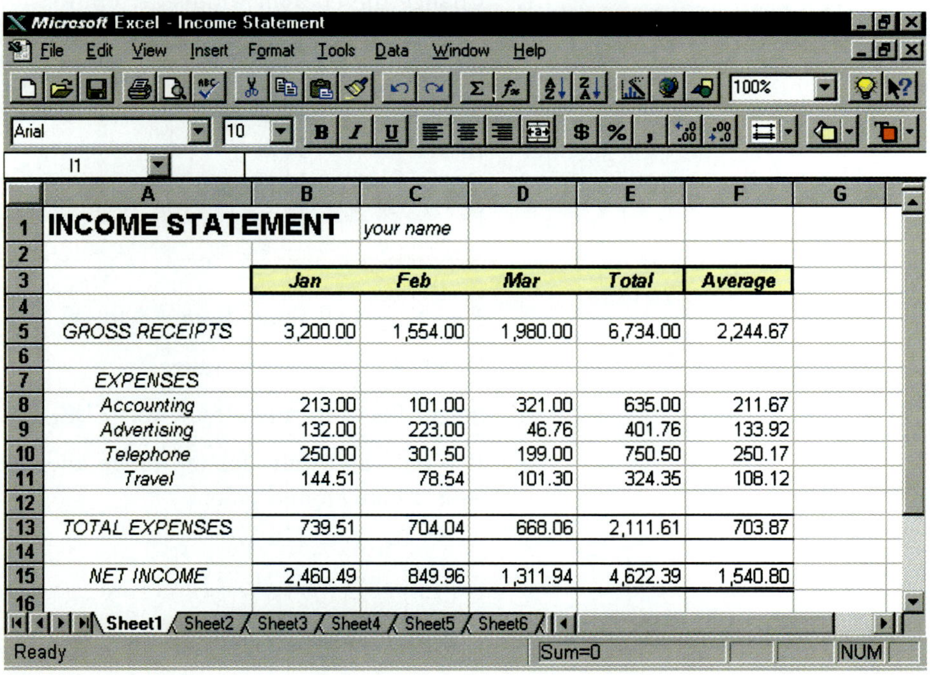

*n.* Print the worksheet.

*o.* Save your workbook as "Income Statement" onto the Advantage Diskette and then close the workbook.

3. In this exercise, you create a workbook from scratch for computing a loan or mortgage table.

*a.* To begin, ensure that you have an empty worksheet.

*b.* Enter the textual information:

| *Move to cell* | *Type* |
|---|---|
| A1 | **MORTGAGE TABLE** |
| D1 | ***your name*** |
| A3 | **Principal Amount:** |
| A4 | **Interest Rate:** |
| A5 | **Years:** |
| C4 | **Monthly Rate:** |
| C5 | **Months:** |
| C6 | **Payment:** |
| A8 | **Payment #** |
| B8 | **Principal** |
| C8 | **Interest** |
| D8 | **Balance** |

*c.* Change the column widths as follows:

| *Column* | *Width* |
|---|---|
| A | 18 |
| B | 15 |
| C | 15 |
| D | 15 |

*d.* Select the cell range from A3 to D8.

*e.* Right-align the entire range.

*f.* Select the cell range from A8 to D8.

*g.* Use bold and italic for the range and then apply an outline border with a background color.

*h.* Enter the numeric information:

| *Move to cell* | *Type* |
|---|---|
| B3 | **150,000** |
| B4 | **7.5%** |
| B5 | **30** |
| A9 | **0** |

*i.* Enter the formulas:

| *Move to cell* | *Type* |
|---|---|
| D4 | =**b4/12** |
| D5 | =**b5*12** |
| D6 | =**pmt(d4,d5,b3)** |
| D9 | =**b3** |
| A10 | =**a9+1** |

*j.* To calculate the amount of interest paid during each period (column C), move to cell C10 and enter the following formula:
TYPE: =**d9*$d$4**
PRESS: ENTER
Notice that the monthly interest rate is an absolute cell reference. Since the formula will be copied down the worksheet, you must enter the formula with an absolute reference to ensure that the expression always refers to cell D4.

*k.* To calculate the amount of principal paid during each period (column B), move to cell B10 and enter the following formula:
TYPE: =**abs($d$6)−c10**
PRESS: ENTER
Again, the formula will always refer to the total payment amount when copied, so an absolute cell address is used in the expression.

*l.* To calculate the amount of principal left (the Balance for column D), move to cell D10 and enter the following:
TYPE: =**d9−b10**
PRESS: ENTER

*m.* Select the cell range from A10 to D10.

*n.* Format the numbers to appear with commas and no decimal places.

*o.* Select the cell range from A10 to D189.

*p.* CHOOSE: Edit, Fill, Down

*q.* Return to cell A1.

*r.* Change the loan principal amount from 150,000 to 175,000. Watch the worksheet recalculate the payments for each period.

*s.* Change the number of years to 25. Note the change in the ratio between the principal being paid back each period and the interest paid on the money borrowed.

*t.* Save the workbook as "Mortgage" onto the Advantage Diskette. Your worksheet should now look similar to Figure 3.14.

*u.* Print the worksheet.

*v.* Close the workbook and then exit Excel.

**FIGURE 3.14** "MORTGAGE" WORKSHEET

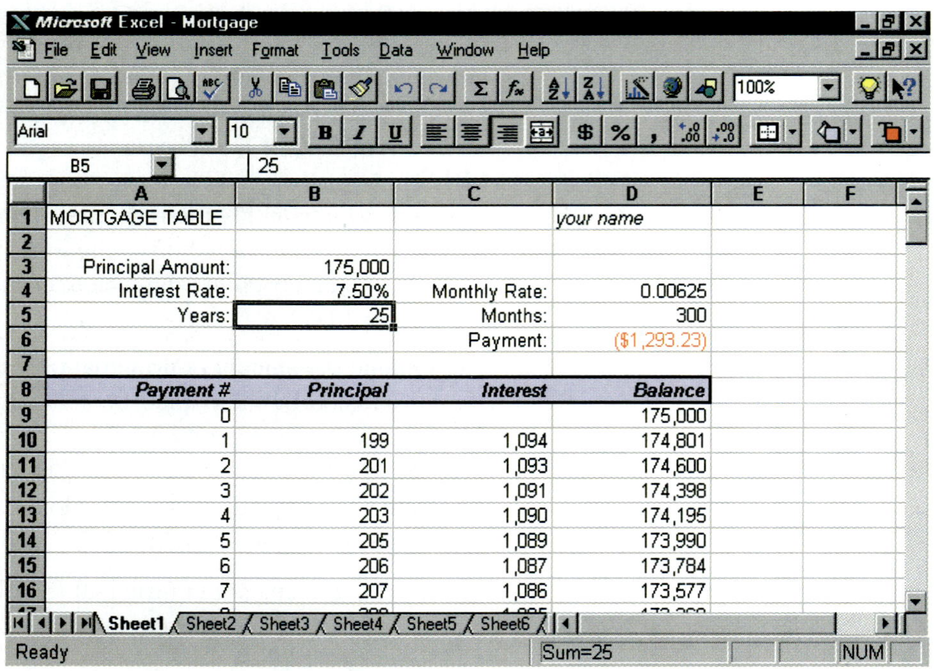


## CASE PROBLEMS

## RIVERSIDE FORD, INC.

(*Note:* In the following case problems, assume the role of the primary characters and perform the same steps that they identify. You may want to re-read the session opening.)

1. Zachary Rempel graduated from college in 1993 with a master's degree in economics. While his friends interviewed for entry-level jobs with larger companies, Zachary accepted the first position offered to him, as business manager for Riverside. Some of the reasons for Zachary's success at Riverside are that he willingly accepts new challenges and constantly looks for better ways of doing things. This was Zachary's attitude when Mr. Davies handed him the responsibility of generating all of the dealership's reports by computer.

   Upon reviewing the previous month's reports, Zachary identifies an opportunity for moving one particular report written in Microsoft Word to Microsoft Excel. The SOFIT report, which is Riverside's own abbreviation for a Summary of Finance and Insurance Totals, summarizes the number of new and used cars that are sold in a given month, including the number of financing, insurance, warranty, and rust-protection packages. Currently, the report is manually typed into a Word document and then printed. All of the calculations are performed using a handheld calculator; so if one number changes, the entire report must be recalculated. Zachary decides that this report deserves his immediate attention.

   Assume the role of Zachary and convert the following SOFIT report for January into an Excel worksheet, complete with formulas for summing the columns. Save the document as "SOFIT - January" onto the Advantage Diskette.

| Product Category | New Cars | New Dollars | Used Cars | Used Dollars |
|---|---|---|---|---|
| Retail Sales | 20 | 492,000 | 15 | 138,000 |
| Financing Packages | 8 | 4,500 | 4 | 2,500 |
| Life Ins. Policies | 4 | 1,250 | 2 | 600 |
| Option Packages | 5 | 2,150 | 0 | 0 |
| Ext. Warranties | 3 | 1,800 | 0 | 0 |
| Rust Protection | 1 | 375 | 1 | 340 |
| Totals | | | | |

2. Now that the original report has been converted into an Excel worksheet, Zachary decides to enhance the report and make better use of Excel's summary and reporting features. Perform the following modifications to the worksheet.

   - Extend the report by two columns for "Total Cars" and "Total Dollars." Enter formulas on the Retail Sales row that add the New and Used values together for both the unit and dollar values. Copy these two formulas into the remaining rows of the table.

- Insert a row for "Accident & Health Ins." between "Life Ins. Policies" and "Option Packages." There are no sales figures for the month of January, so enter "0" in the appropriate cells.
- Insert two rows at the top of the worksheet for the name of the dealership and the name of the report. The first row of the worksheet should contain "Riverside Ford, Inc." and the second row should contain "SOFIT for January 1996."
- Format the worksheet by applying fonts, numeric styles, and borders.
- Below the table, leave three blank lines and then enter the following information:

| Packages: | Average | Total |
|---|---|---|
| New Cars | | |
| Used Cars | | |
| Total Cars | | |

- In the new table, calculate the average and total dollar value of all packages sold with vehicles. (*Hint:* Use the AVERAGE and SUM functions on the values extending from financing packages to rust protection.)

3. Zachary decides to enhance the report by adding the budget figures for Finance and Insurance to the worksheet. That way, Mr. Davies will be able to compare the actual results against the budget estimates on the same report. Having gone through this session, Zachary knows that the easiest method for copying a group of cells on a worksheet is using the drag and drop method. To prepare, he selects the entire cell range (including the titles at the top of the worksheet). He then presses the ALT key and holds it down as he drags the selection over top of the Sheet2 tab. Once the cell pointer is positioned at the top of Sheet 2, he releases the ALT key and the mouse button. He then edits the title on Sheet2 to read "Budget Estimates" instead of "Riverside Ford, Inc."

   Complete the budget area on the worksheet for Zachary by editing the table to contain the figures shown in the following table. As a final step, print the report without gridlines, headers, or footers, and ensure that it appears centered horizontally on a single page. Save the worksheet as "SOFIT - January" back to the Advantage Diskette.

| Product Category | New Cars | New Dollars | Used Cars | Used Dollars |
|---|---|---|---|---|
| Retail Sales | 15 | 300,000 | 20 | 200,000 |
| Financing Packages | 10 | 5,000 | 8 | 2,500 |
| Life Ins. Policies | 5 | 1,500 | 4 | 1,200 |
| Accident & Health Ins. | 1 | 360 | 2 | 900 |
| Option Packages | 5 | 2,500 | 0 | 0 |
| Ext. Warranties | 5 | 1,800 | 0 | 0 |
| Rust Protection | 2 | 750 | 2 | 750 |

4. After explaining the finer points of Excel to Robyn Lombardi, a salesperson at Riverside, Zachary finishes the last bite of his sandwich. "Zak, what you've just finished describing sounds like something we can use on the floor," said Robyn excitedly. "Just imagine, we could calculate loan payments for customers while they are standing right in front of us! Can you design an attractive on-screen form if I provide you with a rough outline?" Zachary thought about what was involved in the project and ended up agreeing to create a simple form. At 4:30 p.m., Robyn drops a handwritten form onto Zachary's desk with the following note. "Thanks, Zak. By the way, I mentioned our idea to Mr. Davies and he wants to see a sample of the form by tomorrow. Good luck!"

   Create an on-screen form from the design sample that Robyn provided below. (*Hint:* Use the PMT function to perform the calculation.) Save your worksheet as LOANFORM onto the Advantage Diskette.

| **Riverside Ford, Inc.** | | | **Loan Calculation** |
|---|---|---|---|
| **Salesperson:** | *Robyn Lombardi* | **List Price:** | *$30,000* |
| **Customer:** | *Mr. Smith* | **Negotiated Price:** | *$25,000* |
| **Year/Make/Model:** | *95 Ford Explorer* | **Ann. Interest Rate:** | *10%* |
| **Serial Number:** | *XLT1001-8808-1* | **Term in Months:** | *48* |
| | **Your monthly payment is: $###.##** | | |

(Zak, this needs to be a formula!)

# *Managing a Workbook*

## SESSION OUTLINE



## INTRODUCTION

What you've already done with spreadsheets is quite sophisticated. Now we introduce some more commands to help you better manage your work. In this session, you will learn how to freeze titles on the screen, open windows to view different parts of a workbook, filter your worksheet data, create multiple-sheet workbook files, consolidate worksheets, and define macros to record and play back keystrokes. All of these features help you manage your workbooks more efficiently.

## CASE STUDY GINO'S KITCHEN

Gino Lerma is the owner of four pizza restaurants in the Boston metropolitan area. Starting with one restaurant 15 years ago, Gino was able to open a new restaurant every few years through hard work and careful planning. Gino now considers himself semi-retired, even though he still works around the clock and requires a full-time assistant, Larry Ingla. Although he is no longer part of the daily activities, Gino fondly remembers his many years working day and night in the restaurants.

Each month, Gino's managers use Microsoft Excel and a custom-developed worksheet to create a financial report of their restaurants' activities. Each manager then sends his or her workbook file to Larry Ingla for consolidation. To date, Larry has been printing each workbook separately and then manually consolidating a report for Gino's review. Hearing much about the consolidation capabilities of Excel, Larry wants to use the computer to combine each individual workbook into a summary workbook. From this one summary workbook, he could then print a monthly consolidated report. It would also be nice if the summary workbook contained a separate sheet for each month and a year-to-date sheet at the end. That way, Larry could analyze and compare sales and costs on a month-to-month basis. Unfortunately, Larry has only heard about Excel's capabilities and doesn't know how to create his dream workbook.

In this session, you and Larry will learn how to manage and extract information from worksheets. In addition, you will learn how to consolidate data using formulas that link separate worksheets and workbooks. To improve the reliability and consistency of your daily procedures, this session also shows you how to compose macros that you can play back in the future.

## FREEZING TITLES

Most worksheets display row and column titles to serve as a frame of reference for information contained in the worksheet. In an address worksheet, the column headings are typically first name, last name, address, city, and phone number. Unfortunately, these titles can scroll off the screen as you move around the worksheet. Using the Window, Freeze Panes command, you can freeze specific rows and columns on the screen so that they appear at all times, regardless of where you move the cell pointer in the worksheet.

Let's demonstrate. Perform the following steps.

1. Make sure that you've loaded Microsoft Excel and that a new worksheet appears in the document window. Place the Advantage Diskette into drive A: or drive B:.
2. Open the file named "Vacation Planner" located on the Advantage Diskette.
3. CLICK: cell B5
4. To quickly move to the end of the row:
   PRESS: CTRL + →
   The cell pointer moves to the end of the row, cell N5. Notice that you can no longer see the titles in column A—they have scrolled off the screen. Assuming that you do not memorize your worksheets, you must return to column A to see what each row represents.
5. PRESS: CTRL + HOME
   The cell pointer moves back to cell A1.
6. By freezing the window **panes,** you can lock the employee names in the first column no matter how far you move to the right. First, you position the cell pointer below the row and to the right of the column that you want to freeze. For this step, move the cell pointer to cell B7.
7. CHOOSE: Window, Freeze Panes
8. Position the tip of the mouse pointer below the elevator scroll box on the vertical scroll bar and click once to move down the worksheet. Notice that the worksheet window scrolls down but leaves the top six rows visible.
9. Position the tip of the mouse pointer to the right of the elevator scroll box on the horizontal scroll bar and click once to move across the worksheet. Again, notice that the worksheet scrolls but leaves the leftmost column of employee names visible. Your worksheet should now look similar to Figure 4.1.

**FIGURE 4.1** THE "VACATION PLANNER" WORKSHEET DIVIDED INTO PANES

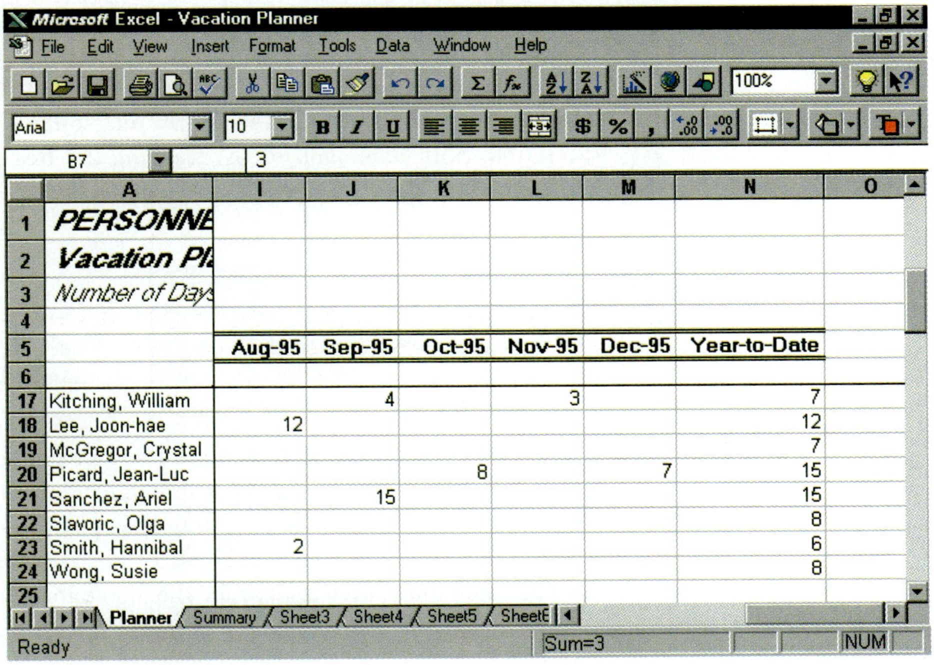


10. To return to your starting screen position and unfreeze the panes:
    PRESS: CTRL + HOME
    CHOOSE: Window, Unfreeze Panes

**QUICK REFERENCE**
Freezing Titles

1. **Position the cell pointer below and to the right of the row and column that you want to freeze.**
2. **To freeze the horizontal and vertical worksheet panes:**
   **CHOOSE: Window, Freeze Panes**
3. **To unfreeze the horizontal and vertical worksheet panes:**
   **CHOOSE: Window, Unfreeze Panes**

When a worksheet is relatively large and is organized under row and column headings, you use window panes to make it easier to work with your data. For a worksheet that is not grouped neatly into blocks or sections, you must use another tool. The next section explores the process of dividing a worksheet's document window into independent panes.

## SPLITTING THE WINDOW INTO PANES

Similarly to freezing titles, you can manually split a worksheet's document window into two or four panes. This makes it easier to view and manage worksheets that cannot fit in a single window. You split the document window using the Window, Split command or by dragging the **horizontal split box** or **vertical split box** at the end of each scroll bar (both are shown below).

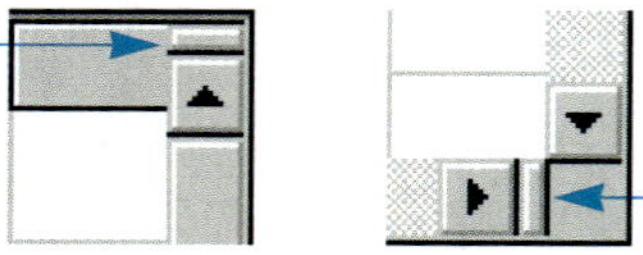


Using the Split command, position the cell pointer below or to the right of the column and row where you want the split to occur—as you would setting titles. If you prefer using the mouse, drag the split boxes to the desired window location. Once in place, you can finalize the positioning of panes by dragging the actual split bars that appear in the document window. To move between two panes or among four panes, you simply click the mouse pointer in the desired pane.

Perform the following steps.

1. Position the mouse pointer over the horizontal split box (above the vertical scroll bar) until the pointer changes to a black horizontal double line split by a two-headed arrow.
2. CLICK: left mouse button and hold it down
   DRAG: the split box downward to split the window in half
3. Release the mouse button. Notice that you now have two vertical scroll bars for controlling both panes independently.
4. Position the tip of the mouse pointer below the scroll box on the bottom vertical scroll bar and click once to move down the worksheet.
5. Position the tip of the mouse pointer below the scroll box on the top vertical scroll bar and click twice to move the viewing area in the top pane. As opposed to freezing titles, notice that you can change the viewing area in both panes.
6. Position the mouse pointer over the vertical split box (to the right of the horizontal scroll bar) until the pointer changes to a black vertical double line split by a two-headed arrow.
7. CLICK: left mouse button and hold it down
   DRAG: the split box to the left to split the window in half

8. Release the mouse button. Notice that you have divided the current worksheet window into four panes.
9. CLICK: anywhere in the bottom left-hand window pane
   PRESS: CTRL + HOME
10. CLICK: anywhere in the bottom right-hand window pane
    PRESS: CTRL + HOME
11. CLICK: anywhere in the top right-hand window pane
    PRESS: CTRL + HOME
12. CLICK: anywhere in the top left-hand window pane
    PRESS: CTRL + HOME
    This example demonstrates that you must click in the pane before moving the cell pointer in the pane. Your worksheet should now appear similar to Figure 4.2.
13. To quickly remove panes from the window:
    CHOOSE: Window, Remove Split
    (*Note:* You can also double-click each split box to remove the panes.)
14. Save the "Vacation Planner" workbook to the Advantage Diskette.

**FIGURE 4.2** DIVIDING THE WORKSHEET'S DOCUMENT WINDOW INTO PANES

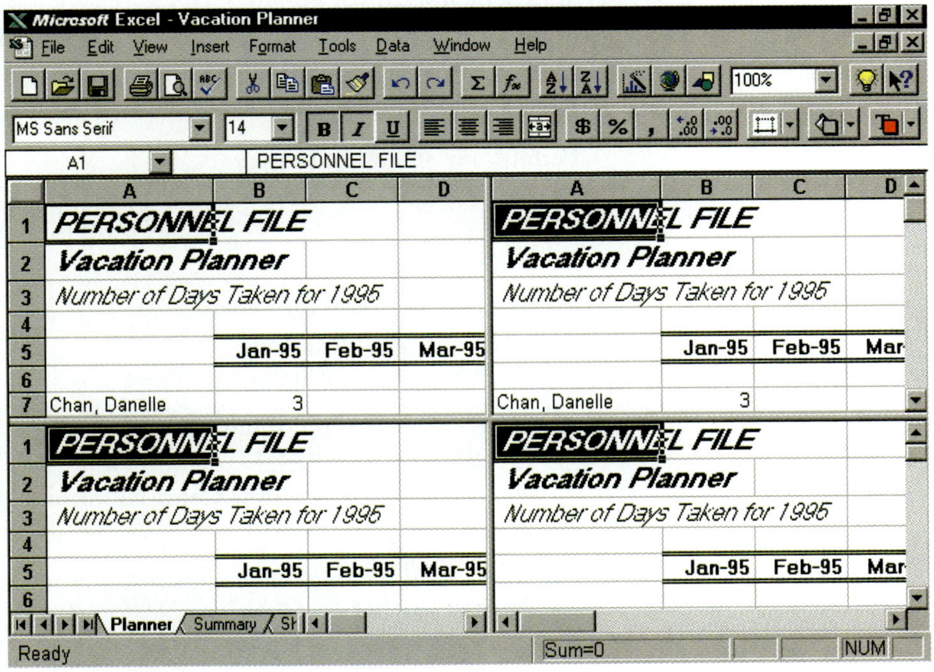

**QUICK REFERENCE**
Splitting the Window into Panes

- **DRAG: horizontal and vertical scroll boxes to divide the current worksheet's document window into two or four panes**
- **To remove panes from the current window:**
  **CHOOSE: Window, Remove Split**

## FILTERING WORKSHEET DATA

Excel 7.0 introduces an exciting new "auto" feature, called **AutoFilter,** that lets you find and retrieve data quickly from a list. To use this feature, you must arrange your data properly in a worksheet. For example, you should leave several blank columns and rows between the data list and any other information in the worksheet. In the first row of a list, enter column headings or labels and then separate these headings from the data using a border. Lastly, you need to design the list so that all columns contain the same type of information, such as text or numbers.

To start AutoFilter, select the desired cell range including the column heading labels and data and then choose the Data, Filters, AutoFilter command from the menu. When executed, AutoFilter analyzes the data and then displays a drop-down list arrow next to each column heading that contains its filtering options. To quickly filter and display data, you select a single criteria for a column from the drop-down list or choose to view a range of data, such as the top ten sales representatives based on units sold.

Perform the following steps.

1. Ensure that the "Vacation Planner" workbook appears in the application window.
2. To start the AutoFilter command:
   SELECT: cell range from A5 to N24
   CHOOSE: Data, Filters, AutoFilter
3. To return to the top of the worksheet:
   PRESS: CTRL + HOME
   Notice that there are drop-down list arrows attached to each of the column headings in row 5.
4. To freeze the column headings in the worksheet window:
   CLICK: cell B7
   CHOOSE: Window, Freeze Panes
5. To move to the Year-to-Date column quickly:
   CLICK: cell B5
   PRESS: CTRL + →
   Notice that the employee names in column A are still visible.

6. To select a filtering criterion:
   CLICK: down arrow (▼) beside cell N5 to display its drop-down list
   Your screen should now appear similar to Figure 4.3.

FIGURE 4.3 USING THE AUTOFILTER COMMAND

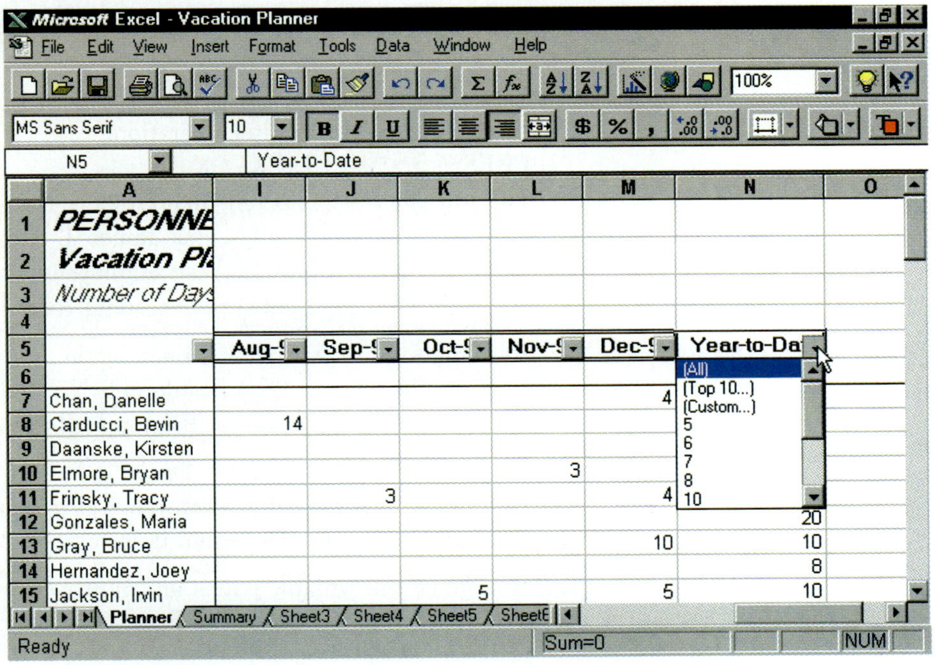

7. To display the three employees with the highest Year-to-Date figures for vacation days taken in 1995, do the following:
   SELECT: (Top 10…) from the drop-down list
   (*Note:* You can filter the list by two or more values, or apply more complex filtering options, by selecting the Custom option from a column's drop-down list box.)

8. In the dialog box that appears, specify that only the top three items (in this case, Year-to-Date vacation days) need to be displayed. Do the following:
   SELECT: 3 in the *Show* spin control text box (Figure 4.4)

**FIGURE 4.4** AUTOFILTER'S TOP 10 DIALOG BOX

9. To proceed with the filter operation:
   PRESS: ENTER CLICK: OK
   The worksheet should now display only the following employees: Bevin Carducci, Maria Gonzales, and James T. Kirk. Also notice that the row numbers appear blue for these employees, as a reminder you are currently viewing a subset of the total records.
10. To display all of the records once again:
    CLICK: down arrow (▼) beside cell N5 to display its drop-down list
    SELECT: (All) appearing at the top of the drop-down list
    All of the records reappear in the worksheet window.
11. To remove the AutoFilter drop-down lists from the worksheet:
    CHOOSE: Data, Filters, AutoFilter
12. To remove the window panes and return to the top of the worksheet:
    CHOOSE: Window, Unfreeze Panes
    PRESS: CTRL + HOME

## QUICK REFERENCE
Filtering Data Using the AutoFilter Command

1. **Create a worksheet with column headings and ensure that each column contains the same type of information (i.e., sales units).**
2. **Select the cell range to be filtered, including the column headings.**
3. **CHOOSE: Data, Filters, AutoFilter**
4. **CLICK: down arrow (▼) beside the column or cell to display a drop-down list box of filtering options**
5. **Select a value from the drop-down list box to filter the list**

**IN ADDITION** MANAGING A DATABASE USING EXCEL

Microsoft Excel is an excellent tool for storing and managing simple lists, especially ones requiring statistical or graphical analysis. In addition to using Excel for sorting and filtering data, you can link Excel with the Microsoft Access database program for sharing data, forms, and reports. For more information, refer to the Help system or Microsoft Excel User's Guide.

## WORKING WITH MULTIPLE WINDOWS

Using multiple document windows, you can load and display different workbook files at the same time or open different views of the same workbook. Multiple window views are useful when you have related information scattered in distant areas or across several worksheets in a large workbook, or perhaps stored in different workbooks. This section explains how to display and organize multiple windows in the Excel application window.

Before you can issue commands to affect a worksheet, its document window must first be active. You activate a window by clicking on it in the document area or by choosing its name from the Window pull-down menu. If there is only one workbook open in the document area, it is active by default. To close a document window, you click its Close button (×) in the upper right-hand corner of the window.

To automatically organize all the open windows in the document area, you can choose the Window, Arrange command to display the dialog box in Figure 4.5. The Arrange dialog box offers several options for arranging windows in the document area. The *Tiled* option lets you maximize the space for each window in a pattern similar to floor tiles. The *Horizontal* option places each worksheet in a horizontal strip in the document area, while the *Vertical* option employs vertical strips. Once you have selected an option, press ENTER or click on OK.

FIGURE 4.5 ARRANGE DIALOG BOX

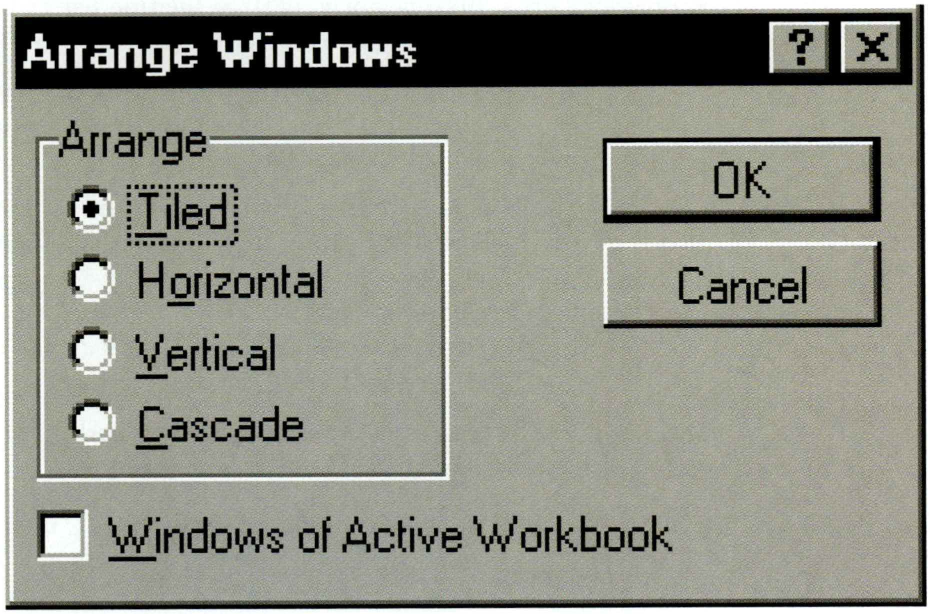

Perform the following steps to practice working with multiple windows.

1. Before proceeding, ensure that the "Vacation Planner" workbook is the only open document window. Do the following:
   CHOOSE: Window
   One entry should appear at the bottom of this pull-down menu called "1 Vacation Planner." If there are more entries, choose each additional workbook option on the menu and click its Close button (☒).

2. Let's practice working with document windows. A document window can be displayed as a window or it can be maximized to cover the entire document area. You can tell the difference by looking at the Title bar. If the name of the worksheet appears next to the words "Microsoft Excel" in the application's Title bar, then the document window has been maximized. If the name of the worksheet appears in its own Title bar within the document area, then the worksheet is displayed as a window. In this step, you practice manipulating the "Vacation Planner" worksheet window. Do the following:

   *a.* If the "Vacation Planner" worksheet is currently maximized:
   CLICK: document window's Restore icon (🗗)
   (*Hint:* When a worksheet is maximized, the Restore icon is located on the second line in the top right-hand corner of the application window.)
   (*CAUTION:* The Excel application window has Restore (🗗), Maximize (☐), and Minimize (_) icons also.)

   *b.* If the worksheet is currently windowed:
   CLICK: document window's Maximize icon (☐)
   (*Hint:* If you accidentally click the Minimize icon (_), you can restore the document window by clicking its Restore icon (🗗) or Maximize icon (☐) in the title bar that appears along the bottom of the document area.)

   *c.* Practice changing the worksheet between a windowed view, a minimized view, and a maximized view. Before proceeding, select a windowed view for the worksheet.

3. Using the Arrange command, you can fill the document area with a single window (and retain it as a window, not a maximized worksheet). Do the following:
   CHOOSE: Window, Arrange
   SELECT: *Tiled* option button
   PRESS: ENTER or CLICK: OK

4. To open a second window on this worksheet:
   CHOOSE: Window, New Window

5. The new document window appears over top of the original window. To view both windows at the same time:
CHOOSE: Window, Arrange
SELECT: *Tiled* option button
PRESS: **ENTER** or CLICK: OK
Notice that the windows are identical, except for their Title bars. There are now two views of the "Vacation Planner" worksheet: "Vacation Planner:1" and "Vacation Planner:2" (Figure 4.6).

**FIGURE 4.6** THE "VACATION PLANNER" WORKSHEET WITH TWO WINDOWS DISPLAYED

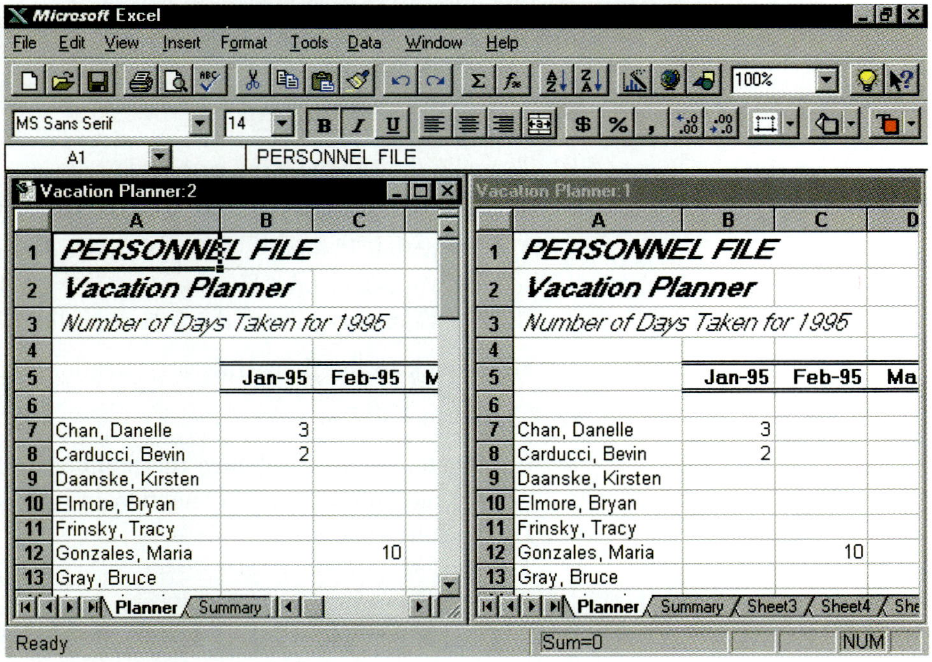


6. For a different window arrangement:
CHOOSE: Window, Arrange
SELECT: *Horizontal* option button
PRESS: **ENTER** or CLICK: OK

7. To change back to the vertical window arrangement:
CHOOSE: Window, Arrange
SELECT: *Vertical* option button
PRESS: **ENTER** or CLICK: OK
(*Note:* With only two windows open, the Tiled and Vertical options produce identical results.)

8. Practice switching between the two open windows using a mouse. Do the following:
   CLICK: any part of a window in the document area to make it active
   SELECT: each open window several times
   With the possibility of having multiple windows open in the document area, it is important to be able to switch among them efficiently. You can execute commands or type information only in the active window, which is set apart from the rest by its solid or dark Title bar.
9. To switch to a window that is covered by one or more windows, perform the following menu command:
   CHOOSE: Window
   CHOOSE: the window name that you want to make active
10. To make the first window active:
    CHOOSE: Window, 1
11. PRESS: CTRL + HOME
12. To make the second window active:
    CHOOSE: Window, 2
13. The "Vacation Planner" workbook has a summary section located on the second worksheet tab. To move to this worksheet:
    CLICK: Summary tab (at the bottom of the document window)
14. Move back to the first window ("Vacation Planner:1").
15. CLICK: cell B7
16. In this step, you will change the number in cell B7 to see the effects of the change on the Summary section in the "Vacation Planner:2" window. Do the following:
    TYPE: **5**
    PRESS: ENTER
    The Average Vacation Days for Jan-96 changes from 3.00 to 3.67.
17. To test the limits of practicality for using multiple windows, open four more windows:
    CHOOSE: Window, New Window four times
18. To arrange the windows in the document area:
    CHOOSE: Window, Arrange
    SELECT: *Tiled* option button
    PRESS: ENTER or CLICK: OK
19. Let's try the Vertical option in this step:
    CHOOSE: Window, Arrange
    SELECT: *Vertical* option button
    PRESS: ENTER or CLICK: OK
    Your worksheet should now appear similar to Figure 4.7.

**FIGURE 4.7** THE "VACATION PLANNER" WORKSHEET WITH SIX WINDOWS DISPLAYED

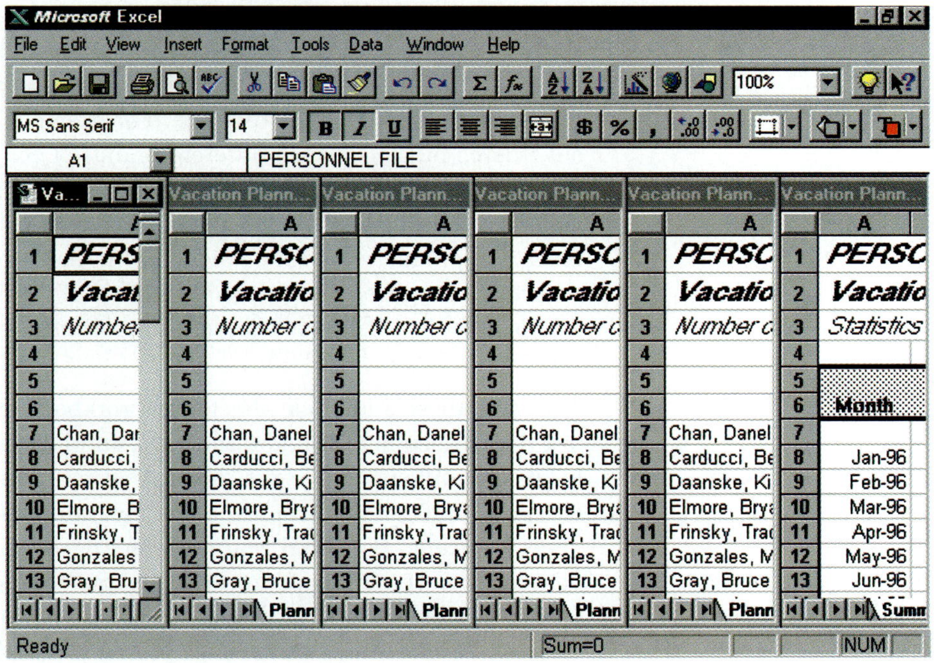


20. To clean up the document area:
    PRESS: SHIFT and hold it down
    CHOOSE: File, Close All
    CLICK: No when asked to save changes
    (*Note:* It is not necessary to use the File, Close All command in this exercise since you are closing only one file, "Vacation Planner". The Close All command is designed to close multiple workbook files that are open in the document area, as opposed to multiple window views.)

## QUICK REFERENCE

Working with Document Windows

- **To create a new window view for the active worksheet:**
  **CHOOSE: Window, New Window**
- **To arrange open windows in the document area:**
  **CHOOSE: Window, Arrange**
  **SELECT: an option button, such as *Tiled, Horizontal,* or *Vertical***
  **PRESS: ENTER or CLICK: OK**
- **To close a window:**
  **CLICK: Close button (X)**

## CREATING MULTIPLE-SHEET WORKBOOKS

In this section, you learn how to create and navigate a multiple-sheet workbook file. Multiple-sheet workbooks enable you to separate related information onto different pages in a single disk file. For example, imagine that you manage the advertising budgets for ten different brands of coffee. In addition to having individual reports for each brand, you need to produce a summary report that consolidates the budgets for the entire product line. Using a workbook, you can place the product summary report on the first worksheet and then each brand report on a subsequent worksheet. This three dimensional (3-D) capability enables you to easily manage and **consolidate** your information.

To access these additional sheets in a workbook, Excel provides tabs at the bottom of the document window. In a new workbook, Excel provides 16 worksheets by default. It may help you to think of a worksheet as a tear-off page on a notepad—the notepad representing the workbook. Although initially labeled Sheet1, Sheet2, and so on, you can enter descriptive names for each worksheet. You can choose any name up to 31 characters including spaces. However, you cannot use the asterisk (*), question mark (?), forward slash (/), backslash (\), or colon (:) in a worksheet's name. To move quickly to a particular worksheet, you scroll the tabs using the tab scroll buttons (shown below) and then click the desired sheet tab. You can also right-click any of the tab scroll buttons for a complete pop-up menu of the available worksheets and then make a selection from the menu list.

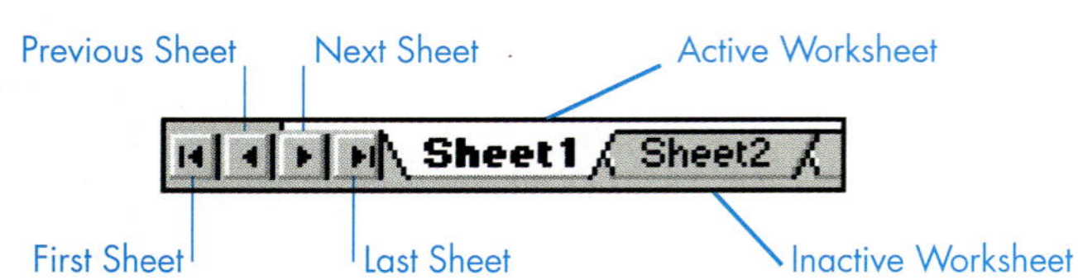


Excel's sheet tabs share the document window with the horizontal scroll bar. You can adjust how much room is devoted to each by dragging the tab split bar that is sandwiched between the two. Similarly to creating window panes using the vertical split bar, the mouse pointer changes to a black vertical double line split by a two-headed arrow when positioned properly over the bar. You drag the tab split bar back and forth to increase and decrease the share of real estate given to each component. If you are working in a single-worksheet workbook, you would normally drag the tab split bar to the far left to hide the remaining worksheets. In this section, you will practice navigating worksheets and executing simple commands.

Perform the following steps to create a multiple-sheet workbook.

1. The document area in the Excel application window should be empty. To create a new workbook:
   CLICK: New Workbook button ()
2. If the worksheet's document window is not maximized:
   CLICK: Maximize button ()
3. To practice moving between the default worksheets:
   CLICK: Sheet3 tab
   CLICK: Sheet5 tab
4. To scroll the tabs to the right:
   CLICK: Next Sheet button () multiple times
   Notice that the active worksheet, Sheet5, remains active (highlighted) as you scroll through the worksheet tabs.
5. To move to the last worksheet in the workbook:
   CLICK: Last Sheet button ()
   Although Sheet16 is now visible, Sheet5 is still the active worksheet.
6. To move to Sheet1 and rename the tab:
   CLICK: First Sheet button ()
   DOUBLE-CLICK: Sheet1 tab
   The Rename dialog box appears, as shown in Figure 4.8.

**FIGURE 4.8** RENAMING SHEET TABS IN A WORKBOOK

7. TYPE: **Australia**
   PRESS: ENTER
8. To rename Sheet2:
   DOUBLE-CLICK: Sheet2 tab
   TYPE: **New Zealand**
   PRESS: ENTER
   (*Note:* You can also right-click a tab and then choose Rename from the shortcut menu that appears.)

9. Position the mouse pointer over the tab split bar until it changes to a black vertical double line split by a two-headed arrow.
10. DRAG: tab split bar to the left so that it rests to the right of the New Zealand tab (as shown below)

11. Although not so important with only two worksheets in the file, let's practice selecting a worksheet using the shortcut menu:
RIGHT-CLICK: any one of the tab scroll buttons (⏮, ◀, ▶, or ⏭)
Notice that the first two menu choices are the new tabs, Australia and New Zealand.
12. To move to the Australia worksheet:
CHOOSE: Australia from the shortcut menu
13. To delete a worksheet in a workbook:
RIGHT-CLICK: New Zealand tab
CHOOSE: Delete from the shortcut menu
PRESS: ENTER or CLICK: OK to confirm the operation
The New Zealand worksheet is permanently removed from the workbook.
14. To insert a worksheet between Australia and Sheet3:
RIGHT-CLICK: Sheet3 tab
CHOOSE: Insert
The Insert dialog box in Figure 4.9 appears. Notice that you can insert different types of sheets into the workbook, including worksheets, charts, macros, and programming modules.

**FIGURE 4.9** INSERT DIALOG BOX

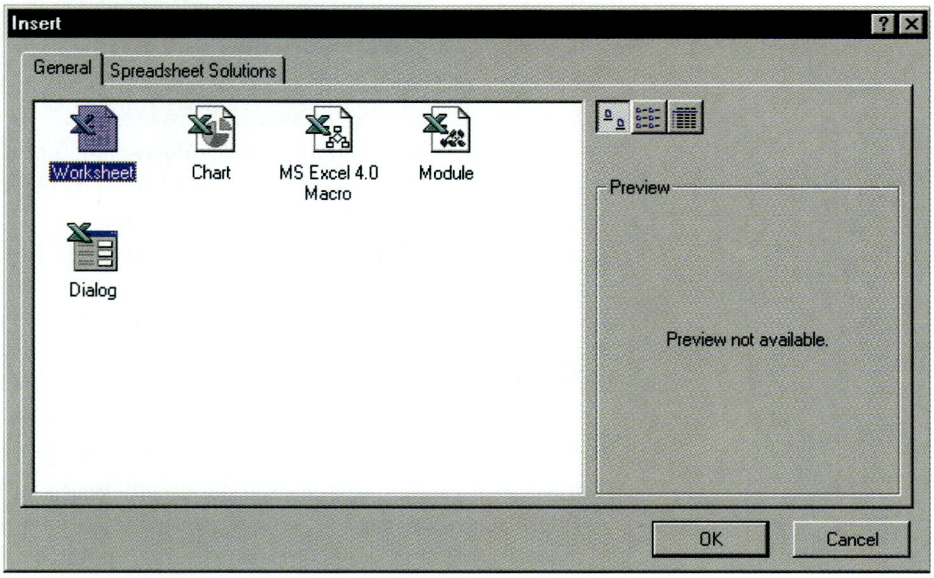


15. To insert a new worksheet:
    DOUBLE-CLICK: Worksheet icon in the Insert dialog box
    A new sheet, called Sheet17, appears next to the Australia tab. You could double-click this tab and rename the worksheet to read something more meaningful. However, we'll proceed to the next section.

16. Close the workbook and do not save the changes.

**QUICK REFERENCE**
Working with a Multiple-Sheet Workbook

- **Use the tab scroll buttons (⏮, ◀, ▶, or ⏭) to move through the available worksheets in a workbook file.**
- **Use the tab split bar to adjust the shared space for the sheet tabs and the horizontal scroll bar.**
- **RIGHT-CLICK: any one of the tab scroll buttons to display a shortcut Go To menu showing all of the sheet names**
- **RIGHT-CLICK: a sheet tab to display a shortcut menu for manipulating (inserting and deleting) sheets in a workbook**

## CONSOLIDATING YOUR WORK

Whether you need to combine revenues from several regions or calculate productivity statistics for several departments, Excel's consolidation tools allow you to better manage, organize, and present your information. In this section, you learn how to consolidate data using two methods. First, you use a single workbook file to summarize information. Second, you consolidate the results of individual workbooks to produce a new summary workbook. To begin our discussion, you are introduced to the Group mode for working more efficiently with multiple-sheet files.

### USING GROUP MODE

In creating a workbook with multiple worksheets, the subsidiary sheets often have a similar, if not identical, layout to the primary or summary worksheet. Therefore, you can copy the layout of the first worksheet to the remaining subsidiary worksheets and then enter the specific figures for each. Excel provides the **Group mode** to assist you in creating and formatting identical subsidiary worksheets. When you select more than one sheet tab, Group mode is automatically turned on and all the commands that you issue affect all the selected worksheets. For example, Group mode enables you to change a column's width in one worksheet and have that same modification made to all worksheets in the file. To understand the effects of Group mode, we will format a multiple-sheet file.

Perform the following steps to practice using Group mode.

1. Close any workbooks that are currently open.
2. Open the "Shift Summary" workbook located on the Advantage Diskette. This workbook summarizes the production results for three shifts in a woodworking operation. The workbook file consists of four worksheets: one summary sheet and three detail sheets for each shift.
3. Let's start by renaming the sheet tabs:
   DOUBLE-CLICK: Sheet1 tab
   TYPE: **Summary**
   PRESS: ENTER
4. To name the Sheet2 tab:
   DOUBLE-CLICK: Sheet2 tab
   TYPE: **Shift 1**
   PRESS: ENTER

5. To name the Sheet3 tab:
   DOUBLE-CLICK: Sheet3 tab
   TYPE: **Shift 2**
   PRESS: ENTER
6. To name the Sheet4 tab:
   DOUBLE-CLICK: Sheet4 tab
   TYPE: **Shift 3**
   PRESS: ENTER
7. To select more than one worksheet at a time for Group mode:
   CLICK: Summary tab
   PRESS: CTRL and hold it down
   CLICK: Shift 1 tab
   CLICK: Shift 2 tab
   CLICK: Shift 3 tab
   Notice that all four sheet tabs are highlighted and the word "[Group]" appears in the Title bar.
8. Release the CTRL key.
9. With Group mode turned on, you can issue commands in the active worksheet which will carry through to the last selected worksheet in the workbook file. To begin, let's format the date headings to make them bold and italic:
   SELECT: cell range from C4 to I4 on the Summary sheet
10. CLICK: Bold button (B)
    CLICK: Italic button (I)
    CLICK: Center button (≡)
    These formatting commands are applied to all the sheets.
    (*CAUTION:* Although the Group mode feature is very handy, it can also be quite dangerous. Remember that you can see the effects of the command only on the current worksheet. Without realizing, you can easily erase or reformat information on other sheets unintentionally. Be careful using this command!)
11. To turn Group mode off:
    RIGHT-CLICK: Summary tab
    CHOOSE: Ungroup Sheets
    Notice that there is no longer the word "[Group]" in the Title bar.
12. Browse through the worksheets to see the effects of the last few steps:
    CLICK: Shift 1 tab
    CLICK: Shift 2 tab
    CLICK: Shift 3 tab
    CLICK: Summary tab

**QUICK REFERENCE**
Turning Group Mode On and Off

- **To turn Group mode on, select multiple worksheets by clicking their tabs while holding down the CTRL key.**
- **To turn Group mode off, right-click any tab and then choose the Ungroup Sheets command from the shortcut menu.**

## CONSOLIDATING A MULTIPLE-SHEET WORKBOOK

With a multiple-sheet workbook, information in one sheet can automatically update information in another sheet. The "Shift Summary" workbook, for example, contains three subsidiary sheets for each shift. You will now create formulas that sum the values from each subsidiary worksheet into a summary worksheet. Thereafter, any changes to values in the subsidiary sheets are immediately reflected in the summary.

Perform the following steps.

1. Move to cell C5 in the Summary sheet.
2. As discussed in past sessions, you enter formulas by typing or pointing to cell addresses. To give you practice entering formulas, the following steps show you how to use several different methods for summarizing data. In a real-world application, however, you would create the first formula and then copy it to the remaining cells. To begin, enter a formula to sum a 3-D range:
   TYPE: `=sum('Shift 1:Shift 3'!c5)`
   PRESS: ENTER
   Notice that you surround the tab range with single quotes and then separate the tabs from the cell address with an exclamation mark (!). If the tab names did not contain any spaces (for example, Shift1 instead of Shift 1), you could leave out the single quotes in the formula.
3. Move to cell C6 in the Summary sheet.
4. To enter the SUM equation, do the following:
   TYPE: `=sum('Shift 1:Shift 3'!c6)`
   PRESS: ENTER
   An answer of 30 appears in the cell.
5. Move to cell C7 in the Summary sheet.

6. Let's create a formula by pointing to the cells:
   PRESS: **=sum(**
   CLICK: Shift 1 tab
   CLICK: cell C7
   PRESS: SHIFT and hold it down
   CLICK: Shift 3 tab
   TYPE: **)**
   PRESS: ENTER
   An answer of 109 appears in the cell.
7. Move to cell C8 in the Summary sheet.
8. Let's perform the same procedure as shown in step 7:
   PRESS: **=sum(**
   CLICK: Shift 1 tab
   CLICK: cell C8
   PRESS: SHIFT and hold it down
   CLICK: Shift 3 tab
   TYPE: **)**
   PRESS: ENTER
   An answer of 406 appears in the cell.
9. SELECT: cell range from C5 through I8
10. To copy these formulas across the remainder of cells in the worksheet:
    CHOOSE: Edit, Fill, Right
    PRESS: CTRL + HOME
11. To select the remaining sheets in the workbook:
    CLICK: Sheet5
    CLICK: Last Sheet button (▶|)
    PRESS: SHIFT and hold it down
    CLICK: Sheet16
    All of the blank worksheets are now selected in Group mode.
12. To delete these worksheets:
    RELEASE: SHIFT
    RIGHT-CLICK: Sheet16 (or any other selected sheet)
    CHOOSE: Delete from the shortcut menu
    PRESS: ENTER or CLICK: OK to confirm the operation
13. To return to the beginning:
    CLICK: First Sheet button (|◀)
    CLICK: Summary tab
    Your worksheet should appear similar to Figure 4.10.

**FIGURE 4.10** CONSOLIDATING A MULTIPLE-SHEET WORKBOOK

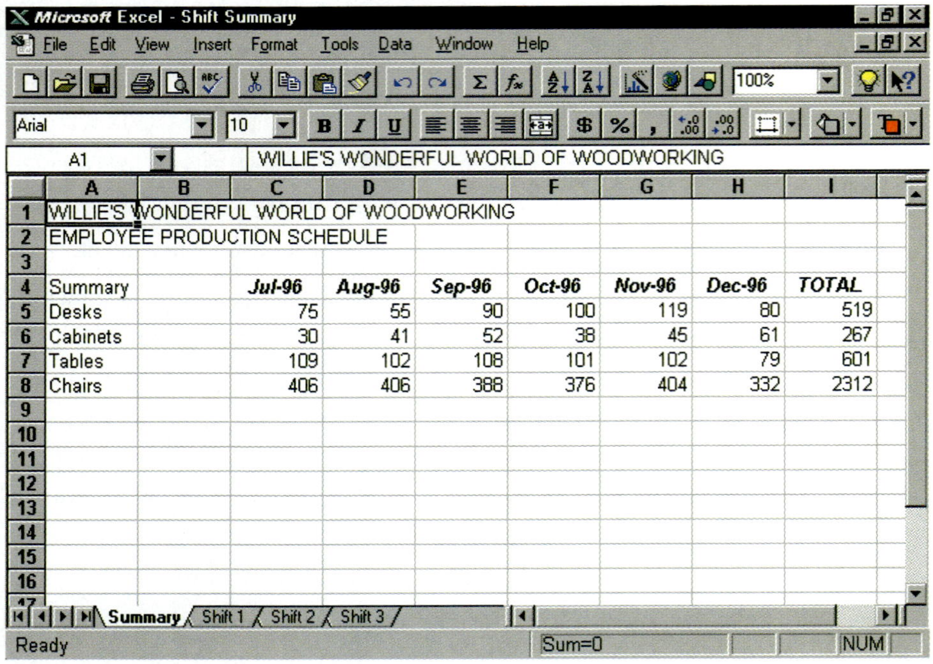


14. For practice, change some numbers in the subsidiary worksheets and then watch their effects on the summary worksheet.
15. Save the workbook to the Advantage Diskette under the same name, updating the old version of the file, and then close the workbook.

## CONSOLIDATING MULTIPLE WORKBOOKS

In addition to consolidating a multiple-sheet workbook, you can link separate workbook files. Linking workbooks has two major advantages over using one large workbook. First, the subsidiary workbooks are smaller in size and therefore are easier to manage on a daily basis. Second, subsidiary workbooks are not restricted to the same computer as the summary workbook. For example, each department may control its own workbook and submit the file once a month for consolidation. To consolidate subsidiary workbooks, you open each file in the document area and then, in a summary workbook, create formulas that reference cells from the subsidiary workbooks.

Perform the following steps to consolidate information from multiple workbook files. In this example, you compile three departmental workbooks from XYZ Corporation into a single summary workbook.

1. Close any workbook files that are currently open.

2. To open four workbook files in one command:
   CLICK: Open button ( )

3. Ensure that the files are displayed in ascending order by Name. If not, do the following:
   CLICK: Name button (appearing at the top of the column) once or twice to sort the list in ascending order

4. In the filename display area:
   CLICK: XYZ Dept 1
   PRESS: SHIFT and hold it down
   CLICK: XYZ Summary
   The four files "XYZ Dept 1," "XYZ Dept 2," "XYZ Dept 3," and "XYZ Summary" should all appear highlighted.

5. To open the selected files:
   CLICK: Open command button
   After a few seconds, the four files are loaded into Excel's document area.

6. To organize the windows within the document area:
   CHOOSE: Window, Arrange
   SELECT: *Tiled* option button
   PRESS: ENTER or CLICK: OK
   Your screen should now appear similar to Figure 4.11.

**FIGURE 4.11** WORKING WITH XYZ CORPORATION'S DEPARTMENTAL WORKBOOKS

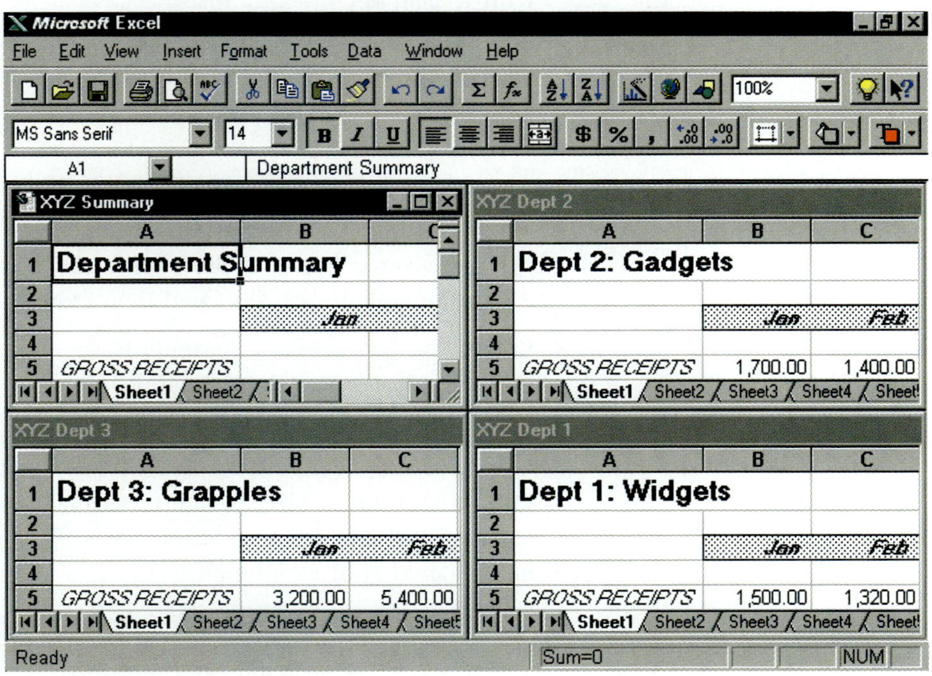

7. To move among the open windows in the document area, you position the mouse pointer on a visible part of the worksheet and click once. To practice, click the Title bars of the four worksheets. Notice that the solid or dark-colored Title bar represents the active worksheet window. When you are ready to proceed, ensure that the "XYZ Summary" worksheet is active.

8. Before you consolidate the "XYZ Dept 1," "XYZ Dept 2," and "XYZ Dept 3" worksheets into the "XYZ Summary" worksheet, notice that the same worksheet structure and design layout were used for all the open worksheets. Although this is not necessary, it provides an instantaneous familiarity with each worksheet and makes entering the consolidation formulas much easier. To begin, you need to select a cell in "XYZ Summary" to enter the first linking formula. Move to cell B5.

9. A formula that links subsidiary workbooks is entered the same as any other formula. To inform Excel that you are entering a formula:
   TYPE: **=**
   CLICK: the title bar of "XYZ Dept 1" workbook to select it
   CLICK: cell B5
   (*Hint:* After selecting the "XYZ Dept 1" workbook, use the scroll bars to move the worksheet window so that cell B5 is visible.) Notice the formula being constructed in the Formula bar.

10. To complete the formula:
    TYPE: **+**
    CLICK: the title bar of "XYZ Dept 2" workbook to select it
    CLICK: cell B5
    TYPE: **+**
    CLICK: the title bar of "XYZ Dept 3" workbook to select it
    CLICK: cell B5
    PRESS: ENTER
    The summary worksheet calculates the answer 6,400.00.

11. Maximize the "XYZ Summary" document window. If the Maximize button (□) is covered by the expression in the Formula bar, you can click cell A1 in the active worksheet and then click the Maximize button (□).

12. Before you can copy this formula to the other cells, you need to remove the absolute references to cell B5:
    DOUBLE-CLICK: cell B5

13. Use the arrow keys or the I-beam mouse pointer to highlight a dollar sign ($) and then press DELETE. Perform this step for each dollar sign that appears in the formula and then press ENTER. When finished, the formula should read as follows:

```
='[XYZ Dept 1.xls]Sheet1'!B5+'[XYZ Dept 2.xls]Sheet1'!B5
                          +'[XYZ Dept 3.xls] Sheet1'!B5
```

14. To copy the formula to the Clipboard:
    CLICK: Copy button (📋)

15. To paste the formula into all the remaining cells at the same time:
    SELECT: cell range from C5 to D5
    PRESS: CTRL and hold it down
    SELECT: cell range from B8 to D11
    RELEASE: CTRL
    PRESS: ENTER
    The formula is pasted to all the highlighted cells. Your worksheet should now appear similar to Figure 4.12.

16. Save and then close each workbook.

**FIGURE 4.12** COPYING THE CONSOLIDATION FORMULA TO THE REMAINING CELLS

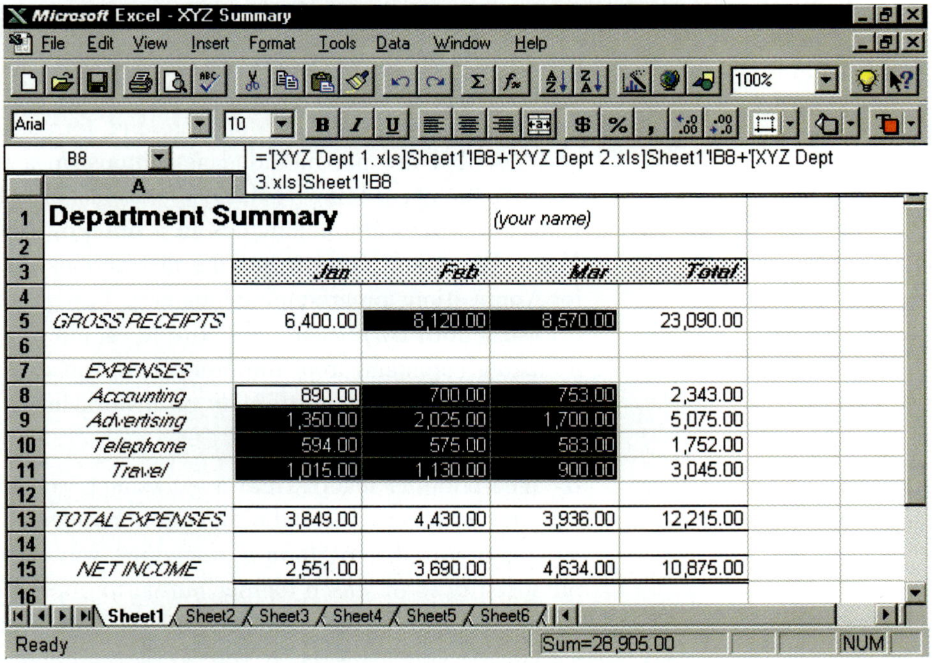


**QUICK REFERENCE**
Consolidating Workbooks

1. **Open the summary workbook and the subsidiary workbooks.**
2. **CHOOSE: Window, Arrange and select the *Tiled* option button**
3. **Enter a formula in the summary workbook that references cells in the subsidiary workbooks.**

USING EXCEL'S CONSOLIDATE COMMAND

Excel provides a Consolidate command for consolidating worksheets. This command was not covered in this section because it introduces new concepts. The formula method for consolidating your workbooks is simply an extension of the skills you already possess. If you would like more information about the Consolidate command, refer to the Microsoft Excel User's Guide or Help system that came with your software.

## WHAT IS A MACRO?

Many spreadsheet tasks are repetitive, such as enhancing titles with fonts and borders, formatting numbers, or printing cell ranges. For our benefit, Excel has assigned many of these monotonous tasks to toolbar buttons and "Auto" commands. However, there are still specific tasks that you may have to perform time and time again, such as entering and formatting your company name and address, that are not included as buttons on a toolbar. To save you time and improve the consistency of these operations, Excel enables you to store and play back keystrokes and commands in a **macro.** Using a special utility called the Macro Recorder, Excel writes the instructions for each task in the Visual Basic for Applications programming language. Using a macro, you can execute a series of instructions by pressing only two keys, clicking a toolbar button, or choosing a custom command from the Menu bar. You can even create custom command buttons and place them directly on a worksheet!

By incorporating macros into a worksheet, you make it easier to use for yourself and for others. Instead of having to remember all of the commands and keystrokes required to perform a procedure, you only have to remember a few simple keystrokes or which toolbar button to click. Furthermore, you can automate complicated tasks for co-workers or temporary personnel who are not familiar with using spreadsheets. If you are so inclined, you can even write your own Visual Basic code for creating menu commands, dialog boxes, and custom applications that don't even resemble Microsoft Excel.

## CREATING MACROS

Macros are created by recording keystrokes or by directly typing in commands. With either method, the results are typically stored in a special sheet called a Visual Basic module. You can specify that macros be stored in the current workbook or in a special file called a **Personal Macro Workbook.** The Personal Macro Workbook is managed by Excel (you don't have to open or close this file) and provides a common area for storing macros that you will use with all your workbooks.

## RECORDING A MACRO

The quickest method for creating a macro is to record the keystrokes that you press and the mouse clicks that you make while performing a procedure. Once recorded, the procedure may be executed again and again by selecting the macro. You turn on the Macro Recorder by choosing the Tools, Record Macro, Record New Macro command. When executed, the dialog box in Figure 4.13 appears.

**FIGURE 4.13** RECORD NEW MACRO DIALOG BOX

After entering a name for the macro, you press ENTER or click on OK. With the recorder turned on, you perform the actions to be included in the procedure. Once finished, you turn off the recorder by clicking the Stop button ( ) or by choosing the Tools, Record Macro, Stop Recording command. Excel automatically writes the macro for you and stores it on a Visual Basic module in the current workbook.

Perform the following steps to create a macro that automatically enters a company name and address and then formats the cell.

1. Close any workbooks that may be open in the document area.
2. CLICK: New Workbook button ( )
3. To create a macro you must first turn on the Macro Recorder:
   CHOOSE: Tools, Record Macro, Record New Macro
   The Record New Macro dialog box appears, as shown in Figure 4.13.
4. In the dialog box, type the name (without spaces) that you want to assign to the macro:
   TYPE: **CompanyName**
   PRESS: ENTER or CLICK: OK
   Notice that the word "Recording" appears in the Status bar and that the Stop button (as shown on the next page) floats above the application window.

5. As the first recorded step in the macro:
   PRESS: CTRL + HOME

6. Now, you can enter the company name and address information:
   TYPE: **Sam's Superior Sailboats**
   PRESS: ⬇
   TYPE: **Suite 100, 2899 Seashore Drive**
   PRESS: ⬇
   TYPE: **Seattle, WA  98004**
   PRESS: ENTER

7. To format this information:
   SELECT: cell range from A1 to E3
   CLICK: Center Across Columns button ( )
   CLICK: Bold button (**B**)
   CLICK: Italic button (*I*)
   SELECT: Times New Roman from the Font drop-down list (Arial)
   SELECT: 14 from the Font Size drop-down list (10)

8. To stop the recording:
   CLICK: Stop button ( )
   And that's all there is to recording a macro! In the next section, you will get an opportunity to play back a macro.

**QUICK REFERENCE**
Recording a Macro

1. **CHOOSE: Tools, Record, Record New Macro**
2. **Enter a name for the macro.**
3. **PRESS: ENTER or CLICK: OK**
4. **Perform the procedure to be recorded.**
5. **CLICK: Stop button ( )**

## PLAYING BACK A MACRO

There are several methods for playing back a macro. You can execute a macro by selecting it from a dialog box, by pressing a keystroke combination, by clicking a toolbar button, or by selecting a custom command from the menu. In this section, you learn how to run a macro from the Macro dialog box. For further information, please refer to the User's Guide and Help system that accompanies Microsoft Excel.

To practice playing back a macro, perform the following steps:

1. CLICK: Sheet2 tab
2. To enter the company name and address at the top of this worksheet:
   CHOOSE: Tools, Macro
   The dialog box in Figure 4.14 appears.

**FIGURE 4.14** MACRO DIALOG BOX

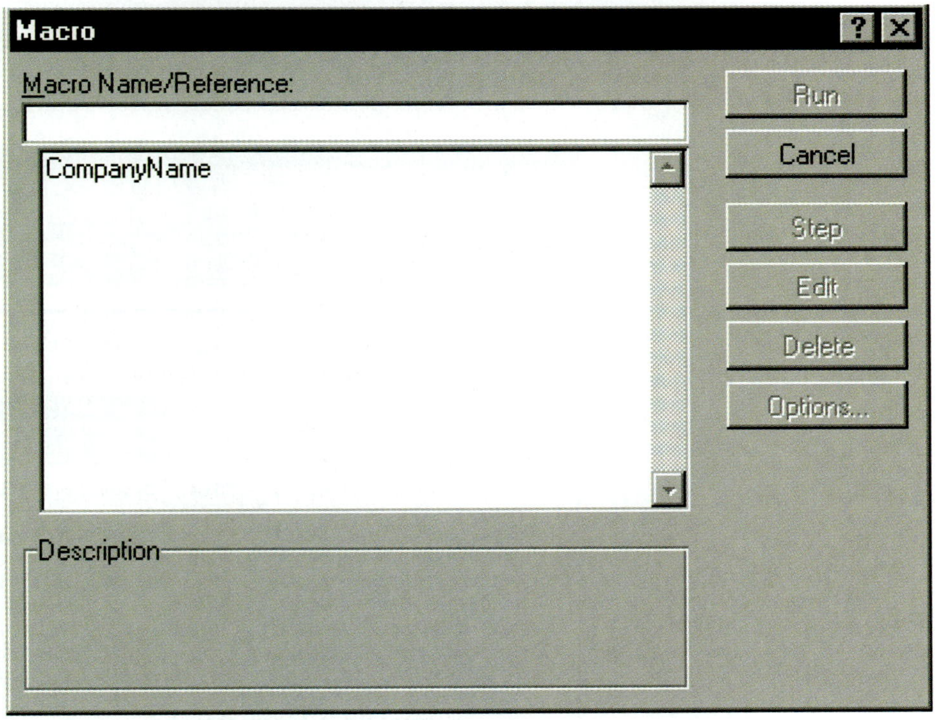


3. To run a macro from the *Macro Name/Reference* list box:
   SELECT: CompanyName macro
   PRESS: ENTER or CLICK: Run
   The company information is automatically entered and formatted in the proper range of the worksheet. (*Note:* You can also double-click a macro name in the list box area to execute the macro.)

**QUICK REFERENCE**
Playing Back a Macro

1. **CHOOSE: Tools, Macro**
2. **SELECT: the desired macro from the list box**
3. **PRESS: ENTER or CLICK: Run**

## REVIEWING YOUR MACROS

Since a macro is stored in a workbook, you can easily review and edit the Visual Basic code that Excel writes. In this section, you learn how to modify Excel's code and play back the new version of your macro. Perform the following steps.

1. To view the Visual Basic module:
   CLICK: Last Sheet button (▶|)
   CLICK: Module1 sheet tab
   Your screen should now appear similar to Figure 4.15.

**FIGURE 4.15** MODULE1 SHEET

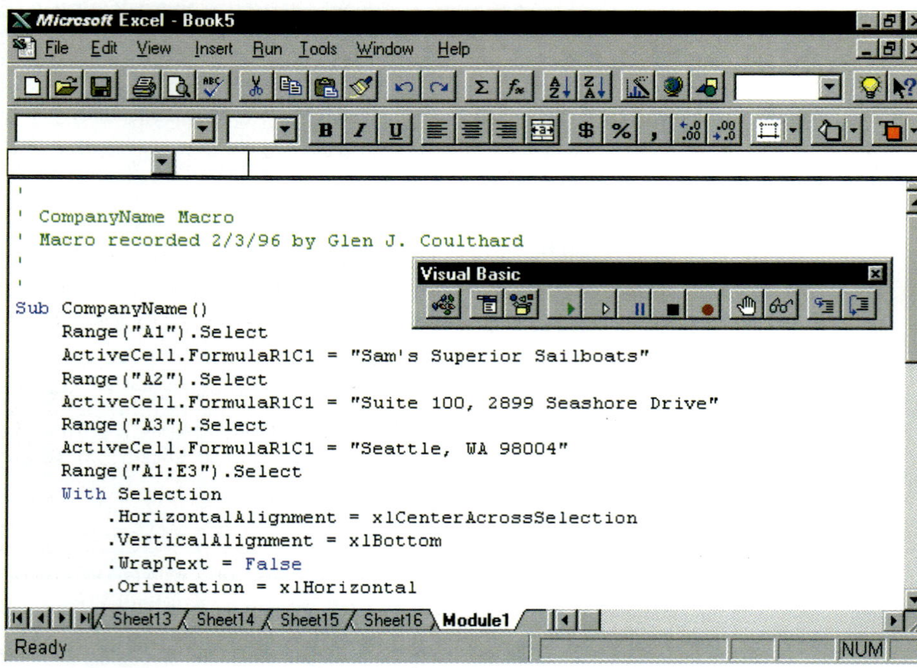


2. You edit the Visual Basic code on this sheet as you would work with a word processing software program. For example, position the I-beam mouse pointer over the word "Suite" in the company's address. To select this text:
   DOUBLE-CLICK: "Suite"
   Make sure that the word is highlighted before proceeding.

3. Let's change the company address:
   TYPE: **Room**
   DOUBLE-CLICK: "Drive"
   TYPE: **Road**

4. To see the results of our editing:
   CLICK: First Sheet button (⏮)
   CLICK: Sheet3 tab
5. To run the macro:
   CHOOSE: Tools, Macro
   DOUBLE-CLICK: CompanyName macro in the list box
   Notice that the new information is entered into the cells. This example demonstrates how quick and easy it is to edit the code created by Excel's Macro Recorder.
6. Save the workbook as "Macros" to the Advantage Diskette.
7. Close the workbook and then exit Microsoft Excel.

**QUICK REFERENCE**
Editing a Macro

1. **Select the sheet where your macro is stored, typically Module1.**
2. **Edit the Visual Basic code using basic wordprocessing keystrokes.**

## SUMMARY

This session introduced you to several commands and procedures that increase your efficiency and productivity when working in Excel. The first part of the session concentrated on dividing the document window into panes for freezing titles on the screen. This technique is useful when your worksheet is organized under static column and row headings. When your application consists of separate but related areas, separating the workbook into multiple window views helps you keep track of the workbook's relationships. You also learned how to filter data and produce "top-ten" lists in your worksheet.

For consolidating worksheets or workbooks into a summary worksheet, the ability to organize and tile multiple windows in the document area is an incredible timesaver. The latter half of the session explored different methods for consolidating worksheet information. You also learned to use macros for automating common tasks and procedures. Excel's easy-to-use Macro Recorder gives everyone the ability to become a programmer in the Visual Basic for Applications language.

The Command Summary in Table 4.1 provides a list of the commands and procedures covered in this session.

**TABLE 4.1**

Command Summary

| *Command* | *Description* |
|---|---|
| Window, Freeze Panes | Lets you lock or freeze rows and columns on the screen so that they appear at all times. |
| Window, Unfreeze Panes | Unfreezes the area that has been locked using the Window, Freeze Panes command. |
| File, Close All | Closes all open documents in the document area. |
| Window, Split | Splits the window into horizontal and vertical panes at the cell pointer. |
| Window, Remove Split | Removes panes created by choosing Window, Split or by dragging the horizontal and vertical split boxes. |
| Window, New Window | Opens a new window in the document area for another view of the active workbook. |
| Window, Arrange | Arranges the open windows in the document area using square, horizontal, and vertical tiling options. |
| Data, Filters, AutoFilter | Analyzes a column's data and produces a filter method that enables you to limit the display of information. |
| Tools, Record Macro, Record New Macro | Records keystrokes, commands, and procedures and saves them as a macro. |
| Tools, Record Macro, Stop Recording | Turns off the recorder to finish creating the macro; you can also click the Stop button (■). |
| Tools, Macro | Executes a macro using the menu. |

## KEY TERMS

**AutoFilter**

In Excel, a software feature that makes it easy for you to select, filter, and display worksheet information quickly and easily.

**consolidate**

In spreadsheets, combining smaller worksheet files into a single summary worksheet. Consolidation procedures make it easier to manage large amounts of spreadsheet data.

**Group mode**

A special mode for working with multiple-sheet workbooks; enables you to perform commands on a single sheet and have those commands reflected in all other sheets in the file.

**horizontal split box**

A small box located at the top of the vertical scroll bar; used to divide a window into panes.

**macro**

A collection of keystrokes, commands, or procedures that can be executed using two keystrokes, a mouse click, or a menu selection. Macros are recorded or written by the user, saved to the disk, and then repeatedly used to perform frequent tasks or commands.

**panes**

When a document window has been divided into separate areas using the Window, Freeze Panes command or the Window, Split command, these areas are called *window panes* or *panes.* A worksheet can have a maximum of four panes at any one time.

**Personal Macro Workbook**

A special workbook file, managed by Excel, for storing macros that you want made available to all your workbooks.

**vertical split box**

A small box located at the far right of the horizontal scroll bar in a document window; used to divide a window into panes.

# EXERCISES

## SHORT ANSWER

1. What is the main difference between freezing titles on a worksheet and dividing a window into panes?
2. What is the purpose of the Window, Arrange command?
3. What are some advantages of linking workbooks?
4. What is the significance of a solid Title bar in a window?
5. How do you change the name of a sheet tab?
6. What is a macro?
7. How do you create a macro?
8. Where are the macros that you create stored?
9. How are macros commonly played back?
10. How can you view the macros that you have recorded?

## HANDS-ON

(*Note:* In the following exercises, save your workbooks onto and retrieve files from the Advantage Diskette.)

1. In this exercise, you retrieve a workbook from the Advantage Diskette and practice freezing titles and viewing the worksheet using panes.

   *a.* Load Microsoft Excel and close all of the open windows in the document area.

   *b.* Open the "Check Register" worksheet located on the Advantage Diskette. This worksheet is an incomplete cash disbursements journal. Make sure that you type your name into cell A3.

   *c.* CLICK: cell A8

   *d.* To see how many checks have been posted in the first quarter:
   PRESS: CTRL + ↓
   Notice how the column text headings have scrolled out of view.

   *e.* Return to the top of the worksheet.

   *f.* Your objective is to freeze the titles in Rows 1 through 6 at the top of the screen. Then, when you move to the bottom of the column to enter new checks, you will still be able to see the column headings. The first step is to move to cell A8.

   *g.* CHOOSE: Window, Freeze Panes

   *h.* To enter more checks into the journal:
   PRESS: CTRL + ↓
   The titles remain at the top of the screen as the cell pointer is repositioned at the bottom of the column.

   *i.* Enter the following checks into the journal:

| *Check* | *Date* | *Amount* |
|---|---|---|
| 51 | 17-Mar-96 | 550.45 |
| 52 | 24-Mar-96 | 300.95 |
| 53 | 31-Mar-96 | 750.25 |

   Your worksheet should now appear similar to Figure 4.16.

**FIGURE 4.16** "CHECK REGISTER" WORKBOOK

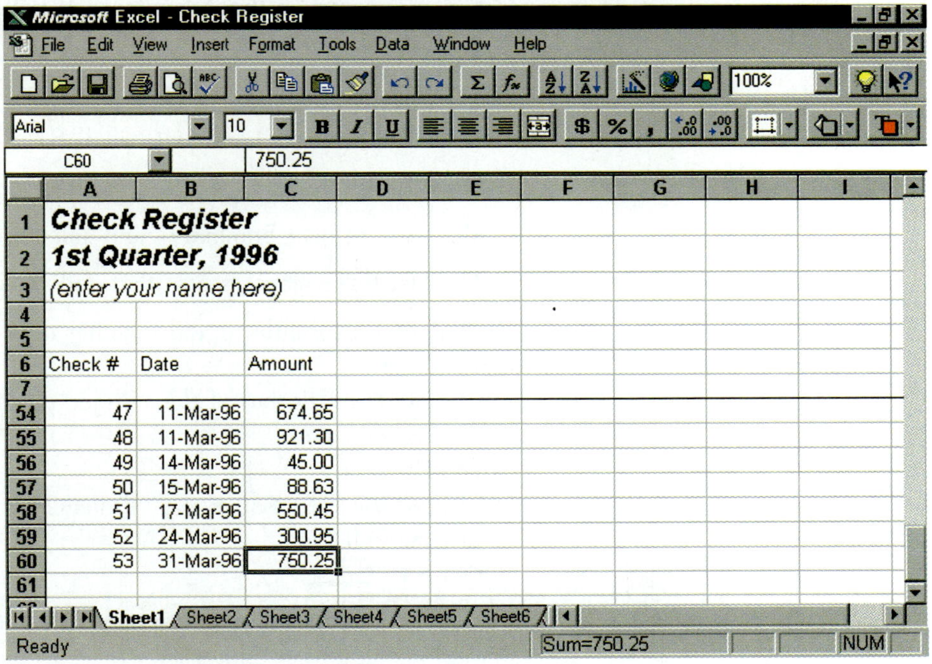

*j.* PRESS: CTRL + HOME

*k.* Unfreeze the row titles.

*l.* To create a new window onto the "Check Register" workbook: CHOOSE: Window, New Window

*m.* Arrange the open windows horizontally in the document area.

*n.* Arrange the open windows vertically in the document area.

*o.* Close the window titled "Check Register:2" by clicking its Close button (×).

*p.* Tile the single "Check Register" window in the document area.

*q.* Save the workbook as "Check Register" onto the Advantage Diskette. Replace the old version of the file.

*r.* Close the workbook.

2. This exercise practices consolidating separate subsidiary workbook files into a summary workbook. The company, XYZ Developments, is currently working on two projects. Each project has a project manager responsible for hiring subcontractors and consultants. Fortunately, XYZ's project managers are experienced in using Excel and have set up tracking workbooks. Your objective is to complete a summary workbook that adds together the data from each project manager's file. (*Hint:* You will use linking formulas to consolidate these workbooks.)

*a.* Close all of the open windows in the document area.

*b.* Open the "Project Summary," "Project1," and "Project2" workbooks that are stored on the Advantage Diskette. Enter your name in cell E2 of the "Project Summary" workbook.

*c.* Arrange the windows using the Tiled option.

*d.* Move to "Project1" and select cell B7.

*e.* Move to "Project2" and select cell B7.

*f.* Move to "Project Summary" and select cell B7.

The last three steps ensure that cell B7 is visible in each worksheet.

*g.* Construct a formula to add together data from the two workbooks:
TYPE: =
CLICK: the Title bar of the "Project1" window
CLICK: cell B7
TYPE: +
CLICK: the Title bar of the "Project2" window
CLICK: cell B7
PRESS: ENTER

*h.* Modify the cell addresses to contain relative cell addresses rather than absolute cell addresses. (*Hint:* Remove the "$" symbols from the formula.)

*i.* Copy the formula in B7 to the cell range from B7 to M16.

*j.* PRESS: CTRL + HOME
CLICK: cell B7
Your screen should appear similar to Figure 4.17.

*k.* Save the workbook as "Project Summary" onto the Advantage Diskette.

*l.* Close all of the open windows.

FIGURE 4.17 "PROJECT SUMMARY" WORKBOOK

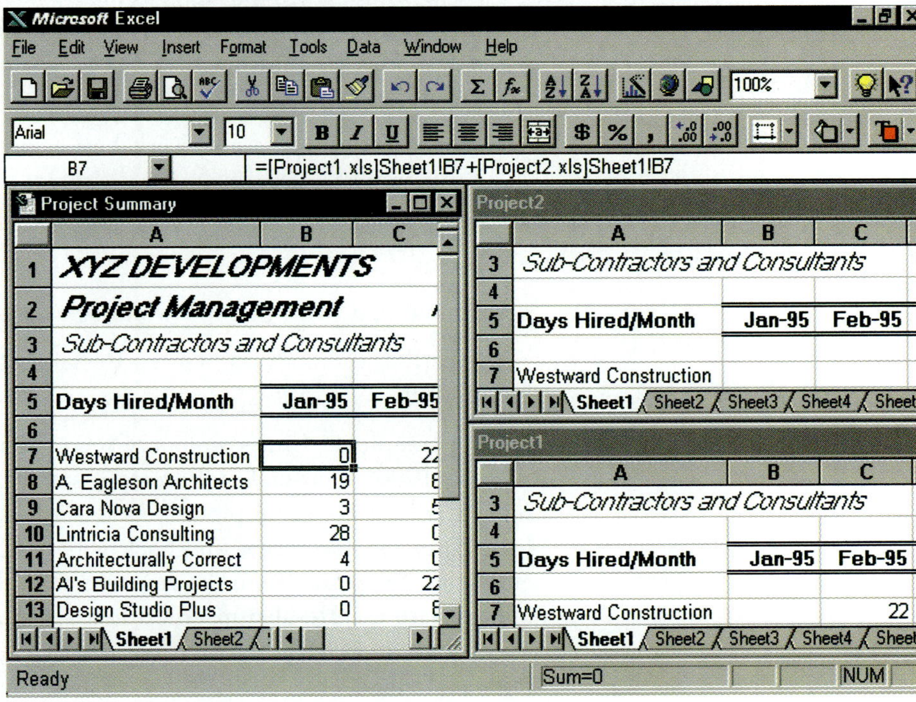


## CASE PROBLEMS GINO'S KITCHEN

(*Note:* In the following case problems, assume the role of the primary characters and perform the same steps that they identify. You may want to re-read the session opening.)

1. After a relaxing Christmas holiday, Larry arrives at the office to find the following note on his desk: "Larry, I trust you had a wonderful time on Nantucket Island. Sorry to be a pain, but I'd like the monthly restaurant report ASAP. Thanks. Gino." With his favorite mug in tow, Larry heads directly for the coffee machine, planning his strategy along the way. When he returns to his desk, Larry turns on the computer, launches Excel, and then locates the four managers' workbooks that are stored on the Advantage Diskette. These files are named "Gino's - North," "Gino's - South," "Gino's - West," and "Gino's - East." He loads all four workbooks into memory and then arranges the windows in a tiled pattern on the screen.

   Leaning back in his chair, Larry ponders the task before him and then writes down the process on a piece of scrap paper. Before proceeding any further, Larry makes sure that the four restaurant workbooks appear tiled on the screen and then he performs the steps outlined in his list.

- Create a new workbook that contains a skeleton copy of the standard restaurant template. In other words, copy the contents of one restaurant's workbook to the new workbook and then delete the specific information. (*Hint*: Make sure that you leave the formulas in the new worksheet and delete only the financial information for the restaurant.)
- Edit the title in the new worksheet to read "Gino's Kitchen - All Restaurants."
- Consolidate the financial information from the four subsidiary workbooks.
- Format and print the new workbook for Gino's approval.
- Save the workbook as "Gino's Restaurants" onto the Advantage Diskette.

2. Having completed Gino's summary report, Larry decides to get a fresh start on 1996's year-end and create a summary workbook for his monthly reports. Using the same process as described in the previous case problem, Larry creates a new workbook with a skeleton copy of the standard restaurant template. Then, he renames the tabs in the workbook Jan, Feb, Mar, and so on. He also inserts a new sheet at the very beginning of the workbook called "YTD" which he will use to sum the contents of the Jan through Dec sheets. Lastly, Larry removes the unused sheets in the workbook.

   Using Group mode, Larry copies the skeleton template to the other sheets in the workbook. Still in Group mode, he makes some formatting enhancements to the worksheet that flow through to all the worksheets in the stack. After previewing the formatting enhancements, Larry ungroups the worksheets. Moving to the YTD worksheet, Larry creates formulas for consolidating the values from Jan through Dec. Pleased with his new summary, Larry saves the workbook as "Gino's YTD 1996" onto the Advantage Diskette.

3. It's 5:30 P.M. and Larry is getting ready to leave the office after a productive day. Just as he closes his briefcase, Gino strolls into his office to share a few ideas. "Larry, you did a good job on that summary report. Marvelous, just marvelous. But Larry, I'm troubled by the numbers that some of our establishments are reporting. I'd like you to develop and print a first-quarter budget for me using these figures." Gino hands Larry a piece of paper with handwritten notes. "I think that I might have to visit our accountant. Can you have this ready for me by tomorrow?" Larry assures Gino as he strolls back down the hallway that he'll finish the budget by tomorrow morning.

   Larry returns to his desk and turns on his computer once again. He loads the "Gino's YTD 1996" workbook and then saves it as "Gino's Budget 1996" onto the Advantage Diskette. Using Gino's information (provided on the next page), he enters the budget estimates, groups the first four sheets (YTD, Jan, Feb, and Mar), and then prints the sheets centered horizontally. Lastly, he saves the worksheet back to the Advantage Diskette as "Gino's Budget 1996" and exits Excel.

| *All Restaurants* | *Jan* | *Feb* | *Mar* |
|---|---|---|---|
| Food Sales | 75,000 | 90,000 | 110,000 |
| Beverage Sales | 95,000 | 120,000 | 145,000 |
| Food Costs | 40,000 | 54,000 | 65,000 |
| Beverage Costs | 32,000 | 40,000 | 52,000 |
| Manager's Salary | 16,000 | 16,000 | 16,000 |
| Wages & Benefits | 26,500 | 30,000 | 36,000 |
| Administration | 2,500 | 4,500 | 5,000 |
| Laundry & Misc. | 9,500 | 12,000 | 10,500 |
| Occupancy Costs | 15,000 | 15,000 | 15,000 |

Microsoft Excel 7.0 for Windows 95

# *Creating Charts*

## SESSION OUTLINE



## INTRODUCTION

Most business people recognize the benefit of using graphics to improve the effectiveness of their presentations. Clearly, a visual display is quicker in conveying information than rows and columns of tiny numbers. This session demonstrates how Excel produces visually stunning charts and data maps from basic worksheet information.

## CASE STUDY H2 UNDERSCAPING LTD.

In 1989 Chip Yee started H2 Underscaping Ltd. (H2U), a landscaping operation that specializes in the installation of underground sprinkler systems. Since that time, H2U has grown from annual sales of $30,000 to its current year's projection of over $700,000. This tremendous growth is due in large part to Chip's sound financial analysis of the landscaping industry. Just the previous year, Chip purchased a competing business, called Xeriscaping, Inc. (*xeriscaping* is a special form of landscaping for desert or low fresh-water areas), that was losing money and turned it around into a profitable business unit at H2U. One of the other keys to Chip's success is his ability to monitor the seasonal trends of his industry.

Having just completed entering a full year's information into an Excel worksheet, Chip wants to take advantage of his slow time this January to analyze the results and trends for 1995. In particular, he wants to compare the dollar sales from his sprinkler installations against his new xeriscaping business. He also wants to plot his combined sales revenues against his expenses for the year to get a feeling for the seasonal trends. Although most of these numbers appear next to each other in the worksheet, Chip feels that he could better understand the results if they appeared in a graph. Ever since he can remember, Chip has been a visual learner and understands charts and pictures better than text or numbers. Unfortunately, Chip's experience with Excel has been limited to entering information into worksheets, formatting cells, using functions, and linking workbooks.

In this session, you and Chip learn about the different charting formats available in Excel and how to create basic charts and data maps using worksheet information.

## FORMS OF BUSINESS GRAPHICS

A graphic representation of worksheet data is far more effective than the numbers alone for the same reason that road maps are easier to follow than written directions. The majority of people are visual learners and seem to remember what they see better than what they hear or read. **Graphics,** which are the pictorial representation of words and data, provide us with a superior method of presentation.

Everybody has seen some sort of business graphic used at one time or another. From interest rates to unemployment statistics, most people prefer to see a picture of the latest trends than study the underlying numbers. Graphics are produced in a variety of formats to suit the specific needs of the business professional. For example, microcomputer images can be displayed on a monitor, photographed, plotted on paper (black and white or color), or made into transparencies to be used with an overhead projector. There are several types of charts available for presenting information to different audiences such as engineers, statisticians, medical researchers, and business professionals.

This section concentrates on the most popular business graphics, namely line charts, bar or column charts, pie charts, and XY or scatter plot diagrams.

## LINE CHARTS

When you need to plot trends or show changes over a period of time, the **line chart** is the perfect tool. The angles of the line reflect variations in a trend, and the distance of the line from the horizontal axis represents the amount of the variation. An example of a line chart appears in Figure 5.1.

**FIGURE 5.1** A LINE CHART SHOWING CHANGES IN TELEVISION VIEWERSHIP OVER A FIVE-YEAR PERIOD

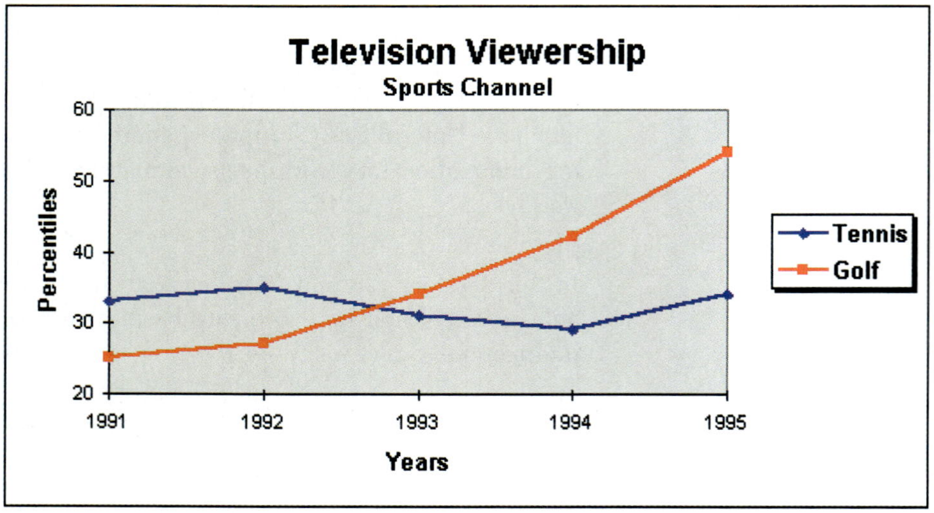


## BAR OR COLUMN CHARTS

When the purpose of a chart is to compare one data element with another data element, a column chart is the appropriate form to use. A **column chart** also shows variations over a period of time, similarly to a line chart, and is one of the most commonly used graphs in business. An example appears in Figure 5.2. A *bar chart* also uses rectangular images, but they run horizontally rather than vertically.

FIGURE 5.2
A COLUMN CHART COMPARING GOLF VERSUS TENNIS VIEWERSHIP OVER A FIVE-YEAR PERIOD

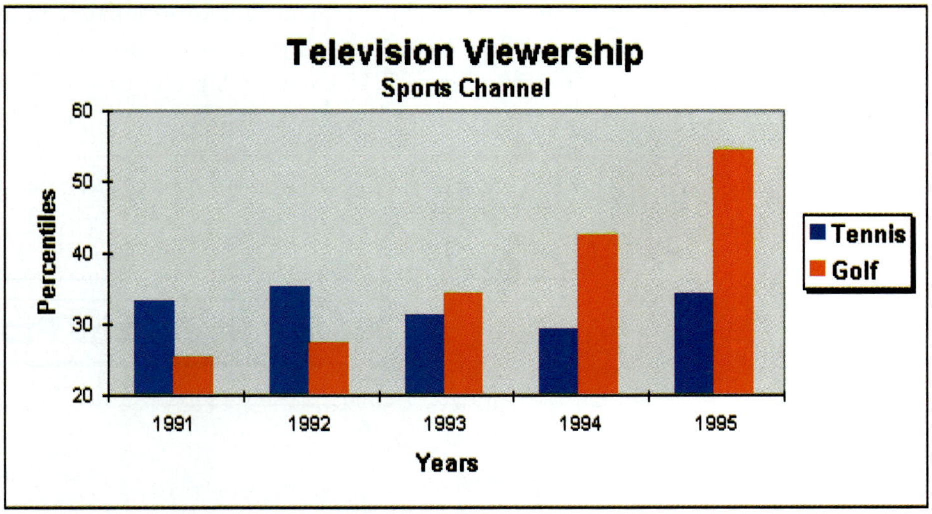


## PIE CHARTS

A **pie chart** shows the proportions of individual components compared to the total. Similar to a real pie (the baked variety), a pie chart is divided into slices. An example of a pie chart appears in Figure 5.3.

FIGURE 5.3
A PIE CHART SHOWING THE BREAKDOWN OF EXPENSES FOR XYZ COMPANY

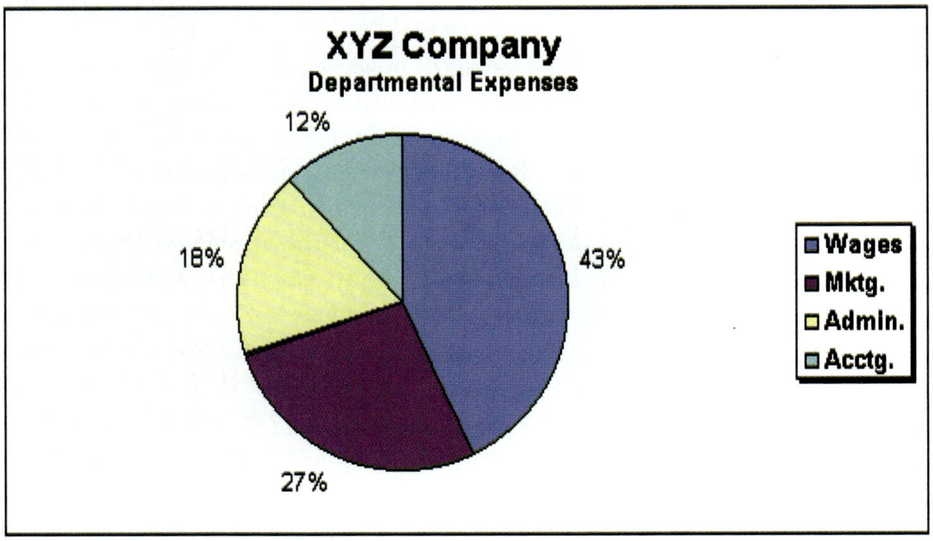

### SCATTER PLOT CHARTS

**XY charts,** which are commonly referred to as *scatter plot diagrams,* show how one or more data elements relate to another data element. Although they look much like line charts, XY charts include a numeric scale along both the X and Y axes. Figure 5.4 shows an XY chart.

**FIGURE 5.4** AN XY CHART SHOWING THE CORRELATION BETWEEN WORKER STRESS AND PRODUCTIVITY

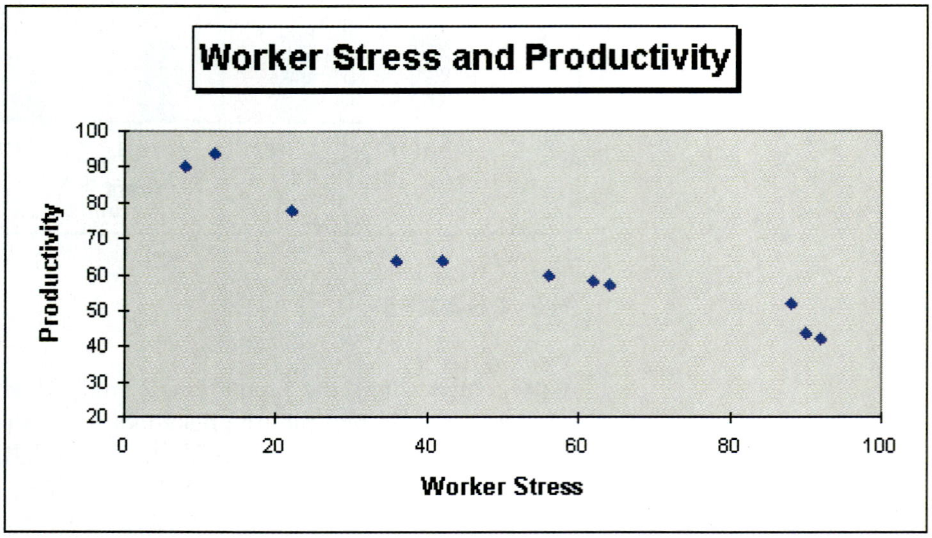


## PRINCIPLES OF BUSINESS GRAPHICS

With graphics programs, there is often a tendency to overindulge in the various formatting and customizing options available. Although a picture may be worth a thousand words, it is probably wise not to test this adage with business graphics. Regardless of the sophistication of your graphics program, do not attempt to tell an entire history using a single chart. To assist your planning for when and how to apply business graphics, there are certain basic principles to follow: simplicity, unity, emphasis, and balance. The following sections describe each of these principles.

## SIMPLICITY

One common problem with graphing is the tendency to put too much information and formatting onto a single chart. For example, using color to differentiate the slices of a pie chart works well. However, using different colors for a chart's title, background, **plot area** (the area for charting values), and legend is distracting. And although it is natural to want to tell the whole story in one chart, trying to do so may defeat its purpose. Charts are used to symbolize numbers or words because most people tend to find graphics easier to understand than straight text and tables. If you include too much text or detail in a chart, the visual aspects become muddled and the symbols become difficult to understand. Always try to keep your charts simple.

## UNITY

A chart must clearly relate the data elements it contains—that is, it must appear as a unit. For instance, if you use too much space between the variables (such as between columns in a column chart), you will probably destroy the unity of your chart.

## EMPHASIS

Use emphasis sparingly and correctly. Emphasis is used to draw one's attention to certain data elements or trends. For example, **exploding** a pie slice emphasizes that particular piece. In the same way, an arrow that points at a column in a column chart focuses the viewer's attention on that data element. Used correctly, formatting and customizing your chart to emphasize certain elements provide viewers with visual cues for focusing their attention.

## BALANCE

Your graph should look balanced—both as a unit and in the context of the rest of the page. One factor that affects balance is the position of descriptive text, including titles, legends, and free-form text. Changing the position of such text affects the balance of the graph. Changing the shading, color, and thickness of the lines used in a graph also affects balance.

These four principles will assist you in developing charts that are easily read and interpreted. The next section introduces the methods for creating charts using Microsoft Excel. The concepts presented in this past section should be applied in the following sections.

## USING EXCEL TO CREATE CHARTS

There are two methods for creating a chart in Excel, differing primarily in the way the chart is output and stored. First, you can create a new chart by selecting worksheet information and then choosing the Insert, Chart, As New Sheet command. This method adds a new chart sheet to the workbook and works well for creating computer-based presentations and slide shows. A second method allows you to create an **embedded chart** that you print and save along with the worksheet page. To create an embedded chart, select the worksheet information that you want plotted and then click the ChartWizard button ( ) or choose the Insert, Chart, On This Sheet command. Because an embedded chart resides directly on the worksheet, you can easily print the chart with its text and numbers. Regardless of the charting method you select, the **ChartWizard** guides you through the entire chart creation process using a series of dialog boxes.

Although Excel's default chart type is a column chart, there are many additional chart types available in Excel's gallery. Table 5.1 explains each type of chart.

**TABLE 5.1**

Excel Chart Types

| *Chart Type* | *Description* |
|---|---|
| Area | Compares the amount of change in data elements over a period of time. |
| Bar | Compares data elements over a period of time. |
| Column | Compares data elements over a period of time. |
| Line | Shows trends in data over a period of time. |
| Pie | Shows the proportion of each individual element when compared to the total. |
| Doughnut | Shows the proportion of each individual element when compared to the total; differs from pie chart in that you can display more than one data series. |
| Radar | Shows each category as an axis or spoke from the center point. |
| XY (Scatter plot) | Plots the relationships between different sets of data. |
| 3-D Area | 3-D version of an area chart. |
| 3-D Bar | 3-D version of a bar chart. |
| 3-D Column | 3-D version of a column chart. |
| 3-D Line | 3-D version of a line chart. |
| 3-D Pie | 3-D version of a pie chart. |
| 3-D Surface | 3-D version of a surface chart. |

In the next section, you will create, print, and save a chart as a separate chart sheet in a workbook.

## CREATING A CHART

You create a chart by selecting a range of cells to plot and issuing a menu command or clicking the ChartWizard button ( ). How does Excel know how to plot the information? What values does it place on the horizontal or **X-axis**? What values does it place on the vertical or **Y-axis**? Excel's decision process is examined in this section, along with the steps for creating a chart as a separate sheet in a workbook.

### CHARTING A SINGLE RANGE

When you select a cell range to plot, Excel examines the shape of the highlighted area to determine which cells contain data and which cells contain headings or labels. If Excel finds text or dates in the left-hand column or in the top row, it then uses this information for the category and data labels. In other words, you should include the column headings and row labels when selecting a cell range so that Excel can automatically generate the labels for the X-axis and the legend.

In determining which information appears where, Excel counts the rows and columns in the selected range and plots the smaller dimension as the **data series** on the Y-axis. Excel always creates a chart based on the assumption that you want fewer data series than points along the X-axis. However, you can change this initial or default assumption in one of the dialog boxes (Step 4 of 5) displayed by the ChartWizard.

Perform the following steps to demonstrate the ChartWizard.

1. Make sure that you've loaded Microsoft Excel and that a new worksheet appears in the document window. Place the Advantage Diskette into drive A: or drive B:.
2. Create the worksheet appearing in Figure 5.5.

**FIGURE 5.5** "EMPLOYED" WORKSHEET

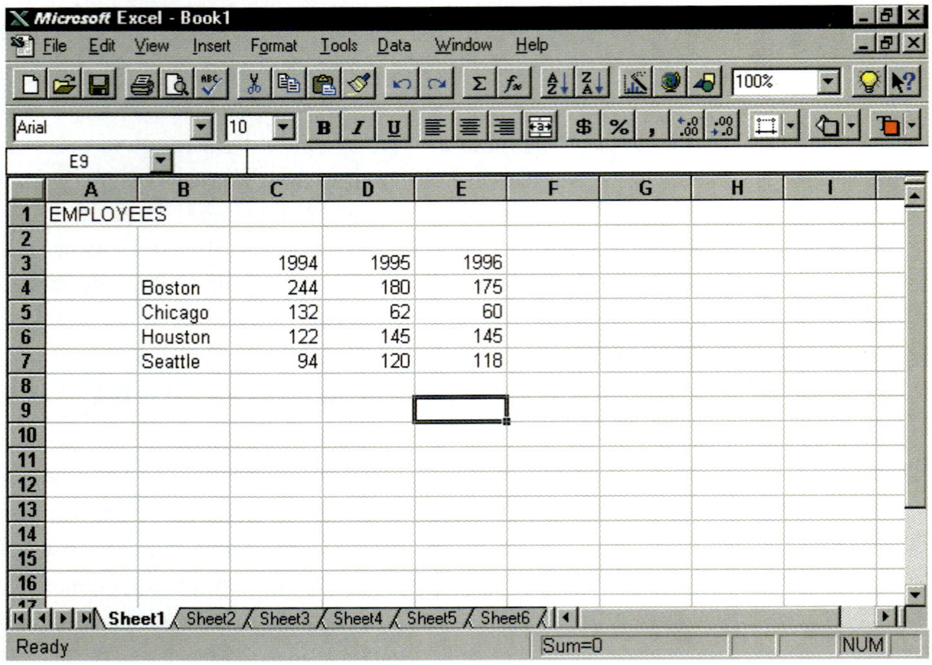


3. SELECT: cell range from B3 to E7
   Notice that there are more cities (4) than years (3) in this selection. Therefore, Excel will place the cities on the horizontal or X-axis and will plot the years on the vertical or Y-axis.

4. To plot the selected range as a new chart sheet in the workbook:
   CHOOSE: Insert, Chart, As New Sheet
   The ChartWizard displays the first dialog box in a series of five, as shown in Figure 5.6.

**FIGURE 5.6** CHARTWIZARD: STEP 1 OF 5

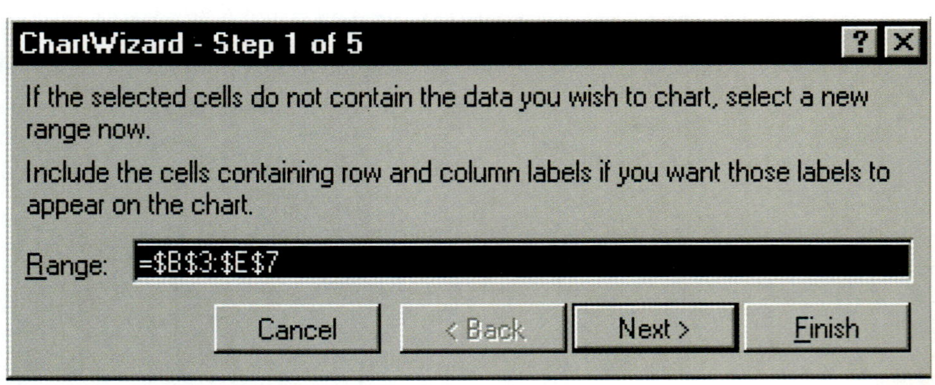

5. In the first dialog box, the ChartWizard confirms the cell range that you have selected. To accept this range as being accurate:
   CLICK: Next > to proceed
   The ChartWizard displays the second dialog box.
6. In Step 2 of 5, you select the type of chart that will best communicate your data (Figure 5.7). To proceed:
   CLICK: Next >
   The Step 3 dialog box (Figure 5.8) appears with alternative formats for the selected chart type.

**FIGURE 5.7** CHARTWIZARD: STEP 2 OF 5

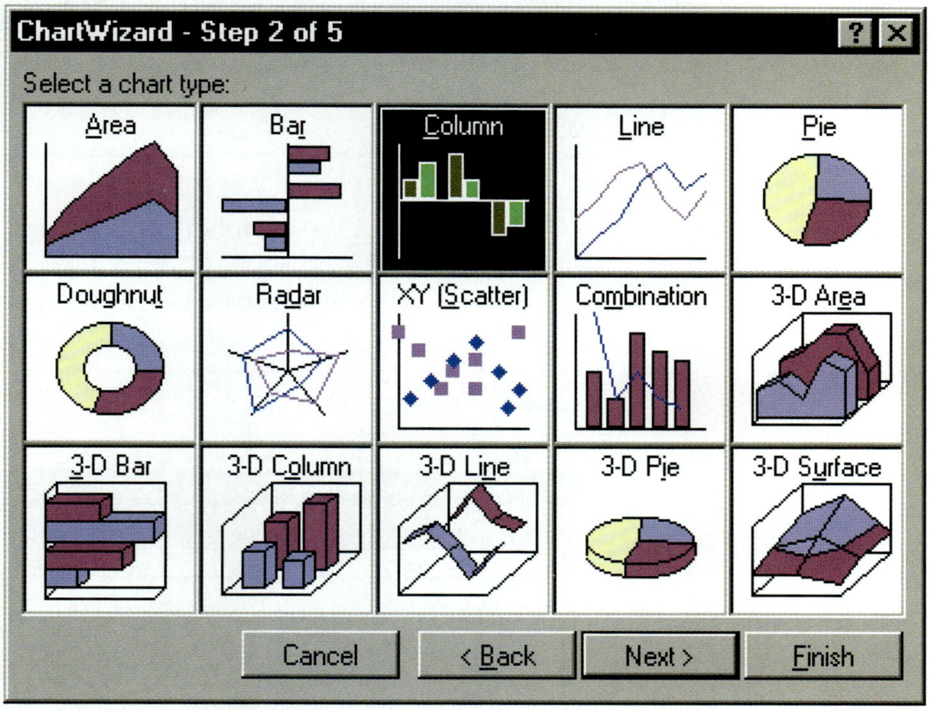

**FIGURE 5.8** CHARTWIZARD: STEP 3 OF 5

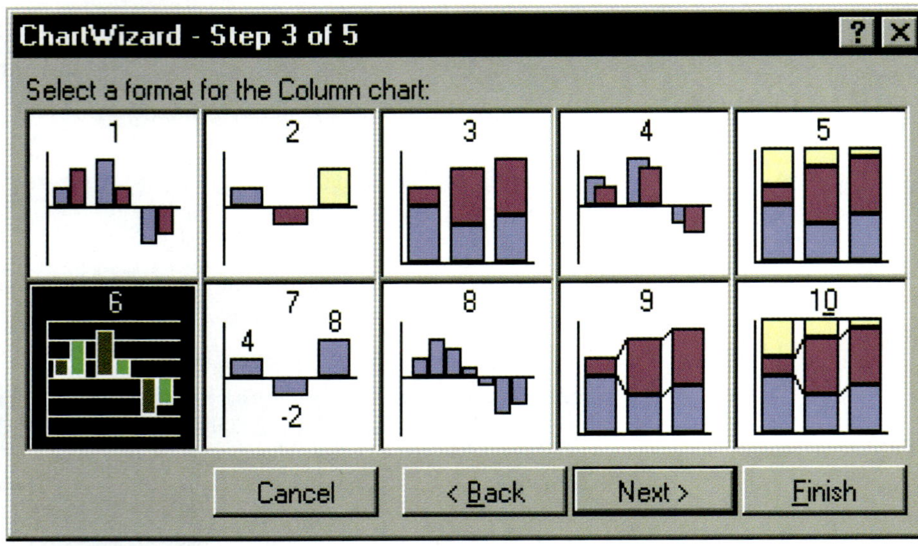


7. To accept the ChartWizard's default settings:
   CLICK: Next >
   The dialog box that appears is called Step 4 of 5.

**FIGURE 5.9** CHARTWIZARD: STEP 4 OF 5

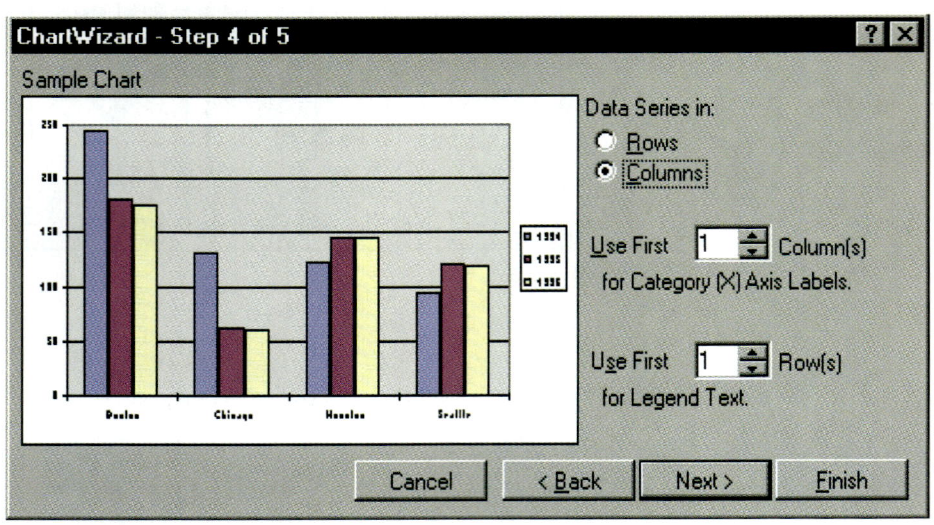


8. In this dialog box (Figure 5.9), you specify whether the column and row orientation is correct. The *Sample Chart* preview area helps you make the right decision. In our example, the orientation is correct:
   CLICK: Next >

**FIGURE 5.10** CHARTWIZARD: STEP 5 OF 5

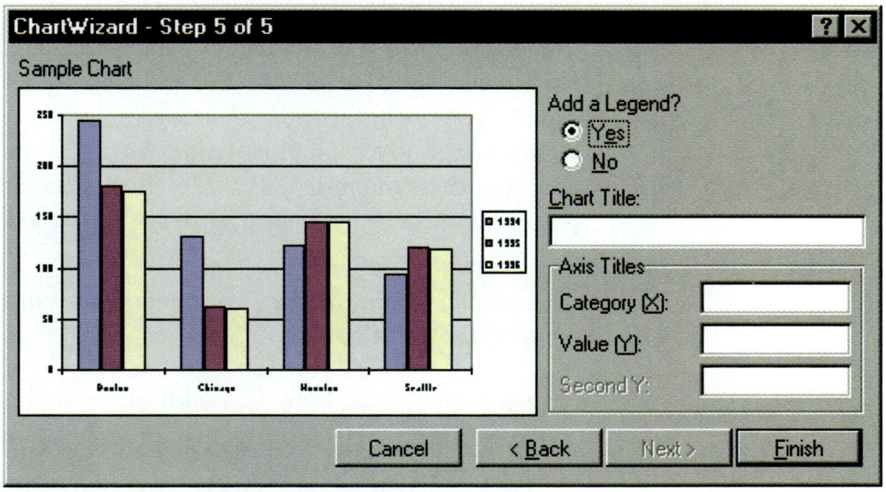


9. In the final dialog box (Figure 5.10), the ChartWizard lets you enter your own titles for the chart and axes as well as providing an option to turn the legend on and off. To proceed:
   CLICK: Finish
   The chart is displayed in a new sheet, called Chart1, in the same workbook file as the selected data.
10. To ensure that you are viewing all of the chart:
    CLICK: down arrow beside the Zoom Control (100%) drop-down list box in the Standard toolbar
    CLICK: Selection
11. Let's demonstrate the link between the worksheet data and the chart. First, take note of Seattle's 1994 bar in the chart. Then, do the following:
    CLICK: Sheet1 tab
    CLICK: cell C7
    TYPE: **300**
    PRESS: ENTER
12. To review the chart:
    CLICK: Chart1 tab
    Notice that the change in the worksheet data is immediately reflected in the chart sheet.
13. Save this workbook as "Employed" to the Advantage Diskette.
14. Close the workbook.

**QUICK REFERENCE**
Creating a Chart as a New Sheet

1. **SELECT: the cell or range of cells to plot in a chart**
2. **CHOOSE: Insert, Chart, As New Sheet**
3. **Respond to the dialog boxes displayed by the ChartWizard.**

## CHARTING MULTIPLE RANGES

You can improve your productivity in Excel by reducing unnecessary keystrokes and commands. One method for reducing keystrokes is to select multiple cell ranges prior to formatting, deleting, or charting worksheet information. This allows you to place information anywhere in a workbook and still select it for charting. Because most worksheets are not as structurally perfect as the example in the last section, you must learn how to take advantage of this flexibility.

Perform the following steps to practice selecting multiple cell ranges for formatting and charting.

1. Open the "XYZ Dept 1" workbook located on the Advantage Diskette.
2. To format the GROSS RECEIPTS line, TOTAL EXPENSES line, and NET INCOME line to display a currency format, you must first select all the cell ranges:
   SELECT: cell range from B5 to E5
3. To select the range of cells from B13 to E13:
   PRESS: CTRL and hold it down
   CLICK: cell B13 and hold down the mouse button
   DRAG: mouse pointer from B13 to E13
   Notice that the original cell selection of B5 to E5 remains highlighted.
4. Release the mouse button and the CTRL key.
5. To select the range of cells from B15 to E15:
   PRESS: CTRL and hold it down
   CLICK: cell B15 and hold down the mouse button
   DRAG: mouse pointer from B15 to E15
6. Release the mouse button and the CTRL key.
7. CLICK: Currency Style button ($)
   Each of the highlighted cells is formatted to the currency format.
8. Let's select some ranges for charting. To highlight the cell range for the horizontal or X-axis:
   SELECT: cell range from A3 to D3
   (*Note:* Column E is not included because it is a summed value and we want to compare the months only.)
9. When selecting the data ranges to plot, you must ensure that they are the same shape (for example, same number of rows and columns) so that they will contain the same number of items:
   PRESS: CTRL and hold it down
   SELECT: cell range from A5 to D5
   SELECT: cell range from A13 to D13

10. Release the CTRL key.
    At this point, there should be three cell ranges selected on the worksheet as shown in Figure 5.11.

**FIGURE 5.11** SELECTING MULTIPLE RANGES TO CHART

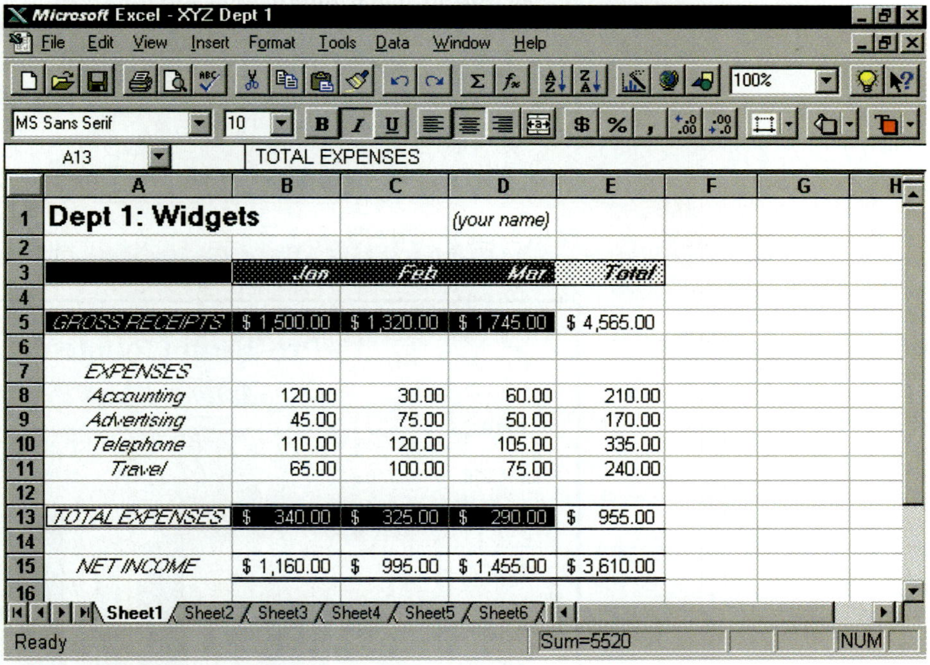


11. To produce a quick chart using the selected cell ranges:
    CHOOSE: Insert, Chart, As New Sheet
12. When the first ChartWizard dialog box appears:
    CLICK: Finish
    A new chart sheet appears in the workbook. Notice that the Y-axis is formatted with dollar signs because of your earlier formatting of the GROSS RECEIPTS and TOTAL EXPENSES lines.
13. Let's rename the chart sheet's tab:
    DOUBLE-CLICK: Chart1 tab
    TYPE: **Widgets**
    PRESS: ENTER
14. Save the workbook as "XYZ Chart" onto the Advantage Diskette.

The next section explains some general features of charts. Do not close the chart or workbook as they are referred to in the following sections.

## WORKING WITH CHARTS

When the chart sheet is active, Excel modifies your work area slightly. In addition to the appearance of the Chart toolbar, you will find additional menu commands specific to formatting and manipulating charts. Because chart sheets are quite different from worksheets, you may find that it takes some time to adjust. For example, you no longer have the familiar rows and columns to guide your entry of information. Before learning how to format and enhance charts in the next sections, take a few moments to study the parts of a chart labeled in Figure 5.12 and described in Table 5.2.

**FIGURE 5.12** PARTS OF A CHART

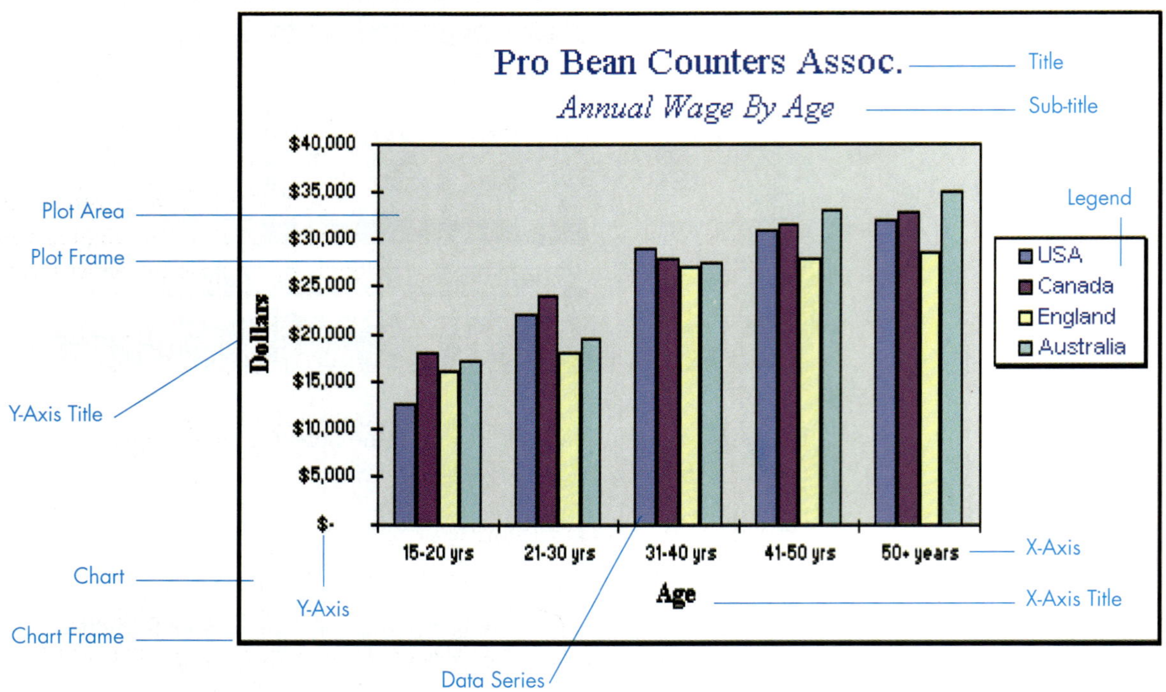

**TABLE 5.2**

Parts of a Chart Window

| *Component* | *Description* |
|---|---|
| Chart and Chart Frame | The area inside a chart, including the plot area, titles, axes, legend, and other objects. |
| Plot Area and Plot Frame | The area for plotting values from the worksheet. The plot area contains the axes and data series. |
| Axes (X and Y) and Axes Titles | Most charts have a horizontal or X-axis and a vertical or Y-axis for plotting values. |
| Data Marker | A single dot, bar, or symbol that represents one number from the worksheet. |
| Data Series | A series of related values from the worksheet. A data series consists of related data markers. |
| Legend | A key for deciphering the different data series appearing in the plot area. |

## SELECTING A CHART TYPE

By default, Excel generates a column chart. However, there are many different chart types and formats to choose from in the gallery, as summarized in Table 5.1. This section shows you how to access these different chart formats.

Perform the following steps.

1. Ensure that the chart sheet is the active sheet:
   CLICK: Widgets tab
2. To select a different chart type:
   CHOOSE: Format, Chart Type
   The dialog box in Figure 5.13 appears.
3. In the Chart Type dialog box, you can customize the chart:
   SELECT: *3-D* option button under the *Chart Dimension* group
   SELECT: *3-D Bar* option in the grid display area
   CLICK: Options command button
   The dialog box in Figure 5.14 appears.

**FIGURE 5.13** CHART TYPE DIALOG BOX

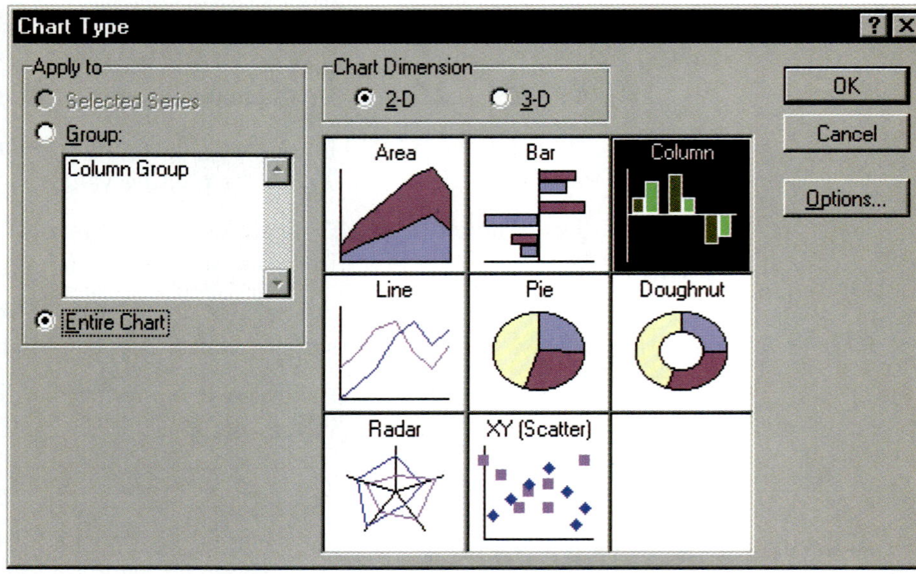


**FIGURE 5.14** FORMAT 3-D BAR GROUP DIALOG BOX

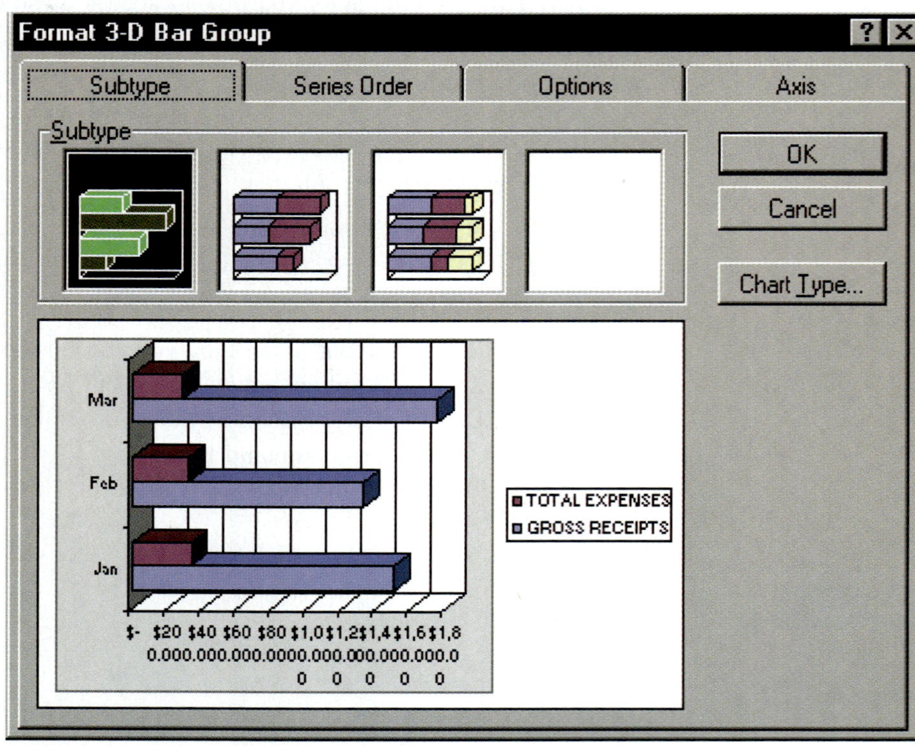

4. SELECT: leftmost (first) subtype
PRESS: **ENTER** or CLICK: OK

5. On your own, practice changing the chart format using the Format, Chart Type command.

6. You can also apply predefined styles to your charts using the Format, AutoFormat command. There are two types of AutoFormat styles: Built-in (provided by Excel) and User-Defined (created by you). To demonstrate this powerful feature:
CHOOSE: Format, AutoFormat

7. In the dialog box that appears, make the following selections:
SELECT: *Built-in* option button under the *Formats Used* group
SELECT: *3-D Column* from the *Galleries* list box
SELECT: 4 in the *Formats* grid display area
PRESS: **ENTER** or CLICK: OK
Your screen should now appear similar to Figure 5.15.

8. Save the workbook as "XYZ Chart" to the Advantage Diskette, replacing the old version of the file.

**FIGURE 5.15** "XYZ CHART" CHART SHEET

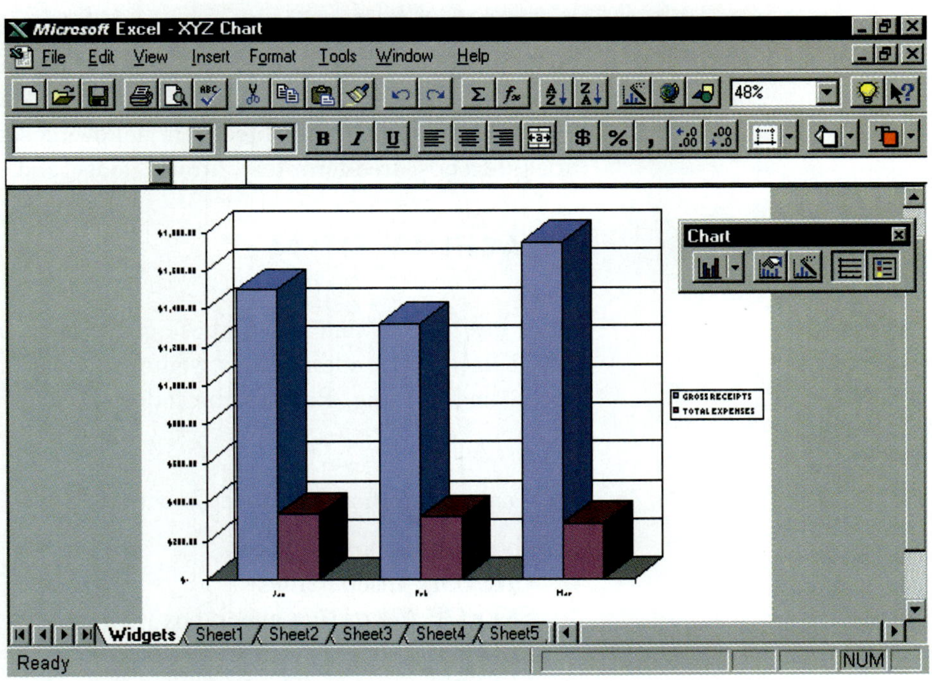

**QUICK REFERENCE**
Selecting a Chart Type Using the Menu

1. **Make the chart sheet active.**
2. **CHOOSE: Format, Chart Type**
3. **In the dialog box, select the chart type.**
4. **CLICK: Options command button**
5. **In the dialog box, select the chart format.**
6. **PRESS: ENTER or CLICK: OK**

## CUSTOMIZING AND FORMATTING A CHART

Customizing a chart involves adding titles, legends, annotations, and arrows which emphasize certain aspects of the chart and improve its overall readability. Formatting a chart refers to setting the display options for each element of a chart. For example, if you are working on a color system, Excel differentiates each data series in a chart by assigning them different colors. When you print the chart to a non-color printer, however, the various colors appear as black or white. Therefore, you need to format the columns using patterns or shades of gray to differentiate the series. This section explores several methods for enhancing your chart.

To customize or format a chart, you must first select the chart item or object that you want to format. To select a single item using the mouse, simply click on the object. Using the keyboard, press the cursor-movement keys until the boxes appear around the object. The following sections demonstrate how to add titles, legends, free-form text, arrows, fonts, and patterns to your chart.

### ATTACHING TITLES

Titles are used to state the purpose of the chart and to explain the scales used for the axes. After adding titles, you can format the text using a variety of fonts, styles, and shading. Perform the following steps to add a title to the Widgets graph.

1. Ensure that the chart sheet is active.
2. To add titles to the chart:
   CHOOSE: Insert, Titles
   SELECT: *Chart Title* check box
   SELECT: *Value (Z) Axis* check box
   SELECT: *Category (X) Axis* check box
   PRESS: ENTER or CLICK: OK
   Excel places temporary text in each title location. (*Note:* If you find it difficult to perform the next few steps because the data appears too small, magnify your view of the chart using the Zoom Control drop-down list box.)

3. CLICK: Title at the top of the chart sheet once to select the object
4. Position the I-beam mouse pointer over the Title text and double-click to select the text.
5. To replace the title text:
   TYPE: **Receipts vs. Expenses**
6. To replace the X-axis title:
   CLICK: X-axis title once to select the object
   DOUBLE-CLICK: I-beam mouse pointer over the text in the axis
   TYPE: **Months**
7. To replace the Y-axis title (appearing as "Z" on the chart sheet):
   CLICK: Y-axis title once to select the object
   DOUBLE-CLICK: I-beam mouse pointer over the text in the axis
   TYPE: **Dollars**
   You will learn how to format the text attributes (for example, font style, size, and typeface) later in the session.

**QUICK REFERENCE**
Attaching Titles

1. **CHOOSE: Insert, Titles**
2. **SELECT: Chart Title, Value, and Category check boxes**
3. **PRESS: ENTER or CLICK: OK**

## ADDING A LEGEND

A **legend** provides a key for the data series plotted in the chart. If you didn't specify a legend in the ChartWizard dialog box, you can add one later using the Insert, Legend command. Excel places the legend at the right-hand side of the chart window. You can move the legend by dragging it using the mouse or by choosing a command from its shortcut menu.

Perform the following steps.

1. RIGHT-CLICK: anywhere on the legend
   CHOOSE: Format Legend from its shortcut menu

2. To change the legend's location on the chart sheet:
   CLICK: Placement tab
   The following options are available:

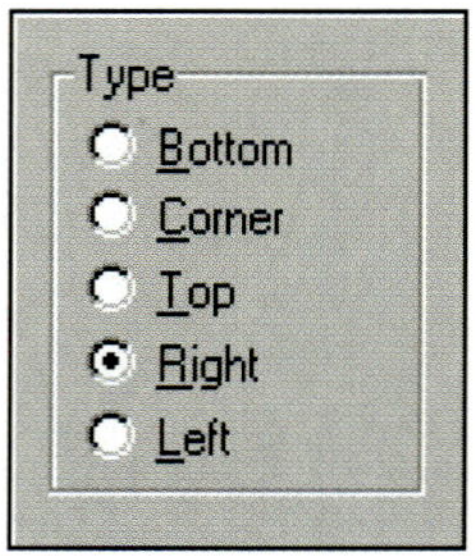


3. To move the legend to the top of the sheet:
   SELECT: *Top* option button
   PRESS: ENTER or CLICK: OK
4. To move the legend to the bottom right-hand corner of the sheet, position the mouse pointer on the legend:
   CLICK: legend once and hold down the left mouse button
   DRAG: legend to the bottom right-hand corner
5. Release the mouse button.
6. Let's finalize the legend's position on the chart sheet:
   RIGHT-CLICK: anywhere on the legend
   CHOOSE: Format Legend
   CLICK: Placement tab
   SELECT: *Right* option button
   PRESS: ENTER or CLICK: OK

**QUICK REFERENCE**
Adding a Legend

- **To add a legend to your chart:**
  **CHOOSE: Insert, Legend**
- **To format the legend:**
  **RIGHT-CLICK: on the legend**
  **CHOOSE: Format Legend**

## ENTERING FREE-FORM TEXT

With free-form text, you can easily emphasize important areas of a chart. Once text is entered, you can move it anywhere in the chart window and apply various fonts and styles.

Perform the following steps.

1. For the next two sections, we access buttons on the Drawing toolbar. To display the Drawing toolbar:
   RIGHT-CLICK: on any button in the Standard or Formatting toolbars
   CHOOSE: Drawing
   The Drawing toolbar should appear on your screen. Figure 5.16 labels the buttons on the Drawing toolbar.
2. If the Drawing toolbar appears in its own window, floating above the chart sheet:
   DRAG: Drawing toolbar to the Status bar so as to dock it near the bottom of the window

**FIGURE 5.16** DRAWING TOOLBAR

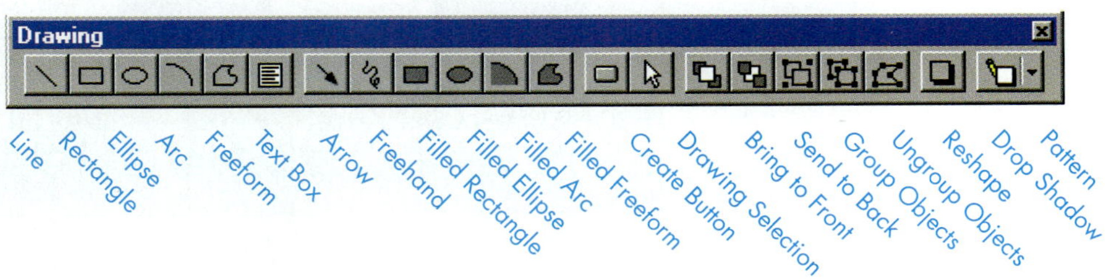


3. To provide a better view of your chart:
   CLICK: down arrow adjacent to the Zoom Control box (100%)
   CLICK: 100%
4. Scroll the window to view the upper-right quadrant of the chart.
5. To enter text, we will use the Text Box button on the Drawing toolbar:
   CLICK: Text Box button
6. Move the cross-hair mouse pointer into the chart sheet and drag a rectangle that is similar to the screen graphic in Figure 5.17.

**FIGURE 5.17** CREATING A TEXT BOX

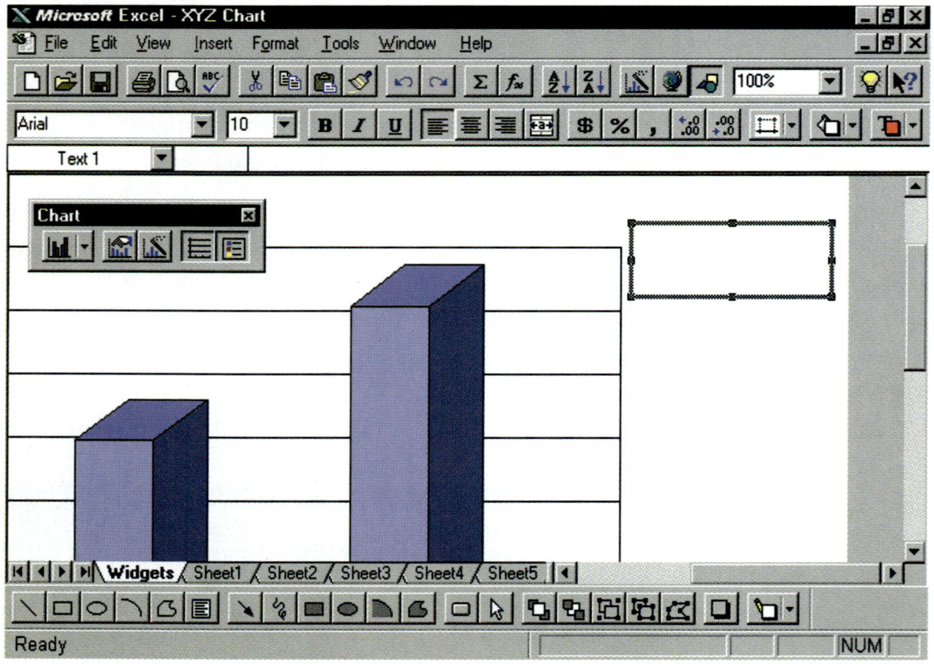


7. When you release the mouse button, you will notice a flashing insertion point. To enter the free-form text:
   TYPE: **After Training**
8. To remove the insertion point and deselect the text box:
   CLICK: on the white or gray area surrounding the chart

**QUICK REFERENCE**
Adding Free-Form Text

1. **CLICK: Text Box button ( ) on the Drawing toolbar**
2. **DRAG: a rectangle in the chart sheet**
3. **TYPE: any free-form text**

## USING ARROWS FOR EMPHASIS

Besides free-form text, you can use other types of objects to direct the reader's attention. Arrows are the most common means for focusing a viewer on certain locations in your chart. Perform the following steps.

1. To add an arrow to the chart:
   CLICK: Arrow button ( ) on the Drawing toolbar
2. Position the cross-hair mouse pointer below and to the left of the letter A in the word "After."

3. DRAG: the cross-hair mouse pointer toward the March GROSS RECEIPTS column (see below)

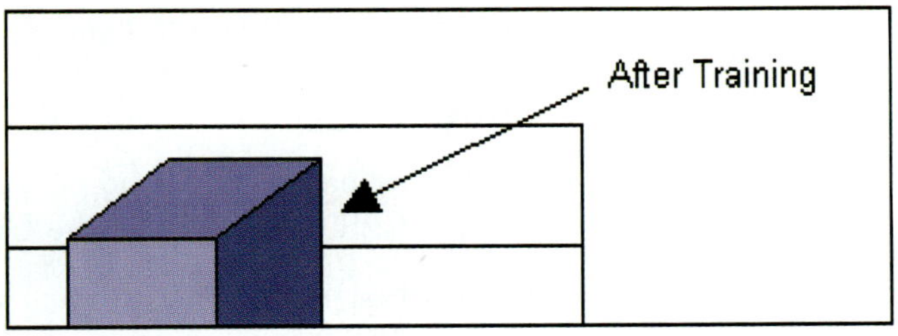


4. Release the mouse button. Your text box and arrow should appear similar to the above example.

**QUICK REFERENCE**
Adding an Arrow

1. **CLICK: Arrow button ( ) on the Drawing toolbar**
2. **DRAG: cross-hair mouse pointer in the chart sheet**

## CHOOSING FONTS AND PATTERNS

Formatting a chart involves changing its background color, choosing fonts for headings and other text, and selecting patterns for data series. In this section, you format the chart title and modify the columns in the plot area for printing on a noncolor printer. Although most commands are available in the Menu bar, you will find that the shortcut pop-up menus are much easier and more convenient to use for formatting a chart.

Perform the following steps.

1. To view the entire chart:
   RIGHT-CLICK: Drawing toolbar
   CHOOSE: Drawing to remove the toolbar from view
   CLICK: on an empty area surrounding the chart to select it
   CLICK: down arrow adjacent to the Zoom Control box (100%)
   CLICK: Selection
2. Position the mouse pointer over the chart title and click the right mouse button to display its pop-up menu.
3. To enhance the text:
   CHOOSE: Format Chart Title
   CLICK: Font tab
   SELECT: Bold Italic from the *Font Style* list box
   SELECT: 18 from the *Size* list box
   PRESS: ENTER or CLICK: OK

4. RIGHT-CLICK: free-form text in the chart sheet
5. CHOOSE: Format Object
   CLICK: Font tab
   SELECT: Italic from the *Font Style* list box
   SELECT: 12 from the *Size* list box
   PRESS: ENTER or CLICK: OK
6. To display patterns, instead of colors, for the data series columns:
   RIGHT-CLICK: any one of the GROSS RECEIPTS columns
7. CHOOSE: Format Data Series
   CLICK: Patterns tab
   CLICK: down arrow beside the *Patterns* drop-down list box
   SELECT: an angled-line pattern
   SELECT: black color
   PRESS: ENTER or CLICK: OK
8. To display patterns for the TOTAL EXPENSES columns:
   RIGHT-CLICK: any one of the TOTAL EXPENSES columns
   CHOOSE: Format Data Series
   CLICK: Patterns tab
   CLICK: down arrow beside the *Patterns* drop-down list box
   SELECT: a shaded pattern
   SELECT: black color
   PRESS: ENTER or CLICK: OK
9. To format the legend box:
   RIGHT-CLICK: legend
   CHOOSE: Format Legend
   CLICK: Patterns tab
   SELECT: *Shadow* check box
   PRESS: ENTER or CLICK: OK
10. Save the workbook as "XYZ Chart" onto the Advantage Diskette, replacing the existing version of the chart. Your worksheet is now ready for printing to a black and white printer and should look similar to Figure 5.18.